Exact Imagination, Late Work

Exact Imagination, Late Work

On Adorno's Aesthetics

Shierry Weber Nicholsen

The MIT Press   Cambridge, Massachusetts   London, England

© 1997 Massachusetts Institute of Technology

This book was set in Baskerville by Wellington Graphics on IBM Pcs using Ventura Publisher and was printed and bound in the United States of America.

Library of Congress Cataloging-in-Publication Data
Nicholsen, Shierry Weber.
    Exact imagination, late work : on Adorno's Aesthetics / Shierry Weber
  Nicholsen.
     p. cm.—(Studies in contemporary German social thought)
    Includes bibliographical references and index.
    ISBN 0-262-14062-4 (alk. paper)
    1. Adorno, Theodor W., 1903–1969. 2. Aesthetics, Modern—20th
century 3. Adorno, Theodor W., 1903–1969. Ästhetische Theorie. I. Title.
II. Series.
B3199.A34N53 1997   97-9398
111′.85′092—dc21   CIP

For Janet and Jeremy, with love

Contents

Introduction: Exact Imagination and Late Work   1

1 Subjective Aesthetic Experience and Its Historical Trajectory   15

2 Language: Its Murmurings, Its Darkness, and Its Silver Rib   59

3 Configurational Form in the Aesthetic Essay and the Enigma of *Aesthetic Theory*   103

4 *Aesthetic Theory*'s Mimesis of Walter Benjamin   137

5 Adorno and Benjamin, Photography and the Aura   181

Notes   227

Bibliography   249

Index   261

Introduction: Exact Imagination and Late Work

The merits of a work, its level of form, its inner coherence, generally become recognizable only when the material becomes outdated or when the sensorium becomes deadened to the most conspicuous features of the facade. . . . For quality to unfold historically, it is not quality alone that is required in itself, but also what comes afterward and sets the older work in relief; perhaps there is even a relationship between quality and a process of dying off.

—*Adorno*, Aesthetic Theory

Of what use is the work of Theodor W. Adorno for an Anglo-American audience now, almost three decades after his death? Certainly, the work is aging, unable to respond to new intellectual currents and issues, and some of its themes have been reiterated to the point of intractable familiarity. And yet one senses that we have still not plumbed the real implications of the work. It is almost as though the sense of familiarity masks an inaccessible core of the work that has so far proved impervious to appropriation.

Consider the contrast between the fates of Adorno and Walter Benjamin in English. The reception of Benjamin's work has been far broader, more diverse, and more imaginative. His work has been taken up in many fields and from many perspectives. He has inspired critical studies as diverse as the essays in *Benjamin's Ground,* the volume edited by Rainer Nägele, and Susan Buck-Morss's *Dialectics of Seeing.*[1] Adorno's reception, in contrast, has remained within narrower bounds (with the exception of his wide-ranging influence in musicological circles).[2] Intellectual historians, philosophers, political scientists, and sociologists with an interest in the Frankfurt School have worked to locate him, to articulate his precise relationship to Marxism and the role of his resignation or his pessimism or his utopianism or his elitism in his political stance, and to define him in relationship to currents in recent French thought, in the process looking at many individual aspects of his multifaceted work.[3] In all this, I think it is fair to say, the emphasis has been more on trying to understand precisely where Adorno stands than on imaginatively appropriating his work. Of course this reflects the difficulty of his work and its strangeness in the Anglo-American context. But beyond that, I think it points to the presence of some fundamental problem in grasping his work that we have yet to overcome.

In retrospect, the path followed by scholarly work on Adorno in the Anglo-American context over the past several decades both reflects the imperviousness of his work and brings us to the point where we can identify it. At the same time, the very aging of Adorno's work, which has occurred as this scholarly reception has proceeded, has allowed the individual character of his work to stand out in contrast to that of other Frankfurt School thinkers. The ground laid by earlier work has made possible two particularly important recent developments in our reception of Adorno. First, in his controversial *Late Marxism* (1990), Fredric Jameson has argued for Adorno's utter relevance to our contemporary situation and has made an attempt at a genuine appropriation of Adorno's work.[4] Second, more scholars have begun to focus directly and in depth on Adorno's aesthetic work.[5] With this new work, accompanied by a revised translation of Adorno's *Aesthetic Theory*, the centrality of the aesthetic for Adorno's oeuvre as a whole is coming to be acknowledged.[6]

The centrality of the aesthetic dimension points the way, I think, to the issue that has blocked a genuine appropriation of Adorno. Adorno himself always insisted that the presentational form *[Darstellungsform]* of his work—which, following Benjamin's lead, he refers to as configurational or constellational form—was inseparable from its philosophical substance. At the same time, he insisted that it was analogous to aesthetic form. Much attention has been devoted to the "negative dialectical" structure of Adorno's thought, but the link between that structure and the aesthetic dimension of his work—in which I include both his work on aesthetics and works of art and the formal dimension of his own texts—has not received the same degree of attention. Yet Adorno's emphasis on the formal structure of his texts marks that link as central. It is in the aesthetic dimension of his work that the inseparability of "form" and "substance" inheres. We all know that one of the most important ideas Adorno has to offer is the notion of a rationality compatible with what he calls the "primacy of the object" *[Vorrang des Objekts]*—a nonconceptual or nondiscursive rationality that might be an alternative to a dominating, systematizing rationality that is the counterpart of an administered world. But this notion of a nondiscursive rationality may ultimately be incomprehensible without the deeper understanding of the aesthetic dimension of his work that we are only now approaching.

To answer the question of Adorno's use to us today, then, we must go more deeply into the connection in his work between the aesthetic dimension and a nondiscursive form of truth. This in turn means looking at an undervalued and underexamined aspect of Adorno's work: the role of the subject and subjective experience. We know that Adorno claims in *Negative Dialectics* that he wants to use the subject to dispel the illusion of constitutive subjectivity.[7] If his work emphasizes the withering of the capacity for individual experience in an administered society that preforms experience—which then only seems to be individual subjective experience, in the sense that it gives the illusion of a constitutive subjectivity—at the same time, the aesthetic dimension of Adorno's work holds out, and indeed is premised on, the possibility of a valid, that is, "adequate" or "authentic," subjective experience.[8] This genuine subjective experience is the correlate of the primacy of the object and the condition for nondiscursive knowledge of the object. By implication, it holds out the possibility of a genuine reading of Adorno's own texts as well.

Adorno's term "exact imagination" *[exakte Phantasie]*[9] marks this conjunction of knowledge, experience, and aesthetic form. The term points provocatively and explicitly to the relationship between exactness—reflecting a truth claim—and the imagination as the agency of a subjective and aconceptual experience. Adorno's use of the term spans the whole of his oeuvre, from the very early to the very late work. In the passage in which it first occurs, the essay "The Actuality of Philosophy," it designates aconceptual or nondiscursive rationality. Adorno is redescribing philosophy as a kind of Baconian "ars inveniendi," a form of empirical experimental investigation. He invokes the exact—as opposed to the creative—imagination as the organon of this art or technique: "An exact imagination; an imagination that remains strictly confined to the material offered it by scholarship and science and goes beyond them only in the smallest features of its arrangement, features which of course it must produce of itself."[10] In emphasizing the imagination's capacity to discover, or produce, truth by reconfiguring the material at hand, Adorno makes knowledge inseparable from the configurational form imagination gives it—in the process, as the reference to Bacon indicates, laying the basis for his conception of essay form. The primacy of the object—the material at hand—produces, as it were, the need for configurational form.

The term "exact imagination" appears again in Adorno's late work, in the 1965 radio talk "Schöne Stellen," or "Beautiful Passages." Here the context is aesthetic experience, and the term is used to justify the primacy of attention to detail. Given the dissociative tendencies in modern music and the demise of master forms, Adorno says, one must be able to experience and interpret music from the details to the whole as well as from the whole to the details: "The instrument of this kind of experience is exact imagination. It discloses the richness of the detail on which it dwells rather than hurrying past it to the whole with an anxious impatience which is bred into the good musician and which currently sours so much interpretation."[11] Like "the speculative ear," a related term derived from Kierkegaard,[12] then, exact imagination spans the philosophical and the aesthetic, the dimension of form and the dimension of experience. It shows us that the primacy of the object is inseparable from reliance on genuine subjective experience, and that configuration is an activity of the subject as well as a feature of form.

The very conjunction of nondiscursive rationality and the aesthetic dimension that I am claiming here as the key to Adorno's potential usefulness to us has been the object of sympathetic but pointed criticism from Jürgen Habermas and Albrecht Wellmer, members of later generations of the Frankfurt School. Their criticisms articulate the central issues with which an attempt to understand this conjunction of Adorno's must come to terms. They put into sharp focus the question whether the aging of Adorno's work has rendered it outdated. In *The Philosophical*

Discourse of Modernity, Habermas argues that in blurring the boundaries between art and reason Adorno is attempting to negate—and possibly regress behind—the modern division of rationality into separate spheres as described by Max Weber. The result is that neither art nor reason can exercise its true function. Adorno's critique of reason extends to the point, Habermas says, that it undermines its own legitimacy as argumentation. Adorno's configurational texts can claim the status neither of knowledge nor of art.[13] Following a similar line of argument in a critique focused on *Aesthetic Theory,* Wellmer points to the "rigid features" of Adorno's aporetic constructions and ascribes them to a systematic flaw, namely, the use of an outmoded subject-object paradigm. He proposes to reconstruct Adorno's aesthetic theory on the basis of a Habermasian intersubjective-linguistic paradigm. In effect, Wellmer construes what for Habermas is a blurring of boundaries between art and reason as a problem of the construal of subjectivity and language.[14]

Wellmer himself, however, acknowledges that it would be premature to dismiss Adorno's work, with its assertion of an inextricable connection between the rational and the aesthetic, as outdated on these grounds. The very aesthetic quality of Adorno's writings on aesthetics, he says, makes them transcend critique to some extent, and Adorno's "incomparable capacity for the philosophical penetration of experience" allows him to transcend the limits of the subject-object paradigm even as he uses it. It may be more accurate to say, however, that Adorno's work transcends Wellmer's attempted Habermasian reconstruction precisely because that reconstruction relies on a premature equation of the subjective with the linguistic or communicative. As Wellmer indicates, the import of Adorno's work could lead to— or is premised on, I would say—a reconstruing of precisely the apparently outmoded subject-object framework within which he seems to be writing.[15] That is to say, the conjunction of truth and the aesthetic in Adorno's work may allow us to understand something about subjective experience and its relation to the object that is not accessible within the Weberian framework as Habermas construes its implications. Similarly, the configurational form of his texts may shed a light on language itself that is not accessible within the framework of a communicative conception of rationality.

At the same time, we would be wrong to disregard the aging of Adorno's work. For, as Jameson remarks, if in Adorno everything leads to the aesthetic, everything in the aesthetic also leads back out to the historical.[16] Adorno would not formulate an exact imagination that was ahistorical and unaffected by its historical context. Our own historical context both makes specific aspects of Adorno's work especially relevant to us now and at the same time makes those aspects difficult to grasp. In fact, Adorno himself has thematized the very issue that makes his work both particularly relevant to us and particularly difficult of access; as his work ages for us, we come to see that his oeuvre as a whole is best characterized by a term that is one of his central concerns: "late work."

A concern with late work and the associated notion of late style runs through Adorno's oeuvre. It reflects the Hegelian aspect of his aesthetics in its concern with the "end of art." It is most in evidence in the writings on music; Adorno was writing about Beethoven's late style as early as 1934. The "new music" inaugurated by Schönberg and his school and continuing into the works that Adorno addressed in "Vers une musique informelle" (1961) is "late" music in general rather than the music of an individual composer's late period.[17] It marks both a radical discontinuity from tonal music and a taking up of the challenges that tonal music posed.

Adorno formulates the essential feature of late work as the disjunction of subjectivity and objectivity, so that as work becomes late it becomes increasingly inorganic. In this sense, late work characterizes the direction the arts take as modernism advances within the context of "late capitalism," a phrase Adorno, too, uses.[18] As an attempt to grasp these "late" phenomena and to give form to the discontinuities between subject and object, Adorno's own work is late work as well, and its difficulties are consonant with its enterprise. It is difficult to achieve an adequate subjective experience of work in which subjectivity and objectivity are disjoined. Within Adorno's oeuvre, *Aesthetic Theory* is the paradigmatic late work in a late style, and if, as Adorno says in "Beethoven's Late Style," late works are the catastrophes in the history of art, embodying that radical discontinuity, then surely *Aesthetic Theory* has been the catastrophe in our reception of Adorno.[19]

"Late work" names the dilemma of subjectivity and subjective experience as Adorno experienced and formulated it, a dilemma that is still more advanced in our own time. If "exact imagination" names the ideal of a genuine subjective experience that can lay claim to nondominating knowledge, then "late work" signals how very problematic the capacity for exact imagination must be today. And if the conjunction of exact imagination and late work is surprising, that is a measure of the degree to which we have barely begun to explore the significance of the aesthetic dimension of Adorno's work.

Exact imagination and late work, then, mark the bounds of the exploration that is needed if we are to use Adorno's work more fully. That they are Adorno's own formulations indicates that our exploration might best be conducted by reading Adorno's work in its own terms, in line with his insistence on the primacy of the object. As Wellmer suggested, we need to look at Adorno's texts stereoscopically in order to see their latent depths.[20] Valuable as the work has been that contextualizes and expounds Adorno and differentiates his ideas from those of others, it may have approached his work from a viewpoint too external to the work and thereby prevented us from penetrating to its depths.

The essays in this volume are attempts to begin this exploration from a vantage point within Adorno's work and on his work's own terms. They attempt to reconfigure aspects of that work, tracing some of its constellations in enough detail and with enough richness that they become clearly visible and available to others for further reflection. The essays make use of material from what I will call, for want of a more elegant term, Adorno's "aesthetic writings": his work on music, literature, and (more rarely) painting and other art forms; his work on aesthetics; and his writings on textual form and the associated themes of reading, writing, and language. They take up the issues I have touched on here: subjective aesthetic experience, the historicity of artworks and our experience of them, Adorno's conception of language, the nature of configurational or constellational form in Adorno's work, and the relation between the artwork, aesthetic experience, and philosophy.

Of particular concern in these essays is the relationship between what Adorno says about language, experience, and textual form and what he actually does in his writing. For the latent depths of Adorno's work are surely to be found in his own writing practices, that is to say, in his own use of language. As Adorno indicates in "The Essay as Form," in the kind of configurational presentation he is concerned with, the rhetorical elements—the "aconceptual transitions" of rhetoric with their verbal ambiguities and equivocations—become a primary carrier of the presentation and are thus fused with the truth content.[21] It is precisely in this way that Adorno's use of the subject-object paradigm puts language itself in a different light than that at work in the Habermasian paradigm of communicative rationality. His is a linguistic but not a communicative rationality.

What this means in practice is that Adorno's configurations are composed not only of individual statements that seem to have a straightforward, if strikingly negative and dialectical, meaning; the figurative dimension of his language is crucial as well and an essential part of the conceptual configurations. Much of what I offer here is composed by means of an attention divided between Adorno's more conceptual statements and the web of figurative language that gives them a body (or a quasi body) and fleshes out their significance.

Cross-referencing is one of the central formal qualities of Adorno's work, and anyone who attempts to write about form in Adorno by reconfiguring his own configurations from within will not escape it. The cross-referencing in the essays in this volume is extensive. Quotations and images from Adorno's works appear and reappear, in shifting contexts, as they do in his own work. While I have tried to reduce the sense of repetitiousness and disequilibrium this can create by pointing the reader to other essays in the volume in which certain themes are more fully expounded, or expounded in other contexts, my hope is that the cross-referencing will help the reader perceive the five essays as a constellation of their own around the central issue of the inseparability of form in its aesthetic dimension and a nondiscursive truth content.

The figure of Walter Benjamin and his relationship with Adorno occupy a place of great importance in these essays. Benjamin is an integral part of the constellation that is the aesthetic dimension of Adorno's work. The concepts that prove to be central to understanding the role of the aesthetic in Adorno's work—mimesis, aura, constellation—emanate from Benjamin's work as Adorno appropriated it. At the same time, the effort to articulate the subtle differences between Adorno's thought and Benjamin's is one of the most effective ways to make the precise nature of Adorno's commitment to the aesthetic visible. As Pierre Missac has rightly pointed out, the widely acknowledged relationship between Benjamin's and Adorno's ideas has rarely been explored in detail.[22] I hope to contribute to that exploration.

The first essay, "Subjective Aesthetic Experience and Its Historical Trajectory," sets Adorno's notion of genuine aesthetic experience in the context of his conception of the way the work of art's truth content unfolds as it ages. It also explores the development of Adorno's own work and the role of subjective experience in it, taking his early writings on late style as a point of departure.

Whereas the first essay draws primarily on Adorno's writings on music, the second, "Language: Its Murmuring, Its Darkness, and Its Silver Rib," articulates his conception of the aesthetic use of language by looking primarily at the essays in *Notes to Literature*. It goes on to examine Adorno's own style in the light of his implicit theory of language.

The following two essays, "Configurational Form in the Aesthetic Essay and the Enigma of *Aesthetic Theory*" and "*Aesthetic Theory*'s Mimesis of Walter Benjamin," address the nature of configurational or constellational form, first as Adorno thematizes it in "The Essay as Form" and then, using Benjamin's concepts of mimesis and aura as points of departure, as it manifests itself in the late work *Aesthetic Theory*.

The final essay, "Adorno and Benjamin, Photography and the Aura," attempts a finer differentiation between Adorno's and Benjamin's conceptions of aesthetic form by way of their contrasting conceptions of photography, shedding light in the process on the "Adorno-Benjamin dispute" of the 1930s.

Earlier versions of the first and third essays appeared in *Theory Culture & Society* 10 (1993) and *Cultural Critique* (spring 1991), respectively. An earlier version of the fourth essay is included in *The Semblance of Subjectivity: Essays in Adorno's Aesthetic Theory*, edited by Tom Huhn and Lambert Zuidervaart (Cambridge, Mass.: MIT Press, 1997). I am grateful for the permission to incorporate those earlier versions here.

The essays in this volume developed from an interest in Adorno's aesthetics that began in Frankfurt in 1965 and was deepened by my work as a translator of Adorno's *Notes to Literature* and *Hegel: Three Studies,* but they would not have been possible without my own explorations of aesthetic experience from the points of view of the maker, the performer, and the receiver. Many colleagues and friends have shared parts of this long involvement with me. In particular, I am deeply grateful to Jeremy J. Shapiro for several decades of dialogue about Adorno and aesthetics, to Janet Pfunder for our conversations on the phenomenology of aesthetic experience, and to Martin Jay for his unflagging support of my work on Frankfurt School aesthetics. In part, this volume is the fruit of a long collaboration with Thomas McCarthy and Larry Cohen of the MIT Press's series Studies in Contemporary German Social Thought. Their encouragement and their faith in my judgment have been invaluable. Linda Rugg and John Davidson of the Ohio State University did me the great service of finding uses for my as-yet-unpublished translation of Walter Benjamin's *Berlin Childhood* and thereby inspired me to incorporate some of it here. Many people both in and out of the academy have read and commented on portions of these essays over the past few years, among them Russell Berman, John Davidson, Joan Fabian, Lynn and Michael Hassan, Karl and Sally Hufbauer, Tom Huhn, Robert Hullot-Kentor, Fredric Jameson, Martin Jay, R. Lane Kauffman, Robert Kaufman, Marllan Meyer, Arden Nicholsen, Maggie O'Neill, Edward Said, Trent Schroyer, Albrecht Wellmer, and Lambert Zuidervaart. Their comments have been much appreciated, although of course I claim full responsibility for the idiosyncrasies and limitations of my work. Finally, I am grateful to Jan Miller of the Antioch College library for her always-friendly assistance with interlibrary loans.

In retrospect, it has become clear to me that Adorno's work itself has been my greatest teacher. As I finish these essays, it is with increasing admiration and amazement at his ability to articulate aesthetic experience philosophically (to echo Albrecht Wellmer). If this book helps the reader to penetrate more fully the rich detail of thought and experience in Adorno's aesthetic writings, it will have fulfilled its purpose.

1
Subjective Aesthetic Experience and Its Historical Trajectory

If Adorno is to be of use to us as subjects in a late-twentieth-century context in which the subject is under siege and the very notion of subjectivity is challenged, we must grasp the sense in which for him a valid subjectivity and authentic experience are still possible, no matter how problematic. The correlate of such a subjectivity in Adorno's work, as we have seen, is the nonidentical, the primacy of the object. In Adorno's aesthetics, the emphasis on the primacy of the object takes the form of an emphasis on the artwork as artifact, and on an aesthetics of production as opposed to the historicist reception aesthetics of the last few decades. This emphasis on Adorno's part has a critical intent, but the reception of Adorno's aesthetics has embraced this productivist emphasis in such a way as to obscure the nonconstitutive subjectivity—and the emphasis on experience—that is its correlate within Adorno's aesthetic work.[1]

As we know from Kant, it is in the aesthetic dimension that the intimacy of subject and object is particularly pronounced, and it is in his aesthetics that Adorno provides us with his most emphatic model of a genuine and valid, if difficult and problematic, subjectivity. The work of art may be objective, both in being object—artifact—and in embodying an objective relationship to societal dynamics, and in this sense nonsubjective in that it is not simply an expression of some purportedly unique and original personality exercising its creativity, but the objectivity of the artwork is nevertheless mediated both by the subject who produces it and by the subject who experiences it. This is the "objective mediatedness of art through the subject," in Adorno's words.[2] It is this quality of kinship within difference between artwork and subject that makes the subject-object dialectic particularly acute in the case of the aesthetic. This is why it is crucial for Adorno to work within the subject-object paradigm rather than the paradigm of a communication between human subjects that arises after the linguistic turn in philosophy. The artwork is object rather than subject in a way that another human being can never be. And yet the subject experiences the artwork in a way that is completely different from the experience of an object that is more fully external to the self.

Adorno insists that the subject-object dialectic is a historical one. The artwork and our experience of it unfold in history. A genuine aesthetic experience must be able to grasp the specific conjunction between the aging work of art and the historical moment in which it is experienced. In this chapter, I attempt first to elucidate the structure of genuine aesthetic experience as Adorno conceives it and then to explore the complexities of its historicity, with its implications for our changing perceptions of Adorno's own work.

Aesthetic Experience as Mimesis and Self-Transcendence

When the work is recomposed by the ear in accordance with its own logic, repainted by the eye . . .

—*Adorno, "Presuppositions"*

If one reads Adorno's aesthetic works with an eye to the role of the subject in aesthetic experience, one soon sees that a particular notion of mimesis is at the core of his conception. Art itself is mimetic, and in accordance with the primacy of the object, the subject's activity in genuine aesthetic experience, following the dictates of its object, is mimetic as well. The subject mimes the object both in its mimetic activity as such and in following the dynamics of the work. "If works of art imitate nothing but themselves," Adorno says, "then the only person who can understand them is the one who imitates them" (*Aesthetic Theory*, 190/183). The idea that experience imitates or follows the tensions and motions inherent in the work of art recurs constantly in Adorno's work. His term for this form of imitation is, variously, *mitvollziehen* or *nachvollziehen* or *nachfahren*. That is, the experiencing consciousness reaccomplishes or co-enacts or follows along after the internal dynamics of the work. The term invokes musical scores, which, Adorno tells us, should be regarded as "congealed imitations of the works," but the imitation is not limited to actual performance from a score or to music alone; rather, the experience "finds its ideal form in a mute internal experience" (*Aesthetic Theory*, 190/183). This notion is so fundamental that Adorno asserts that the unity of art lies in the fact that the diverse artistic media are laws for their own imitation. The score and the work itself are both demands for mimetic experience: "Such imitation reads the coherence of meaning from the signs of works of art and follows them the same way it follows the curves in which the work of art manifests itself" (*Aesthetic Theory* 190/183).

The primacy of the object that is reflected in this mimetic activity shapes the dialectic of subjectivity and objectivity in aesthetic experience at every point. If the object is not to be dominated by preformed categories of the understanding, for instance, it must be experienced spontaneously—naively, Adorno says provocatively. "A naive stance toward art is a ferment of illusion; anyone who lacks it completely is truly narrow-minded, trapped in what is pushed on him" (*Aesthetic Theory* 401/380). At the same time, genuine aesthetic understanding *[Verstehen]*, which emerges "only in an extremely mediated way; namely, in that the substance grasped through the completed experience is reflected and named in its relationship to the material of the work and the language of its forms," requires reflection. Such reflection, however, Adorno emphasizes, is not subsumption under the categories of a dominating conceptual understanding, not "something external to the contemplation *[Anschauung]* of works of art, but rather something always already required by their contemplation and something that terminates in contemplation."[3]

The mimetic activity that moves between these poles is both passive and active, both an immersion and an active effort. As such, it is neither an activity of sensuous perception nor an activity of logical understanding but rather a kind of intermediary, quasi-sensuous and quasi-logical activity. "Art is the most drastic argument against the epistemological separation of sensuousness and understanding" (*Aesthetic Theory* 260/249).[4] In the essay "Presuppositions," Adorno describes the mimetic activity of *Nachfahren* or *Mitvollzug* in such terms: "One does not understand a work of art when one translates it into concepts . . . but rather when one is immersed in its immanent movement; I should almost say, when it is recomposed by the ear in accordance with its own logic, repainted by the eye, when the linguistic sensorium speaks along with it" (97). The experiencing subject carries out quasi-logical operations with material that is quasi-sensuous: the ear recomposes in mute immaterial experience with the logic of hearing; the eye repaints in mute immaterial experience with the logic of vision.

Similarly, countering popular anti-intellectualism and its defense of passive cultural consumption as more "feelingful," Adorno insists that genuine aesthetic experience involves a mediation of intellect and feeling:

The going notions of intellectual and feeling-toned music are a facade that must be torn down. What is called intellectual is for the most part only what demands work and effort on the part of the hearing *[Gehör]*, what demands strength of attention and memory, what demands, in fact, love; and what is called feeling is for the most part only the reflex of a passive attitude that samples music as a stimulus without having any specific, if you will, naive relationship to it, to what is concretely heard.[5]

The same imaginative movement that follows the immanent movement of the work, in other words, can be called feeling; it is a work of love. The relevant distinction, then, is not between intellect and feeling but between a loving effort to understand imaginatively and the leveling liquidation of the individual subject in passive repetition.

The correlated terms "exact imagination" and "the speculative ear," mentioned in my introduction, indicate how, for Adorno, aesthetic experience is both rigorously determined by the primacy of the object and wholly dependent on a genuine, spontaneous subjective response. The term "exact imagination" designates the experiencing subject's ability to follow the quasi-logical relationships in the artwork with accuracy and precision. "Such imagination discloses the richness of the detail on which it lingers instead of hurrying over it toward the whole" ("Beautiful Passages," 699). Grasping detail in this way conjoins authenticity of experience to the authenticity of the work itself, which can afford a glimpse of the nonidentical only by means of such details: "Details on this level of dignity are the text's seals of authenticity; one could compare them to the Name." When the details are absent, as in the case of the music of Max Reger, Adorno notes, we see how much music owes them; the "inextinguishable and unrepeatable eludes the music along with them" (700).

The capacity for such fresh "spontaneous receptivity" (a term Adorno borrows from phenomenology) must coexist with the subject's ability to move back and forth not only between the whole and the parts and between the various moments within the work but also between the work and the subjective associations that arise. Hence Adorno also speaks of a "productive" imagination[6] and uses the Kierkegaardian phrase "the speculative ear" ("Beautiful Passages," 718) to evoke the associative activity of the subject that accompanies or alternates with contemplative immersion in the details of the object. The experiencing subject fantasizes and speculates, producing associations from the subject's own experience, which are then matched against what is perceived of the object. The process is as crucial to intellectual experience as it is to aesthetic experience; in fact, Adorno expounds it in greatest detail in "Skoteinos," his essay on reading Hegel: "No one can read any more out of Hegel than he puts in. The process of understanding is a progressive self-correcting of such projections through comparison with the text. The content itself contains, as a law of its form, the expectation of productive imagination on the part of the one reading" (139). What might thus seem to be undisciplined subjectivity, the precise opposite of exact imagination, is a means to objective understanding of the work. Adorno emphasizes how necessary this aspect of aesthetic experience is: "The more the observer contributes, the greater the energy with which he penetrates into the work of art, and he gains access to objectivity. He participates in objectivity where his energies, including the energy of his deviant subjective 'projections,' are extinguished in the work of art. The subjective digression may completely miss the work of art, but without it no objectivity becomes visible" (*Aesthetic Theory* 261/250).

Subjectivity and objectivity in aesthetic experience, then, are completely interdependent. On the one hand, it is through subjectivity that objectivity is attained. On the other hand, if the subject's experience imitates the dynamics crystallized in the artwork, then subjective aesthetic experience is very much like the work of art itself (and like the activity of the maker or performer of the work as well, as Adorno points out). The subjective experience of the "receiver" of the work is subjective/personal and objective/impersonal at the same time. Adorno expresses this fusion—or perhaps better, this reversal[7]—of the poles of subjectivity and objectivity in the image of the receptive subject becoming an arena for the work of art while the work of art in turn comes alive and speaks: "The thinker does not actually think but rather makes himself into an arena for intellectual experience, without unraveling it" ("Essay as Form," 13). He also describes this process as one in which the subject enters the interior of the work of art through imitation: "If for Kant discursive knowledge was prohibited from access to the interior of things, then works of art are the objects whose truth can be conceived only as that of their interior. Imitation is the path that leads into this interior" (*Aesthetic Theory* 191/183). What Adorno describes as a contained space—an arena—is at the same time the interior of the work in which its life processes occur. What is experienced is experienced as the objective life of the internal processes in the work: "The experience of works of art is adequate only when it is alive. Aesthetic experience becomes alive in terms of the object at the moment in which works of art themselves come to life under its gaze. . . . Through contemplative immersion, the immanent processual character of the work is released. In speaking, it becomes something animated in itself" (*Aesthetic Theory* 262/252).

Genuine or adequate aesthetic experience, then, transcends itself and moves into the work of art. In coming alive, the work of art in turn becomes subject rather than object: "The linguistic character of art leads to reflection on what it is that speaks out of art; that, not the one who produces it and not the one who receives it, is actually its subject" (*Aesthetic Theory* 249/239). In this assertion about the speaking quality of the work, we see that the quasi-logical and quasi-sensuous characteristics of subjective aesthetic experience inhere equally in the artwork itself. Hence Adorno can speak of the "logicity" *[Logizität]* of the work of art. He often describes this quality in musical rather than linguistic terms—thus further emphasizing its quasi-logical nature—as when he says of Georg Trakl's poetry, which might seem to be merely a string of images, that "logical categories play into it indirectly and obscurely, like the categories of the—actually musical—rising or falling curve of the individual moments, of the distribution of values, of the relationship of characteristics like positing, continuation, conclusion" (*Aesthetic Theory* 431–32, 405).

Further, by its very nature, subjective aesthetic experience, which seems to have understanding the individual work of art as its end, extends the subject beyond itself and beyond the individual work. The dialectic of subjective aesthetic experience opens out into intersubjectivity, history, and utopia. Of the essay form, for instance, Adorno notes that, although it seems to be based on individual experience, "the relation to experience—and the essay invests experience with as much substance as traditional theory does categories—is the relationship to all of history. Merely individual experience, which consciousness takes as its point of departure, since it is what is closest to it, is itself mediated by the overarching experience of historical humankind" ("Essay as Form," 10). This mediation between the individual and the intersubjective/historical occurs in the process of associating, as the experiencing subject reaches beyond the individual work to bring to it human experience in general and the experience of other works of art as well. Although aesthetic experience is crystallized in the individual work, Adorno says, "nevertheless no experience can be isolated, none is independent of the continuity of the experiencing consciousness. . . . The continuity of aesthetic experience is colored by all other experience and all the knowledge of the one experiencing; confirmed and corrected, to be sure, only in comparison with the phenomenon" (*Aesthetic Theory* 400/379).

At the same time, when the work of art comes alive through being experienced, it alters the experiencing subject, literally shaking the subject out of its distance from the work and its contingency. Adorno refers to this shaking as "Erschütterung," which connotes being moved emotionally—perhaps to a shattering extent—as well. In the moment of *Erschütterung*, the subject experiences himself as taken beyond the limits of subjectivity:

The experiencing subject, from whom aesthetic experience moves away, returns in it as a trans-aesthetic subject. The experience of being shaken draws the distanced subject back into itself. . . . The truth of the work dawns on the viewer as the truth that ought also to be the truth about himself. The moment of this transition is the highest in art. It rescues subjectivity, even subjective aesthetics, through their negation. The subject shaken by art has real experiences; now, however, by virtue of his insight into the work of art as work of art, they are experiences in which his hardening within his own subjectivity dissolves and his self-positing becomes aware of its limitations. (*Aesthetic Theory*, 401/379–80)

In this moment, not only has the subject become the arena in which the interior of the work of art comes alive and speaks; at the same time, the subject recognizes the interior of the work of art as the interior of himself, a subjecthood that goes beyond the contingent individual subject that he is. In this moment, something that is capable of being experienced but is yet more objective and more free than the individual subject is glimpsed: "The pain experienced in view of beauty is the yearning for that which is barred to the subject by the subjective block—that which, however, he knows to be truer than he is himself. Experience that would be free of that block, but not through coercion, is practiced in the submission of the subject to the law of aesthetic form" (*Aesthetic Theory* 396/375). We see here what Adorno is striving for when he claims to be trying to use the force of the subject to dispel the illusion of constitutive subjectivity. His intuition of utopia is located precisely here, in the dialectic of subjective aesthetic experience.

Early Works and the Traces of Experience

I thought of Richard Strauss as a music loud, dangerous, extremely bright, and like industry.
—*Adorno, "Motifs"*

Once we become aware of the centrality of subjective aesthetic experience to Adorno's work, it becomes obvious that his own writings, works of critique and philosophy though they are, must have begun in, and emerged from, subjective aesthetic experience—his own, which is the experience he has reflective access to—in its ongoing dialogue, so to speak, with reflection. We see the traces of Adorno's aesthetic experience, its tracks or *Spuren*, as he would say, everywhere. In this light, the familiar statement that there is no Archimedean point from which Adorno could make his critique of civilization does not make sense. At least in the aesthetic realm, at each point his own direct subjective experience necessarily serves as the touchstone for his philosophical and critical reflections. It makes sense to assume, in fact, that all Adorno's theoretical statements about art and aesthetics and all his specific comments on individual works of music or literature are attempts to articulate that experience and to mediate it with categories from aesthetics and criticism.

The old academic convention of not speaking about oneself may limit the degree to which even the unconventional Adorno refers explicitly to his experience, but reference to it is particularly clear in some of his later essays and talks. It is as though by that point in his work both the movement between experience and reflection and its correlate, the relationship between subjective contingency and objectivity, could be taken for granted. A case in point is the radio talk "Beautiful Passages," referred to earlier. Adorno notes there that he is using passages that he personally finds beautiful. He acknowledges that his choice is contingent, in that another individual would have selected other passages: "My selection has the contingent quality of biographical destiny. It is dependent on the beautiful passages that have remained with me since my earliest musical memories. Others have loved completely different passages, and one could not dispute about which has preeminence" (700). But the selection is also objective, in that, as details, the passages attest to the beauty of the music from which they are taken. Indeed, he continues, "If I may venture a supposition, it is that from a central perspective, in music that is itself beautiful in the emphatic sense, there are in fact also innumerable beautiful passages; the only thing that is required is that one assure oneself of the beauty, that one lose oneself in the details unreservedly, in that which nothing else can substitute for" (700). If, as Adorno notes in "Beautiful Passages," in a historical period in which larger, prestructured forms have lost their validity, movement toward the whole needs to proceed from details, this means in turn that Adorno's subjective nominalism, if we may call it that—the use of individual aesthetic experience as the point of departure for the movement between reflection and further experience—has a special historical justification, which in turn makes this aspect of Adorno's work particularly relevant now.

"Beautiful Passages" shows us that when subjective aesthetic experience—which, as the reader will remember, is the work of "exact imagination," mediating between sensuousness and intellect to produce an experience that is quasi-sensuous and quasi-logical—is articulated in language, it is expressed in figurative language, in imagery. Thus, in the Bach example in "Beautiful Passages," the end of the fugue is described as "detaching itself from the objective structure and illuminating it from above." In the Beethoven example we hear "the rising of hope," and in the Schubert example a "shifting of aspects that results in a feeling of almost spatial depth." The final example, no doubt the one that inspired the whole talk, is the music that accompanies the words "Ich fühle Luft aus anderen Planeten" [I feel air from other planets] in Schoenberg's String Quartet opus 10. Here, Adorno says, we have something "unerhört," never heard before. At the last syllable of the word "Planeten," "the speculative ear has, almost physically, the feeling of having crossed abysses and reached a firm ground, light-years away and yet a place in which it arrives in utmost safety" (718). This particular imagery, that of stars and light, depths, empty spaces, and earth, is the imagery with which Adorno cites the utopian dimension throughout his work, and it signals very directly how for Adorno the possibility of utopia is grounded in this quasi-sensuous dimension of aesthetic experience.

Adorno's "Im Jeu de Paume gekritzelt" ["Notes Scribbled in the Jeu de Paume"] (1958), one of the few instances in which he writes about paintings, provides dramatic confirmation of this connection between genuine aesthetic experience and figurative language, as well as showing the transition from experience to reflection very clearly. In these notes, Adorno writes explicitly and unabashedly about his contingent subjective responses. What we see is that the less the works "speak" to him or in him, the less he uses figurative language for the experience and the more the associations that arise in his mind are the *kunstfremd,* or "art-alien," gestures of a commodity culture and its culture industry. Here, for instance, is Adorno looking at Renoir:

These late, rosy Renoirs, fruit-bodies, round to the point of unsensuousness, truly *jeunes filles en fleurs* but not Albertine—I resist them, as though they were manufactured for export, and I simply cannot put them together with the genial landscapes, figure groupings, and portraits from his earlier period. Are they the autonomous painterly consequence of the feeling for the vegetative that Samuel Beckett considered central to Proust and that may define the unity of Jugendstil and Impressionism—or are they truly witnesses to the loss of tension in a form of painting at the moment in which it achieves success? . . . I don't know; if it were music I would know.[8]

Adorno's reflections involve posing alternative possibilities. His resistance to these late Renoirs is his point of departure, but it may not persist; there may be an autonomous aesthetic development here that he simply has not yet grasped. But since in any case the present aesthetic experience is not a successful one—he does not like these paintings—it is not described in the quasi-sensuous figurative language we saw in "Beautiful Passages" but rather in negatives ("unsensuousness" and "not Albertine") and in references to the commodity sphere ("manufactured for export").

In another piece from "Notes Scribbled in the Jeu de Paume," in contrast, where Adorno is more certain of his negative aesthetic judgment, the moment of aesthetic failure is articulated directly through reference to a phenomenon of bourgeois culture. The passage in question deals with Toulouse-Lautrec:

> I tried to figure out why I cannot really get into contact with the indescribably virtuoso and original painting of Toulouse-Lautrec. His specific talent, presumably, is the cause: that verve and dash that for me is fatally reminiscent of what in music we call "musikantisch," musician-like. It is the quick painterly eye that through its affinity with things announces its affinity with the world, awaiting the "aha" response: we should have seen it like that long ago. One imagines a father who with the inexperienced sovereign gesture of the expert points to a poster like these and says, "Now, that man knows what he's doing." (45–46)

Here the word "fatal" signals that the experience is not a genuine one and the work has not come alive and begun speaking. If the work that is genuinely experienced speaks in figurative language, the work that cannot be experienced because it was never subject, never spirit, elicits clichés.

Adorno tells us that the passages discussed in "Beautiful Passages" had "remained with [him] since [his] earliest musical memories." Although the examples we have just seen are from Adorno's later work, this evocation of childhood memory signals that the quasi-sensuous and figurative moment plays an even more prominent role at earlier stages in the developmental trajectory of subjective aesthetic experience. This trajectory is beautifully illustrated in a short early piece, written in 1929, on Adorno's childhood experience of Richard Strauss's music. Adorno describes the aura that the name of the composer Richard Strauss had for him as a child, when, as he puts it, he knew Strauss's music only by hearsay and not by hearing:

> I thought of Richard Strauss as a music loud, dangerous, extremely bright, and like industry—or, as I thought of it at the time, factories; it was the child's images of modernity that the name set off. . . . More than anything else it was the word "Elektra" that fed my imagination. This

word was turbulent and artificial, full of attractive evil smells like a great chemical plant in my city with a name that sounded very similar; an electrical set of gears that gleamed and emanated chlorine and that only adults were allowed to set foot in—luminous, mechanical, and unhealthy.[9]

When he actually heard Strauss's music for the first time, as an adolescent, Adorno reports, he was concerned only with identifying the instruments used. It was only later and with further experience that he realized that his original fantasies about the music were far more adequate to it than the instrumental analysis he attempted then. This observation is the springboard for his comment on the developmental trajectory of subjective aesthetic experience:

Thus it may be that the latent content of art communicates itself only in the aura into which one stumbles when one comes into contact with the work when one is unfamiliar with it, whereas in the dense core of its form it is too encapsulated to become apparent to us until the form has disintegrated; that aura, however, takes form in a radiant emission; it hovers before us as the sign of the material stuff that our eye may be able to partake of in fluid particles but not in a dense mass; it dies out and finally blazes up again when we see through the work and its form. ("Motifs," 35)

This image anticipates those in which Adorno will articulate his understanding of the aging of works of art and the historical moment in our understanding of them. At the same time, like the link we have seen between beautiful figurative language and genuine aesthetic experience, it indicates why the layer of figurative language remains so important in all of Adorno's own writings; it marks the layer of aesthetic experience on which they are founded.

Adorno's early writings in general have something in common with that childhood grasp of the aura. They transmit the essence they perceive in figurative language without detailed analysis of the works themselves. In a sense, they themselves are quasi-logical, quasi-sensuous structures of metaphor and association. They display, as Adorno says in his preface to *Moments Musicaux,* in which a number of his early essays on music are reprinted, the "breakthrough force" *[Durchschlagskraft]* of initial formulation, but at the same time they are "schlecht abstrakt" abstract in the bad sense, as Hegel says,[10] in that they have not yet been extended into analysis of details; the movement from experience to reflection and back is incomplete.

A short piece on Chopin, which also dates from 1929, when Adorno was in his mid-twenties, offers an almost paradigmatic example of this feature of Adorno's early style. It locates Chopin within the context of the nineteenth-century problematic of achieving a relationship between the whole and the parts once an autonomous bourgeois subjectivity has arisen. Chopin, Adorno says,

> handles the contradiction [between parts and whole] by setting himself outside the compositorial flux, as it were, and directing it from the outside. He does not construct form autocratically; he does not let it disintegrate before the assault of his themes. Rather, he guides the themes through time. The aristocratic nature of his music may have its basis in the melancholy chivalry of his formative mode, in which subjectivity renounces full ascendancy, rather than in the psychological tone. With eyes shut, like a bride, the objective theme is led in safety through the dark woods of the self, through the stream of onrushing feeling. ("Motifs," 17)

Here the aura of Chopin's music is expressed in the image of chivalry, which is the crystallizing force in this short piece. What will remain with the reader is not any detailed analysis of individual works, for there is none, nor any technical musical explanation of what Adorno means by his imagery, but the association of Chopin's aristocratic melancholy with the image of the knight leading the lady through the dark woods. The image, however, though subjective in the sense that it arises from Adorno's associations and his experience of Chopin's music, and though romantic in being drawn from the image stock of the romantic era, is neither organic nor psychological. Not only does Adorno explicitly state that the melancholy is a matter of form rather than expression, not only does he portray feeling as a danger in Chopin's music, but the image itself is a kind of baroque conceit complete with props, in keeping with the baroque topos of melancholy. It is only the mention of the lady's closed eyes that endows the image with a note of utopian gentleness.

The Inorganic Aging of the Work of Art

What I have just said about a developmental trajectory of subjective aesthetic experience points to the much larger issue of the historical trajectory of subjectivity in art. For if Adorno's aesthetics are grounded in his subjective aesthetic experience, that experience registers its shifting reception of older works in comparison with its experience of contemporary works, and it is in constant dialogue with his historico-philosophical perspective on the historical dynamics of modern Western European civilization.[11] On this basis, Adorno attempts to articulate a self-reflective perspective on the historical trajectory of subjectivity in art, which will include the perspective of the maker of art as well as that of the receiver of art and that of the subjectivity embodied within the work of art itself—all of which, as we have seen, are in some respects homologous for Adorno. I will sketch some key features of this perspective, relying again primarily on Adorno's writings on music.

The situation in which Adorno began to articulate this perspective, around 1930, provided him with a powerful experiential standpoint for reflecting on these issues. He had a deep familiarity with nineteenth-century European music but was also inti-mately acquainted, from the composer's, the performer's, and the listener's point of view, with the music of Schoenberg and the Vienna School at a time when its revolutionary character had been consolidated into a distinct development but it had not become a cultural commodity; and he had a strong basis in philosophy and social criticism to bring to bear on his musical experience. This is the experiential basis on which Adorno attempts to articulate the historical trajectory of subjectivity in art. His project involves several interrelated theoretical intentions. It attempts to extricate conceptions of greatness and historical progress in art from bourgeois notions of progress, on the one hand, and the ahistorical immortality of great works, on the other. And it attempts to extricate subjectivity from organicist, expressivist, and biographical notions that focus on the creator's inspiration and expression, on the one hand, and the fiction of the work as a harmonious organic totality, on the other. For the aesthetics of organicism and expression are contrary to Adorno's experience of the fate of works of art over time: what happens to older works in experience is not what one might expect to happen to something organic or to something that is a pure expression of the psyche. Organicism also runs contrary to Adorno's experience of the music of his own time, which is moving away from the illusion of a harmonious totality and toward the difficult enterprise of structuring intelligibility without the support of the conventions of tonality. At the same time, Adorno attempts to keep his perspective grounded in the dialectic of subjectivity, including the genuine and living subjective experience of both older and newer works, and the factors that make such experience difficult to achieve, and objectivity, which itself includes historical and technical moments.

Adorno is attempting, one might say, to create a theory of "musical materialism" (a phrase he uses in one of his 1929 essays) or musical enlightenment (see "Reaction and Progress," from 1930)[12] and a criticism based on it. In these terms, individual works of art do not constitute a continuum of progress in which later works are better than earlier ones, nor do historical and technical developments in art determine the nature of the works of art produced. But—this is the thesis of the essay "Reaction and Progress"—in terms of the composer's subjective freedom and expression, the composer is indeed constrained by history to deal with the most advanced musical material available. The "musical material" does not mean the state of musical technology, although that is not irrelevant to it, but rather what has already been created for musical experience that is not yet eroded. In other words, it is what most provides the experience of increasing freedom, openness, newness—what most demythologizes musical conventions that were formally accepted without question.[13] The composer is not free to ignore this state of the musical material if his music is to be authentic; he is constrained to deal with it. But he is constrained to deal with it in freedom and not by conforming to a currently accepted "style"; in other words, he is constrained to deal with it concretely and not abstractly. "Reaction," in these terms, would mean attempting to arbitrarily return to some earlier or allegedly primordial state of the musical material.

The early musical essays in which Adorno lays out his conception of the historical trajectory of subjectivity in art are indeed, as he called them, "schlecht abstrakt"—abstract in the bad sense, as in the abstract transfer of constructs from dialectical materialism to music in "Reaction and Progress"—and they are often apodictic in tone. They are also abstract in being composed of associative linkages of imagery expressed in figurative language without immanent analysis of musical works. But the imagery Adorno uses has a great deal of evocative power and recurs throughout his later work in connection with these ideas. It is as though here, in these early essays, he intuitively grasped the "aura" of his theory of the historical trajectory of subjectivity in art, and he set it down in images whose content he could elaborate at length in the following decades. This imagery, in other words, contains the experience which will be increasingly mediated with theory and further experience.

In these early essays, we find images of the work of art and the way its contents, including subjectivity, figure in it, as well as images of the work of art as it appears to the listener in historical perspective. These are images of matter and energy that might seem susceptible of interpretation in organic terms but that quickly reveal their inorganic—materialist—qualities: we are dealing with bodies and landscapes of stone and crystal, starlight and voids, and constellations. In the piece on Richard Strauss, for instance, although Adorno is talking about a childhood experience, he is specifically concerned to counter a psychologistic or organicist conception of aesthetic experience and the work of art in history. This concern is reflected in the imagery of his experience of Strauss, which though specific to Strauss's music is also consonant with Adorno's conception of the work of art as more artifact than organism. The light and energy that the child perceived as the essence of Strauss's music is a chemical and technological light, a light that is emphatically not organic. And the "body" of the music, as opposed to its immaterial aura, in Adorno's description is more like the nucleus of an atom that disintegrates and becomes transparent than it is like an organic body. The contrast between the "fluid particles" of the aura that one perceives at first contact and the dense core that disintegrates later suggests the history of physics and chemistry more than it does the natural life cycle of a living being.

Perhaps Adorno's most fundamental image for the work of art, considered in terms of its inorganic historical trajectory, is that of the work of art as a container into which certain contents, *Gehalte,* have been sunk or embedded. Although the work may have originally seemed to form a unity with itself and with those contents—a closed unity with a unified surface, a solid mass, as it were—in the course of history, which changes the meaning of the contents and our relation to them, the work disintegrates. The unity of the surface is seen to be illusory, as is the unity of form and content. The contents come to the surface, are exposed, and depart, becoming external to the work and rendering interpretation problematic:

The contents which interpretation tries to grasp have changed completely in reality and thereby in the works as well, which stand within history and participate in real history. History has uncovered and made evident the original contents within the works; they are visible solely by virtue of the disintegration of their gestalt-like unity in the form of the work, and it was only the closed unity of the two that provided the space for adequate interpretation. Today interpretation wanders around lost among the fragments. It can recognize the contents, to be sure, but it cannot draw them back into the material from which history has dislodged them.[14]

In this process in which the contents of the work become externalized, different layers appear at different historical points. There is, however, no "work in itself" that remains when this process is complete. When all the contents have departed, Adorno says, the work is dead.

The disintegration of the work and the departure of its contents are also and especially an externalization of the subjectivity that was contained in the work. The work of art, which in the nineteenth century seemed the epitome of subjective creation, becomes objective. Our own subjectivity too, the subjectivity of those experiencing the work in the present, moves outside it, so that we no longer regard a work of art from the inside, as though it were a safe, secure house in which we lived. This affects earlier works:

The decline of musical subjectivism is, historically, such that the subjective component disappears in works that were originally constructed subjectively. In actuality there is no purely subjective music, and behind the subjective dynamics there have only been long forgotten and menacing objective qualities hiding, which are now finally breaking through. For the disintegration of works is the disintegration especially of their inwardness. The contents that depart are above all the personal contents and with them the constitutive subjective contents, those which are structurally removed from the vicissitudes of private psychological subjectivity. ("Night Music," 65)

What we are left with when both the subjective contents and we ourselves as experiencing subjects move outside the work is a mute, inorganic form, a form of contours and lines. This means, on the one hand, that the work becomes enigmatic and uninterpretable; it no longer speaks to us. The only thing we can do with Bach's preludes and fugues, for instance, is to "trace the enigmatically muted contours of their form" ("Night Music," 59).

This externalization opens up certain possibilities, however, as Adorno suggests in some developments of this image of fragmentation and mute contours. A constructivist subjectivity that reexamines the work from the outside may discern new configurations in the shrunken and fragmented work. This is how Adorno explains the tendency to play older musical works faster over time. What is no longer progressive in content no longer needs as much time to be heard; it cannot be lingered over. Instead, a constructivist interpretation can bring the parts, now particles, together to let a composed—certainly not an organic—whole emerge for the listener: "The true meaning of the currently inevitable hastening of tempo may be in reproducing the unity of the work, lost as an organic unity, constructively, as the dissociated parts in the disintegrated work of art move closer together and seek refuge with one another."[15]

If there is no such thing as a work of art in itself, outside of history and immortal the way the system of bourgeois cultural prestige would have it, neither can there be any one ahistorical, "authentic" interpretation of the work. (Similarly, the genuine or authentic aesthetic experience Adorno speaks of is presumably subject to historical transformation.) It is the kind of constructivist interpretation described earlier that has contemporary relevance. Such interpretation, Adorno argues, is more faithful to the aging work than any "original" interpretation the work was given when it was first created. The constructivist interpretation demands a close and careful reading of the work, for the disintegrating work does not simply become passive and impotent, subject to arbitrary interpretation. Rather, specific historical changes in the work orient interpretation:

Knowledge of an interpretation of the work that would have contemporary relevance is rigorously negotiated between the text and history. To interpret a work with contemporary relevance, that is, in accordance with the objectively current status of truth in it, to interpret a work more adequately and more correctly, always also means to interpret it more faithfully, to read it better. History causes latent contents in the work to come to the surface, contents that have been put there objectively rather than subjectively, and the guarantor of their objectivity is the gaze that looks more closely at the text and becomes aware of features in it that were previously hidden in the work and lay scattered about and that now present themselves in the text—that can present themselves, to be sure, only at their appointed historical moment. ("New Tempos," 75)

Or, in a variation of this idea, as the internal contents and the formerly internalized experiencing subjectivity move outside the work so that its "true outside is restored," subjectivity can illuminate these enigmatic muted contours so that they form a constellation that hints at truth: "No work is inside truth, and the disintegrating work is far removed from it. But the contents that were previously embedded in the work now illuminate it brightly from the outside, and in their light the external lineaments compose themselves to become figures that may be the ciphers of truth" ("Night Music," 66). Here the faint possibility of salvaging the work's link to a longer-lived truth appears. This inorganic imagery, which is specifically designed to evoke materiality and to represent the dialectic of subjective inwardness and material exteriorization, has a face that is strikingly dynamic. The dynamic quality, however, is that of unfolding and shifting perspectives rather than that of an amorphous flux. Indeed, there is nothing amorphous whatsoever about this portrayal of the work's historical trajectory, and the image of the constellation reflects that: though the creature of the perceiver's standpoint and interpretation, a constellation is also composed of long-lived inorganic bodies.

In Adorno's 1928 essay on Schubert, which he says was his first attempt at extended musical analysis, we can see this imagery used to interpret a composer's oeuvre. Schubert, whose lyrical work with its preoccupation with death, standing at the beginning of the romantic period in music, has been particularly subject to psychological and biographical interpretation, poses an important test case for Adorno's antiorganicist and antipsychologizing musical hermeneutics. And indeed Adorno makes the connection between death and the inorganic the crux of the analysis he embeds in his imagery. This shift from associating death with organic mortality to associating it with an inorganic imagery is announced in the startling epigraph from Louis Aragon: "The whole useless body was invaded by transparency. Little by little the body turned to light. The blood shone. The limbs, in an incomprehensible gesture, became rigid. And the person was no longer anything but a sign among the constellations."[16] Further countering a conception of Schubert's work as the expression of personal feelings about death, Adorno describes the work as a landscape, a material configuration. Using the imagery of Schubert's texts, "Die Winterreise" in particular, he describes the music as a landscape not of flowers but of death, a landscape of ice, snow, and crystals. Even if we think of Schubert's music as "grown" rather than "made," he says, its growth is "not vegetable but crystalline" (23). What seems to be organic form is a thin illusory layer covering a "second form," which is crystalline. And the earth that appears in Schubert's work is not earthy but rather an underworld: "Nature here is not the sensuous object of internal human nature-feeling; rather, the images of nature are likenesses of the chthonic depth-space itself, and no more adequate to it than the poetic word" (31–32).

Formally speaking, Schubert's work is characterized by a lack of thematic development that differentiates it strikingly from Beethoven's. Short phrases are even repeated literally. Adorno links this, on the one hand, to the endless cyclic repetitiveness of the wanderer's wanderings and, on the other, to the repetitions in the crystalline layer. This objective death layer in Schubert's work is a particular stance toward history, a negation of history, and it allows one to see why Schubert's music would be so readily incorporated by the culture industry; it is already clearly akin to the culture industry's nineteenth-century precursors, the potpourri and the miniature landscape. At the same time, particles—here crystals or cells—can be assembled into figures, and Adorno draws on this aspect of his image in explaining the role of subjective feeling in the creation of the work's truth content. Subjectivity is portrayed as a means to produce objectivity in the work rather than something that enters directly into the work as expression:

The lyric contents [of Schubert's landscape] are not produced: they are the smallest cells of existing objectivity, as the image of which they stand, after the great objective forms with their authoritarian legitimacy have long since gone to ruin. These images do not fall into the soul of the lyrically open person like rays of light into vegetation: in no respect are works of art creatures. Rather, they are "hit" by the person like targets in a shooting gallery. If one hits the right number, they reverse themselves and let something real shine through. The force that hits them is human, not artistic: it is human feeling that moves it. This is the only way to understand the null point between subjectivity and objectivity in the lyric work. The lyricist does not depict his feeling in the work directly; rather, his feeling is the means by which to draw truth in its incomparably tiny crystallizations into the work. (20)

This small-scale form, with its rejection of the great architectonic forms, can be both the vehicle of an infernal depravation into sentimentality and the vehicle of a transcendence of nature in an image of reconciled intimacy. In the latter case, the music becomes the vehicle of an enigmatic *Erschütterung:* "We weep without knowing why; because we are not as the music promises we could be, and in the unnamed happiness that it only needs to be the way it is to assure us that we will be that way someday. We cannot read them, but it holds up before the flooded and reeling eye the figures of ultimate reconciliation" (36). If Schubert's music remains alive for us, it is because it has already incorporated death, like a poison, and has not needed to go through a period of historical decay; "in its origins it is already the inorganic, discontinuous, fragmented life of stones, and death is too deeply embedded in it for it to have to fear death" (25).

Late Works and Difficult Experience

For Adorno, Schubert's music was inorganic from the beginning. But works may also prove to have a long afterlife because a long historical trajectory is contained within them, or because the composer has traversed a long historical trajectory within the course of his oeuvre. The notion of a composer's "late works" or "late style" is important in this regard. The late style of Beethoven—for whom "late style" has become a topos of criticism—is particularly important, given that for Adorno Beethoven is the paradigmatic composer of the autonomous, bourgeois compositorial subjectivity that established the terms of nineteenth-century music, which endured until the demise of tonality with Schoenberg. Hence, Adorno's early essay on Beethoven's late style ("Beethoven's Late Style," 1934) is an important statement on the historical fate of subjectivity in music. In it we find the same images and the same concern with countering an organic or psychologistic portrayal of the relationship between the subjectivity and the objectivity of the work: "The ripeness of the late works of significant artists does not resemble that of fruits. They are generally not round but furrowed, or even ripped to shreds; they tend to be devoid of sweetness" (13). These images are now, however, set in a developmental context.

Here, too, the issue is death and mortality. The popular view holds that in Beethoven's late style we see subjectivity given free rein to ignore form and contemplate death, fate, and mortality. But for Adorno, mortality is part of human beings' life as natural creatures, and it cannot enter into the inorganic work of art as such. Hence, although what we see in Beethoven's late style is indeed a response to human mortality, it is not an expression of subjective feeling about impending death. Rather, what we in fact see in the music is the return of musical conventions, such as the extensive trills in the late piano sonatas, now untampered with by the compositorial subjectivity that subordinated all elements of musical form to itself in the middle-period works. Adorno's interpretation of Beethoven's late style turns on this return of conventions: "The relationship of the conventions to subjectivity must itself be understood as the formal law that gives rise to the substance of the late works" (15). This relationship is once more expressed in terms of the imagery of a landscape, in this case a landscape from which subjectivity is in the act of departing. This is a landscape of catastrophe, a landscape strewn with ruins, petrified, with vast fissures and holes, illuminated by fiery flashes of lightning—in short, another version of the idea of the external contours of the work being illuminated from the outside by the subjective contents that have left it; "objective is the fragmented landscape, subjective is the light in which alone it glows" (17). In this case, however, we can almost hear the explosive force with which subjectivity, knowing itself mortal and at the end of human life, leaves the work. If "late works are the catastrophes in the history of art," Adorno says, this is because

the force of subjectivity in late works of art is the abrupt gesture with which it leaves the works. It explodes them, not to express itself but to throw off—without expression—the semblance of art. It leaves behind the ruins of the works and communicates itself as with ciphers, only by means of the empty spaces through which it breaks out. Touched by death, the master hand lets go of the masses of material that it hitherto formed; the gaps and fissures in them, evidence of the ultimate impotence of the self in the face of what exists, are its last work. (16)

The ruins and fragments left behind take on an expressive quality, not of subjectivity but of the "mythic nature of the creature and its fall," portrayed emblematically by the conventions in the illumination of the departing subjectivity. Here, too, the work becomes a figure. If the trills are placed as petrified monuments to what has been, the caesuras, the most characteristic moments in the late Beethoven, are the points at which subjectivity departs and the work falls silent. The next fragment then appears, to be linked to the one before: "The mystery lies between them, and it cannot be conjured up except in the figure they form together"

(17). Beethoven, in other words, has already incorporated within the trajectory of his own oeuvre the historical stages to come: the departure of subjectivity, the petrification and silence of the work, its return to mute emblematic images, the configurations into which, with the help of an interpretive subjectivity, it may enter.[17]

These conceptions of the historical trajectory of subjectivity pose certain difficulties for the mimetic activity of "following along," discussed earlier. How does subjective experience, with its moment of naïveté, grasp a work from which subjectivity has departed in the course of its historical unfolding, or a late work blasted by the departure of subjectivity, or indeed a contemporary work in which the composer is struggling with the most highly developed state of the musical material? How can the listeners' associations bring the continuity of humankind's historical experience to bear on the experience of a music whose aging process is precisely one of disintegration?

The early essays we have just looked at suggest a partial answer to such questions: the receiving subjectivity in the present reconstructs—reconfigures—a constructed totality from the mute fragments that the work has become in the course of history. In this context, it is interesting to note that although the material on the nature of genuine aesthetic experience presented earlier stems primarily from writings of the late 1950s and 1960s—from Adorno's later work, in other words—Adorno also indicated that most of what he ever wrote about music was already conceived in his youth, prior to 1933 (*Moments Musicaux,* 7). His emphasis on, and dialectical conception of, genuine aesthetic experience seems to have emerged through and in the course of his lifetime of working out what he early grasped in "auratic" form.

In writings from the last decade of his life, Adorno combines his insistence on the necessity of genuine aesthetic experience with an attempt to articulate the difficulties such experience faces given the historical trajectory of subjectivity and art. Thus, in that last decade, we see a number of essays devoted explicitly to the question of aesthetic understanding and to problems that arise for aesthetic understanding in the contemporary period. Examples are the essay "Skoteinos" (1963), a kind of prolegomenon to reading Hegel; the essay "Presuppositions" (1960), occasioned by the reading of a contemporary literary work that resists understanding; and "Alienated Masterwork" (1959), an essay on the difficulties of understanding Beethoven's *Missa Solemnis*.[18] In all of these pieces, Adorno uses his own experience and his own difficulties as the basis for his exposition. As he says in another essay of the same period, "Vers une musique informelle" (1961), someone of an older generation cannot either claim that advances ended with the avant-garde of his youth and one should not go beyond that, or that whatever is new is thereby also advanced and good; rather, one needs both to look to one's experience of contemporary works *and* to articulate the difficulties experience faces.

Particularly important in this regard is a pair of essays from 1964 and 1966 respectively on the difficulties in composing and in grasping contemporary music.[19] They demonstrate how much Adorno's writing has changed to accommodate uncertainty and at the same time how well suited his original conceptions are to deal with the contemporary situation. From the perspective of the mid-1960s, with the musical landscape occupied by serial music and its descendants on one side, aleatory music on another, and some emerging form of "aserial," or, in Adorno's term, "informal" music, which hopes to compose works that are free rather than presystematized in every aspect, on yet another, it is clear that the situation of music has become even more difficult than in the period around 1930. Although traditional ("classical") music has been adopted by the system of cultural prestige, it has in many respects not been genuinely understood; at the same time, contemporary music, which abandoned tonality with the early Schoenberg and continues to leave it behind in more and more ways, has lost its audience and its social place. In retrospect, Adorno says, one sees how much staying power the system of tonality in the broad sense of major and minor has, how much it still maintains its dominance for listeners. The loss of tonality is equivalent to the loss of a musical language. One sees now how tonality, though itself a historical phenomenon, has provided, probably for much longer than musicology has tended to think, a set of forms within which the composer can generate particular details. Without such a set of forms, music must be both completely individually formed at every point and completely internally coherent, since there is no preestablished language to provide the coherence.

The loss of the language of tonality creates a very difficult situation for the composer. Authentic achievement depends on the composer's subjectivity being—unconsciously—in tune with the most advanced possibilities that history presents through the process of grappling with the available musical material. Without the support provided through convention and tonality, this requires tremendous concentration. The degree to which such concentration becomes increasingly burdensome becomes apparent when we listen to the music of Mozart and Beethoven and hear in retrospect how much schematic support tonality provided them. In this situation, the subjective consciousness of the contemporary composer cries out for relief from the tremendous burden of being alone and unsupported in the task of grappling with the historical situation. In support of this notion of the overwhelming burden of authentic composition for the contemporary composer, Adorno cites Webern's very short pieces and

Berg's very limited output, as well as Schoenberg's long silence after the intense short period in which he composed the *Erwartung*. In this light, systematization and rationalization along the lines of serial music become a form of relief for the composer, as does aleatory music with its randomization. In both cases, the moment of subjective grappling with the material is liquidated, which achieves the same result as the assimilation of the dead totemic "classics" to the prestige circuits or the culture industry. Music becomes what Adorno calls *ichfremd*—"ego-alien." But given that the compositorial subject must still have some intention of creating something coherent, even if it is the coherence of fragments, something that the responding subject in turn can "follow along" with, it is not clear what is possible:

Today music sees itself faced with the alternative between the fetishization of material and technique on the one hand and unrestrained contingency on the other. I am reminded of a maxim of Christian Dietrich Grabbe's that once made a big impression on me: "For nothing but desperation can save us." Everything depends *quand même* on spontaneity, that is, the involuntary response of the compositorial ear. But if one takes composition deadly seriously, one must ultimately ask whether it is not as such becoming ideological today. Hence, unmetaphorically and without the consoling idea that things could not possibly stay like this, one must now face the possibility of becoming silent. ("Difficulties," 273)

This should be taken not as a pronouncement of doom but as a statement of uncertainty and an attempt to articulate the difficulty of the situation.

Similarly, the listener, who must be able to follow the particular in its quasi-logical relationship to the whole at any point, likewise without the support of tonality, must have a degree of concentration that will be as overwhelming a burden on him as it is on the composer. There is no longer any preestablished harmony between the general and the particular such as tonality once afforded: "The perceiving ear, attuned to that harmony, feels itself overwhelmed when it has to follow unaided the specific processes in the individual composition in which the relationship of the general and the particular is articulated at any particular point" ("Difficulties," 283). This demand for increased concentration comes at a point and in a cultural system in which there is an increasing demand for sameness and repetition and a correlated hatred of otherness and difference. In this context, Adorno notes that the demand for "feeling" in music, which he sees as, in reality, a demand not for feeling but for sameness, is a version of the anti-intellectual *ressentiment* that is both the expression of the individual's leveling and a response to the individual's being overwhelmed. In this situation, then, as the demands and difficulties entailed by enlightenment in the sense of increasing freedom from convention and the past become apparent, there is an increasing temptation to regress and to retreat to some kind of apparent security.

If "Difficulties" and, similarly if perhaps more optimistically, "Vers une musique informelle" lay out the options and the problems for contemporary music, then "Alienated Masterwork," on Beethoven's *Missa Solemnis,* shows us some of the retroactive force that this situation has on our perception of works of the past. Adorno's inability to achieve a genuine aesthetic contact with this work, despite Beethoven's statements about its importance, was the sticking point, he tells us, in the project of a philosophical treatment of Beethoven that he had planned since 1937.[20] But in fact the attempt to articulate the difficulties of understanding the *Missa* leads him to note some resemblances between the *Missa* and the informal music he saw emerging in the late 1950s, and he finds himself in the same position of uncertainty regarding both.

In the *Missa Solemnis,* Adorno confronts a work that has been canonized in such a way that not only is it not understood, but even the fact that it is not understood is obscured. To even attempt to contemplate the work, it is necessary to alienate it from the sphere of official culture that has appropriated it; hence the title of the essay, "Alienated Masterwork." Adorno attempts to describe the particular quality of the *Missa* that makes it repel understanding: for the most part, it is not even recognizably by Beethoven; it certainly does not share the secure religious objectivity of Bach; instead, it has an archaic, almost medieval quality, distanced both from expression and from subjective dynamics. Nor can it be seen as an expression of some broader kind of religiosity; rather, it is enigmatic yet conveys a sense of leveling:

Whereas in other places the category of totality, which is definitely predominant throughout Beethoven's work, results from the autonomous movement of the individual moments, in the *Missa* it is maintained only at the price of a kind of leveling: the ubiquitous stylistic principle no longer tolerates anything truly particular and sloughs off individual features to the point of seeming academic; these motifs and themes make do without the power of the Name. (180)

The fate of subjectivity in the *Missa,* Adorno says, differs from its fate in others of Beethoven's late works. Whereas both the *Missa* and the late quartets refrain from a false reconciliation of subjectivity and objectivity, the *Missa* does so by barring subjectivity's access to the work altogether. The individual psyche seems to submit to a kind of voluntary subordination: "Pseudomorphosis to alienated form, which is one and the same as the expression of alienation itself, is to achieve something that could not be achieved otherwise. Beethoven experiments with a bound style because formal bourgeois freedom as a stylistic principle is inadequate" (184). This is deliberate archaism, which Adorno interprets as a deliberate sacrifice to the future. Whether it is successful is not clear, but he notes that, given that development as a compositorial principle has come to an end, one can now see a resemblance between the *Missa* and contemporary music with its layering of sections and its articulation of "fields" and the resulting difficulty in achieving an integral coherence of the whole.

Here, as in some of the other essays of this period, we see Adorno deliberately and explicitly pushing against the boundaries of his own understanding and his ability to conceptualize. Perhaps the *Missa* has deliberately incorporated a kind of poison, both as a sacrifice and as an attempt to survive. Perhaps this is a sign of its objective impotence: the "impotence not of the most powerful of composers as much as of a historical situation of the spirit in which it can not yet, or can no longer, say what it is attempting to say" (182). Earlier works, with the explosive power of the breakthrough, may be greater by virtue of that power. But that does not mean that one can simply return to them and take up where they left off. They, too, are heard differently in the light of the contemporary situation.

I do not want to leave the topic of late works without broaching the subject of the difficulties of *Aesthetic Theory*. Certainly *Aesthetic Theory* is a work of Adorno's own late style. In contrast to the vivid figurative language of his early essays and the highly polished dialectical constellations of his "middle period" essays (which Adorno continued to write on into the 1960s), and also in contrast to the sometimes more informal and more personal essays of his last decade, *Aesthetic Theory* offers a more fieldlike presentation in which the figurative language has virtually disappeared and been replaced by a flatter, almost compendium-like dialectic without detail, in which one idea shifts into the next virtually without boundaries.

There is little in *Aesthetic Theory* that is new within the totality of Adorno's work, but it seems as though the historical forces that are shifting the relationship between the whole and the parts—

forces making for a "late" situation in general—are making themselves felt in the form of his work. Adorno said that *Aesthetic Theory* had to be written differently from any of his other works, "concentrically, as it were, in paratactic parts of equal weight arranged around a central point that they express through their constellation" (*Aesthetic Theory* 541/497). If the ideas seem more plain and blunt, a little eroded, they also seem more utterly interconnected, and the whole more total but less articulated in its structure. In his essay on the last scene of Goethe's late work *Faust* II, Adorno comments that the "forced" elements in Goethe's late style, including the archaisms and the apparent clichés, are the "scars poetic language acquired in defending itself against communicative language."[21] As with the developments he discusses in "Vers une musique informelle," the impersonal and fieldlike quality of *Aesthetic Theory* may reflect Adorno's attempt to accommodate to and survive the forces of leveling, in the hope that the invisible constellation at the center will be visible from another vantage point.

If in earlier years what we valued in Adorno was the nonreductionist connections he made between works of art and historical-cultural dynamics on the one hand, and his analysis of the culture industry and the administered world on the other, what now emerges as most salient is the added and mediating dimension of subjective experience in its historical transformations and its complex relationship to the shifting reception of works in history. Adorno insists on the subject and on living, current subjective experience as the fulcrum of any cultural analysis, recognizing at the same time that this experience in both its content and its form is subject to historical transformations that in turn cannot be grasped without reference to subjective experience. He insists that we examine the problems and difficulties entailed by this reference to indispensable subjective experience, and that the necessary activity of reflecting on our own presuppositions and pushing the limits of our understanding requires in turn a continual reference to changing experience. Adorno insists that living experience be distinguished from the abstract and repetitive, reified schemas of pseudoexperience offered by any dimension of culture, including the system of cultural prestige, and that to be genuine, experience must be accurate, achieved through contact with the object in its current state of historical unfolding. And finally, Adorno insists that, like the artist, our cultural criticism—of whatever cultural phenomenon—must be situated, not in being predetermined by our situation but in proceeding on the basis of experiential struggle with the "most advanced state of the material" of culture, which includes the unfolding and not yet comprehended dimensions of older works and the possibilities for increased freedom that become visible in their light. Among these older works are now Adorno's own.

Coda: Person and Spirit, Star, Fame and Name

The concept of personality cannot be saved. In the age of its liquidation, however, something in it should be preserved: the strength of the individual not to entrust himself blindly to what washes over him, nor to blindly level himself to it. . . . Only if the individual incorporates objectivity within himself and in a certain sense, namely consciously, adapts to it, can the individual develop resistance to it.

—*Adorno, "Gloss on Personality"*

Just as Adorno presents us with a picture of the historical fate of subjectivity in works of art, so he presents us with a picture of the historical fate of the individual person. If the bourgeois system of cultural prestige propagates the illusion of an untouched immortality for works of art, it does the same for individuals, the converse being the glitter of a fadlike cult of personality in the present. But just as the dialectic of subjectivity and objectivity in works of art does not exclude the role of individual subjective awareness, so the dialectic of subjectivity and objectivity in the individual person does not exclude individuality. If Adorno attacked the cult of personality, he also fought the liquidation of the individual. Here again, what is crucial is that the mortal human being—who is not art, not objective, not immortal—become an arena for the "life," in that other sense, of what Adorno, following Hegel, calls "spirit," *Geist*. As with subjective aesthetic experience, within that arena, individual awareness or experience is, as it were, the transforming point or process through which mortal humanity and spirit are mediated. Since part of the problem with Adorno's continuing reception is in fact the glitter and prestige that accumulated around him and other figures associated with the Frankfurt School, such as Walter Benjamin, perhaps a sketch of this dialectic of private individual and objective spirit will help us see another layer of Adorno's work that we can use in the current period.

The person becomes spirit by abandoning the self to what is not self. This is the process of *Entäusserung* or externalization, which is also a process of alienation or divestiture of the self; it is perhaps the key concept in Adorno's dialectic of the person and personality. We see it in his defense of Thomas Mann and Hegel against the notion that they were "solid citizens," archetypical bourgeois individuals. What we see in them is in fact, Adorno says, a lack of narcissism, a flexibility in the boundaries of the self that allows one to spread one's net wider, the bourgeois virtue of sobriety *[Nüchternheit]* that Benjamin thematized in his *Deutsche Menschen*—all of which are, in reality, the divestiture of self in favor of objectivity. In his portrait of Thomas Mann, whom he knew in the glittering world of Southern California, Adorno notes that "in a world of high-handed and self-centered people the only better alternative is to loosen the bonds of identity and not become rigid."[22] And we see this theme in Adorno's depiction of Hegel's self-divestiture as the self-renunciation or self-externalization that is practiced for the sake of one's goal: "Hegel's demeanor, full of suffering, his countenance ravaged by thought, the face of one who has literally consumed himself until he is no more than ashes, bear witness to this self-divestiture."[23] This self-divestiture is really the means by which one gains experience and translates it into spirit, and the fire through which this is accomplished is the opposite of the "flashiness" of personality and lifestyle:

Like the subject of his theories, the man Hegel had absorbed both subject and object into himself in spirit; the life of his spirit is all of life again within itself. . . . The almost tradesmanlike dryness and sobriety [Nüchternheit] to which the most extreme pathos shrivels in Hegel gives the idea a dignity it loses when it provides its pathos with a fanfare. The meaning of Hegel's life is tied to the substance of his philosophy. No philosophy was so profoundly rich; none held so unswervingly to the experience to which it had entrusted itself without reservation. Even the marks of its failure were struck by truth itself. ("Aspects of Hegel's Philosophy," 51)

In Walter Benjamin, who of his contemporaries or near-contemporaries was perhaps the most important to Adorno personally, and whose work is so close to Adorno's in the themes I have been concerned with here that it is difficult to specify the precise location of the boundary between them, the dialectic of individualization and spiritualization is, if anything, even more spectacular in its manifestations, providing, perhaps, the occasion for the aura that surrounds Benjamin now. Benjamin, Adorno says in his essay "Benjamin the Letter Writer," was "designed by nature to express the universal through extreme particularity, through what was peculiar to him."[24] The arrogance one sees in Benjamin's youth, accordingly, represents Benjamin's intuition of the difference between his potential and his state of development, so that just as early intuitions and images capture the aura of a work of art so powerfully, Benjamin's early letters, "for the most part clouded, are shot through with touches of imperiousness, like flashes of lightning trying to strike; the gesture anticipates what his intellectual power later accomplished" (237). In the mature Benjamin, it is as though the person has been given over to spirit: "The predominance of spirit in him had alienated him from his physical and even his psychological existence to an extreme degree" (232). Benjamin's extreme idiosyncratic privateness is a measure of this impersonality, manifesting itself in graciousness rather than arrogance. Accordingly, in the period of exile and danger at the end of his life, Benjamin's "almost impersonal quality worked to the benefit of his attitude. . . . He understood himself to be the instrument of his ideas, and did not think of his life as an end in itself, despite or precisely because of the wealth of substance and experience he embodied, and similarly he did not lament his fate as a private misfortune" (239). Again, as with Hegel, immersion in the reality outside oneself, but mediated through consciousness, produces a wealth of experience that is translated into spirit rather than an inflation of the private self, the personality.

This notion of self-divestiture for the sake of spirit leads to some subliminal ironies in Adorno's work. Just as the notions of "star" and "name" are central to the culture industry and the cult of personality, so the images of star, constellation, and name are linked with hope and truth in Adorno's writing. Playing on Benjamin's treatment of the theme in his essay on Goethe's *Wahlverwandtschaften*, Adorno links the image of the star with hope; the constellation, as we have seen, represents the discontinuous and inorganic but spiritual figure that may be the figure of truth; and the name evokes, again in allusion to Benjamin, the true or divine, though also hidden, Name. Hence, for instance, Adorno says of Benjamin's concept of truth, "No more than for Hegel is this for him the mere adequacy of thought to its object. . . . Rather, it is a constellation of ideas that, as he may have envisioned it, together form the divine Name."[25] But of course the Name has become problematic in a world in which, as Adorno says at the beginning of his essay on *Faust* II in justification of the reading of classical texts, the sacred has migrated into the profane and concealed itself there. This theme is beautifully elaborated in the short and deliberately inconspicuous essay "Titles." "The title is the work's fame," Adorno writes, but, again echoing Benjamin's notion of the true Name, "the work itself . . . no more knows its true title than the zaddik knows his mystical name."[26] Instead, works have become unnamable, as Beckett indicated in the title of his novel *The Unnamable*.

If it is the historical dynamics of the modern period that have made works unnamable, the same dynamics have produced the "damaged life" that is the subject of Adorno's *Minima Moralia*. But those same dynamics still contain an element of hope. One might call it the star of oblivion; perhaps it is the star that rises over late works. Adorno touches on this theme of forgetting in his essay on *Faust* II. Perhaps it is the sleep of oblivion with which that work opens, he says, that is the key to the reconciliation at the end: "Perhaps Faust is saved because he is no longer the person who signed the pact; perhaps the wisdom of this play, which is a play in pieces, a '*Stück in Stücken*,' lies in knowing how little the human being is identical to himself, how light and tiny this 'immortal part' of him is that is carried off as though it were nothing. The power of life, as a power of continued life, is equated with forgetting" ("*Faust*," 119–20). At the end, a memory appears across the abyss of oblivion, and Adorno's conclusion reads, "Hope is not memory held fast but the return of what has been forgotten." Again, the self is not one continuous or solid or organic thing; identity is in fragments, but just as in the course of history subjectivity comes to illuminate works from the outside after it has abandoned them, so the fragments of identity—and even, as in *Faust,* memories linked with past crimes—can pass over into spirit and there be seen anew, and illuminate us anew, as constellations.

If we think of fame as the opposite of oblivion, and of the damaged life as damaging for the kind of rounded lifework that might lead to name and fame in a positive sense, then we are led to the figure of the émigré, a figure intimately linked to the damaged life for both Adorno and Benjamin. This figure is at the center of Kafka's novel *Amerika,* and one of Adorno's most poignant comments in "Titles" deals with Kafka's original name for that work: *Der Verschollene,* the one who was never heard of again. "*Der Verschollene,*" Adorno says, is a "blank space for a name that cannot be found. The perfect passive participle *verschollen* . . . has lost its verb the way the family's memory loses the emigrant who goes to ruin and dies." (7) But the émigré also appears elsewhere in Adorno's writing in more hopeful contexts, just as Kafka's *Amerika* also contains images of utopian hope. Adorno was of course himself an émigré, and the figure of the émigré learning a new language appears and reappears in his work.[27] For the émigré who learns the new language through immersion in it, words come to be known in a many-sided way, through their use in different contexts. In this process, there is an element not only of self-externalization but also of the erotic, as we see in Adorno's impassioned defense of the use for foreign words in his writing: "Love drives us to foreign words. . . . What lures us is a kind of exogamy of language, which would like to escape from the sphere of what is always the same."[28] And if we think of Adorno's scathing criticism of Heidegger's interpretation of

Hölderlin's reference to the "brown women" of France as "really" meaning a love for the homeland,[29] it becomes clear that Adorno's notion of the damaged life and its link with emigration and oblivion is inseparable from his deep conviction of the need for self-externalization and immersion in what is other and foreign.

This despite the fact that the foreign words are in fact inorganic, unnatural, technical: Adorno recalls Benjamin's image of the author "inserting the silver rib of the foreign word into the body of language" ("Words from Abroad," 187). We saw the same dialectic in the imagery used of music in Adorno's essay on Schubert. The metallic, the crystalline, the inorganic are true to the fact that art, language, and identity are not harmonious wholes, not organic totalities: "By acknowledging itself as a token, the foreign word reminds us bluntly that all real language has something of the token in it. . . . Not the least of what we resist in the foreign word is that it illuminates something true of all words: that language imprisons those who speak it, that as a medium of their own it has essentially failed" ("Words from Abroad," 189). Similarly, Walter Benjamin wrote the *Berlin Childhood ca. 1900* in exile to immunize himself against nostalgia for his homeland,[30] but in it he describes how, from the first, language had made him identify with the cultural landscape around him. He learned to disguise himself in words, he says, which exercised a compulsion on him to become and act like things around him—not models of good behavior, but dwellings, furniture, clothing: "I was disfigured by everything that surrounded me." (417) Similarly, the child in his hiding places becomes what he hides in; he is "enclosed in the world of matter." (418) Just as it is the scars of poetic language's battle to come to terms with the artificial language of communication that we see in the language of *Faust* II, so the peculiar, the discontinuous, and even the repetitious qualities of Adorno's work may represent the hope that, through incorporating the poisonous and the inorganic, something will pass over into spirit. It may be that at least in the present age there is no alternative but to externalize oneself in the world of historical dynamics and the cultural dynamics they bring with them. One's own "self" and one's "identity" will suffer, and one's work will bear the scars of the damage one sustains through the immersion.

2

Language: Its Murmuring, Its Darkness, and Its Silver Rib

No fixed abode, he says, and laughs; but it is only the kind of laughter that has no lungs behind it. It sounds rather like the rustling of fallen leaves.

—*Kafka, "The Cares of a Family Man"*

The figure of Odradek, to which, or whom, these sentences refer, was the kind of enigmatic and indeterminate phenomenon that held great meaning for Adorno. Neither organic nor inorganic, not alive yet surviving, both relic of the past and prolegomenon of the future: like the aura of the aesthetic or the constellation of figures in a void that is Adorno's fundamental image for his own writing, such a figure has indeed "no fixed abode." It is compounded of negation and indeterminacy and for that very reason at the same time signifies also reconciliation and transcendence.[1]

Kafka describes Odradek's laughter, which is not fully identifiable, somewhere between a human sound and a noise, as like the rustling *[rascheln]* of fallen leaves. A similar German word, *Rauschen,* used for the rustling of leaves, the murmuring of flowing water, the roar and surge of surf or wind, appears repeatedly in Adorno's writings on literature, where it stands for a similarly enigmatic and indeterminate phenomenon, namely, the appear-

ance of an authentic poetic dimension of language. Just as
Adorno saw Odradek as a key figure in Kafka, he saw *Rauschen*
as a key image for language. "Ich habe nichts als Rauschen"—I
have nothing but murmuring, said the poet Rudolf Borchardt,
in a line Adorno likes to quote.

Although Adorno's work does not present a conspicuous or
systematic theory of language, it contains an implicit theory of
language that is interwoven with the other central philosophical
themes of his work.[2] If, for instance, Adorno speaks of the languagelike character of art to indicate the quasi-sensuous and
quasi-logical character of aesthetic experience, then conversely
he also indicates the ways in which language itself shares the
languagelike character of art and the ways in which the language
used by human subjects participates in the subject-transcending
character of genuine aesthetic experience. Adorno is a producer
of texts whose medium is language, and his comments on language indicate its role in the configurational or constellational
form that is inseparable from the substance of his thought.

As early as the first years of the 1930s, in his "Theses on the
Language of the Philosopher," Adorno defined the philosophical
potential of language in terms of configurational form. The philosopher's only hope in this era of linguistic decay, he says in that
essay, is to "place words around the new truth in such a way that
their configuration yields the new truth."[3] The counterpart of
this configurative use of language is what he calls *Sprachkritik*, or
linguistic criticism, in which the philosopher tests the capacity of
a word to enter into such a configuration. Such a use of language
alters the words in turn, creating "a unity of concept and thing
that is dialectically intertwined and cannot be disentangled
through explication" (369). In other words, configuration and
language's potential for authenticity and validity—for a movement toward the nonidentical object and away from a conceptual

hierarchy in which the object is subsumed under the concept expressed in language—are interdependent.

"Theses on the Language of the Philosopher" indicates how foundational in Adorno's work is the role of language in the configurational form that reflects the primacy of the object. Adorno's implicit theory of language is further elaborated in the essays in *Notes to Literature,* which stem primarily from his middle and late periods. But it is rarely foregrounded. In contrast to the more programmatic formulations on literary form in relation to thought or society that we find in "The Essay as Form" or "On Lyric Poetry and Society," Adorno's conception of a more authentic use of language tends to manifest itself in *Notes to Literature* as an inconspicuous background murmuring or rustling—as *Rauschen,* in fact. In the constellation of ideas and images that make up his implicit conception of language, then, *Rauschen* is a key word. It indicates both the substance of the conception and its enigmatic manifestation in Adorno's work.

The question of an authentic literary language is inseparable from that of an authentic critical or philosophical use of language; surely it is no accident that Adorno uses Borchardt's line "Ich habe nichts als Rauschen" as the epigraph for "Skoteinos," his essay on reading Hegel. The word *Rauschen* is alien to the vocabulary of the philosophy of language, and that essay on Hegel (as well as "The Essay as Form") instructs us in how to reach an understanding of such an alien and enigmatic word as *Rauschen.* The émigré, prototype for Adorno of the person who needs to learn an alien language, does not use a dictionary, with its narrow and isolated definitions, but instead compares the many contexts in which the foreign words appear. In that way, words that are at first surrounded by indeterminateness begin to "decipher themselves through the abundance of combinations in which they appear." This method of language study, which we might call the configurational method, allows for a fuller grasp of the word's substance. "The linguistic configuration, and the gaze focussed intently on the individual word," Adorno tells us, "complement one another. Together they explode the layer of mediocre tacit agreement, the sticky layer between understanding and the matter at hand."[4] Let us proceed, then, like the émigré, to look at *Rauschen* in its contexts.

This is the passage in his essay on Borchardt's poetry in which Adorno introduces the line "Ich habe nichts als Rauschen":

In everything he wrote Borchardt made himself an organ of language. His incomparable line "Ich habe nichts als Rauschen" . . . leads deep into his spiritual modus operandi—to use Borchardt's words, deep into the "Schmerz, in dich zu lauschen" [the pain of listening into you]. Language murmurs and rustles through him *[durchrauscht ihn]* like a stream. He reaches for language and learns to deploy it in order to serve it; he made his work an arena for language. He was borne by the experience his whole literary oeuvre was striving for—the experience of language itself speaking, to use a baroque expression. The speaking gesture of almost every line he wrote is not so much the gesture of a person speaking but rather, in its intention, the epiphany of language.[5]

Rauschen, then, is how we experience the movement and sound of language itself speaking. It is the appearance of language as such, language in its autonomy, something that may be manifested in poetry. It is language not subordinated to anything else. But what does this mean? In this and other contexts, Adorno gives *Rauschen*, this speech of language itself, negative definition; we learn what it is not, what it is not subordinated to, what it therefore requires a certain negation of. Language itself speaking, we learn, is not human speech, nor the expression of human subjectivity or intention, nor nature or sensuousness, nor communication or meaning.

Despite the word "speaking," and despite *Rauschen*'s suggestion of the murmuring of human voices, language itself speaking is to be distinguished from human speech and the human voice. Just as Odradek's laughter has no lungs behind it, Borchardt's "speaking gesture" is not the gesture of a person speaking. It is reminiscent of human speech, certainly, as is *Rauschen* in its murmuring, but the word "gesture" differentiates it from speech, just as the phrase "language itself speaking" needs the word *Rauschen,* with its lack of distinctness and its connotations of nonhuman nature, to indicate that it is not human speech. Nor is language itself speaking the expression of human subjectivity, despite the fact that the word *Rauschen* can also include such connotations of expressiveness as the notion of the wind sighing in the trees. On the contrary, for language itself to speak, a certain voluntary renunciation or sacrifice is called for on the part of the human subject, what Adorno calls "self-alienation" or "self-divestiture" *(Selbstentäusserung).* Thus Borchardt makes himself an "organ of language" and his work an "arena for language." The essay on Eichendorff, whose favorite word, Adorno tells us, was *Rauschen,* turns on this antisubjectivism. In the subject's "self-extinction in the service of language," Adorno says there, the subject "turns itself into *Rauschen,* the rushing, rustling, murmuring sound of nature: into language, living on only in dying away *[verhallen].*"[6] The subject becomes the container, or better yet the empty space, in which this movement of language can occur.

Does *Rauschen,* then, suggest that when language itself speaks it becomes not human so much as material, sensuous, organic, natural? Here too, Adorno, acknowledging the reminiscences, stresses the difference. Borchardt's poems, for instance, "are not objects of contemplation, especially by the criterion of visual concreteness, but linguistically they are fully of sensuousness; the paradox of non-sensory contemplation" ("Borchardt," 193–94). And in Eichendorff the romantic, where the cliché might lead one to think of poetry as fusing with nature, just as one might tend to think of it as subjective, Adorno reminds us that *Rauschen* is not a tone *[Klang]* but a noise *[Geräusch]*, more closely akin to language than to sound. Eichendorff himself, he notes, presents it as similar to language and compares the rustling in the trees to "a continual secret perceptible whispering" ("Eichendorff," 69). Linguistic "sensuousness," then, is nonsensory; and *Rauschen* as the sound of nature is so only through its reminiscence of language.

Adorno lets the early–twentieth-century aesthetician Theodor Meyer articulate this point emphatically for him. Language cannot create sensory images, Meyer says, but rather creates psychic images perceived in inner representation. Hence it is through "language itself and the structures created by it and peculiar to it alone," Meyer says, that we receive the substance of poetry ("Eichendorff," 68). In other words, language does not become nature or sensory reality, even in its images. Rather, says Adorno, "the act in which the human being becomes language, the flesh becomes word, incorporates the expression of nature into language and transfigures the movement of language so that it becomes life again" ("Eichendorff," 69). The same movement in which the subject extinguishes himself in the service of language allows language to incorporate something of nature without becoming nature at all. Rather, language as *Rauschen*, as language itself speaking, becomes a kind of "second nature," in which "the objectified nature that has been lost to the subject returns as animated nature" (69).

Language speaking for itself, then, is neither subjective nor natural. Nor is it meaning, in the ordinary sense in which language is used to communicate meanings. Language itself has substance or import *[Gehalt]* rather than meaning. The indistinctness that is inherent in *Rauschen* should alert us to that. "Kein Deutliches erwarte dir"—May nothing distinct await you, continues Borchardt's poem. "What is meant or intended is secondary in comparison with linguistic form," Adorno comments. "Substance crystallizes in language as such, as though it were the authentic language Jewish mysticism speaks of" ("Borchardt," 193). For Adorno, meaning implies the gap between thing and concept, and the relationship between nature and language we have just seen requires a distance from meaning in this sense. This alone makes the speech of language itself not symbolic, as the cliché would lead us to expect of romantic poetry, but allegorical, as Adorno's mention of the baroque would suggest. Eichendorff's romantic clichés, his castles and mountains and nightingales, are allegorical rather than symbolic. But in his writing "the allegorical intention is borne not so much by nature . . . as by his language in its distance from meaning. It imitates *Rauschen* and solitary nature. It thereby expresses an estrangement which no thought, only pure sound, can bridge" (69). To elaborate one aspect of what Adorno is saying here, the second, animated nature that language becomes when it speaks for itself is an imitation, achieved through an act of mimesis rather than a process of equivalence. Imitation in the sense of mimesis is not something lesser or inferior. What it implies is both a disjunction from what language imitates and also a nonconceptual relationship with it.[7] Hence the inevitable estrangement from meaning, which relies on concepts.

Thus *Rauschen*, which might originally have seemed the epitome of continuity and lack of differentiation, turns out to be the manifestation of something inherently allegorical, something shot through with disjunction and differentiation, something that is more like this than that in one context and more like that than this in another, having "no fixed abode," not only because it moves and flows but also because it is always not something else. The romantic is the baroque and life is death, as with Odradek. How can we explain this incursion of negativity, of the allegorical, into *Rauschen* and language speaking for itself? Two answers come to mind, ultimately related but requiring separate elaboration. First, *Rauschen*'s indistinctness is a manifestation of its alienness. If language itself speaking is not human speech, then it is inevitably alien to us who attempt to understand it. It requires our self-extinction in some sense, and thus a negation stands between us and it. Second, this indistinctness is an indication that language itself cannot attain what it—or the poet on behalf of it—strives for. It cannot fully escape human subjectivity and intentionality, for language can never be fully separate from meaning and communication.

Meaning, Music, and the Name

A central tenet of Adorno's implicit theory of language is that language has two distinct but inseparable dimensions. One of these he refers to as the communicative dimension and the other as (among other terms) the poetic or expressive dimension. A second tenet of the implicit theory is that a historical process of deterioration has taken place in which the communicative dimension, through its involvement with social domination, the market, exchange and other processes loosely associated with the development of capitalism, has overrun or colonized the poetic dimension, so that, for instance, in the twentieth century Borchardt is dealing with "a language devastated by commerce and communication, by the ignominy of exchange" ("Borchardt," 194).

The term "communication," then, which Adorno uses consistently as a negative foil for an authentic literary language, amalgamates two ideas: first, the idea that meaning as such, or signification as opposed to substance, is dependent on the disjunction between words and concepts expressed in words, on the one hand, and things, on the other, so that meaning is implicated in the dominating and leveling that is inherent in the rigidities of conceptual categorization and logical judgment. As communication, that is, language has the same flaws Adorno finds in rationality as such.[8] The second idea is that communication serves as a form of social control in which human beings are treated as potential customers, reduced to their function within an exchange society. In this sense, language as communication must be seen as a failure, alienating human beings from one another rather than facilitating their relationships: "Language imprisons those who speak it; . . . as a medium of their own it has essentially failed" ("Words from Abroad," 189). We can see the relationship between these two ideas in Adorno's description of the linguistic situation faced by the late Goethe in the early decades of the nineteenth century:

In his late period Goethe found himself facing a contradiction which has now become an unreconcilable divergence, the contradiction between a language with literary integrity and communicative language. The second part of *Faust* is wrested from a deterioration of language whose course had been set at the point when a reified, facile discourse invaded expressive discourse. The latter proved so incapable of resistance because the two antagonistic media are nevertheless still one, never completely separate from one another. ("*Faust,*" 112)

The vulnerability of the "other" dimension of language is clear here. It is as though the more authentic, poetic dimension of language is hidden within, and dependent on, the same features of language, the same words and syntactic structures, through which ordinary communication takes place; without words and syntax and their potential for specific meanings and logical judgments, there is no language at all. And this communicative potential of language, which implies commonality and equivalence, and accordingly also the lowest common denominator of the "layer of mediocre tacit agreement," works against the recognition and naming of things in their nonidentity that a more authentic language might hope—but in fact be unable—to achieve.[9]

For while Adorno states emphatically that there is no such thing as an ontology of language; that language is a human, mediated phenomenon rather than something natural and cannot be restored to a state of natural purity or integrity; and that any divine language of names in which words and their objects are not alienated from one another is inaccessible to human beings, whether because it is hidden or because it was lost or because it never existed—still, these notions of the divine Name echo negatively through Adorno's writings on literature, as allusions to Jewish mysticism and Benjamin's theories of language attest. The coincidence of word and thing in the Name is the impossible ideal that language strives for and fails to attain. And when language itself begins to speak, when it moves farther from meaning and closer to mimesis, even briefly, it comes closer to names and thus to things as well. "Things, which have grown cold, are brought back to themselves by the similarity of their names to themselves, and the movement of language awakens that resemblance," says Adorno of Eichendorff's language ("Eichendorff," 69). This does not mean that language attains this ideal. If things are reawakened by the similarity between their names and themselves, this similarity is not an identity; what is achieved is not a return to a divine language in which names and things are identical. Language remains double and divided, unable to completely free itself of its communicative dimension, however much literary language moves toward hermeticism in an attempt to break with communication. Adorno's comment on the awakening of the similarity of names and things in Eichendorff immediately follows his interpretation of Eichendorff's romanticism as allegorical. Indeed, this striving on the part of language is a kind of necessary madness, and Adorno refers elsewhere to "the abyss into which language plunges when it tries to become name and image."[10]

Insofar as names stand for this impossible ideal, they cannot be thought of as individual words, which, as concepts, will also be divided from the things they refer to. When proper names or titles—whose idea is the nonidentical, the individual person or thing they name—have been subjected to what Adorno calls "the primacy of communication," literary language may be most authentic when it tries to capture namelessness. Hence Beckett's title *The Unnamable* "embodies the truth about the namelessness of contemporary literature. Not a word of it has any value now if it does not say the unsayable" ("Titles," 12), Adorno says in an essay that explores this dialectic of names and titles.[11] Just as "titles, like names, have to capture it, not say it," the true name is approached through configuration, thus mimetically, rather than through individual words that correspond directly to it. Indeed, the similarity Adorno refers to is all that language achieves, and, as he makes clear in his comments on the émigré learning to understand foreign words, similarity and its richness are achieved through configuration.[12]

In many of the essays in *Notes to Literature,* music seems to stand in for this impossible ideal for which language strives. Reading these essays, one comes to expect that, at some point in each one, Adorno will compare the literary work with music as a kind of seal of its authenticity. Indeed, the title *Notes to Literature [Noten zur Literatur]*, originally intended to be *Words without Music*, in a play on Mendelssohn's *Songs without Words*, as Adorno tells us in "Titles," refers explicitly to "the constellation of words and music" (6). One obvious way to conceive what happens when language itself speaks is that it becomes, or comes close to being, music. Just as the use of the word *Rauschen* for language suggests a kind of self-transcendence on the part of language, so does the suggestion that language approaches music. We see this idea in Adorno's description of Schumann's *Eichendorfflieder*. Schumann's songs, Adorno says, "bring out a potential contained in the poems, the transcendence into song that arises in the movement beyond all specificity of image and concept, in the rustling and murmuring of language's flow" ("Eichendorff," 73).

It is crucial to understand the precise sense in which language moves toward music. Language does not come to be "musical" in the sense in which that word is commonly used of language. "The speaking energy that holds language to its objectivation in [Borchardt's] poetry," Adorno says, "causes the poems to approximate music. Compared with Rilke or Trakl, they repulse music-like effects in favor of linguistic articulation" ("Borchardt," 194). "Music-like effects" connotes the sensuously pleasing aspect of sound, and we have already seen that when language itself speaks it is not assimilated to the sensuous or natural but rather becomes something nonsensory. Indeed, Adorno also reminds us that "to associate *[Rauschen]* all too quickly with music . . . would be to miss the sense of [it]. *Rauschen* is not a sound in the sense of a musical tone *[Klang]* but a noise *[Geräusch]*, more closely akin to language than sound" ("Eichendorff," 69). Again, it is not the sensory aspect of music that is important here. In fact, it would be false to think of music as such as the ideal of language. Rather, music and language stand in complementary relationships to that ideal, thus indeed forming part of a constellation, as Adorno's comments on the title *Notes to Literature* indicate. Music and language come to resemble one another as parts of the constellation around that ideal by renouncing more superficial resemblances between them. Hence Adorno's warning against too quick an association between *Rauschen* and music.

In what sense, then, does language come to approximate music? Here it is helpful to refer to Adorno's "Music and Language: A Fragment," collected in *Quasi una fantasia,* his volume of essays on modern music, which elaborates at some length on the question in what sense music comes to resemble language. Of course music resembles language in many ways, as the use of such terms as "idiom" and "phrase" in speaking of music indicates. And although music is fundamentally different from language in that it does not operate with a system of signs or symbols in which particulars stand for specific other things, music does manifest some of the most fundamental features of what Adorno here calls "intentional language," or what I have been referring to as the "communicative dimension" of language. Accordingly, the difference between music and language can be understood only when one regards them as totalities. Both are attempts to mediate the absolute, to name the Name. But music works toward (and fails to attain) this ideal in a different way than language does. Although the particulars in music are interconnected in that they point to one another through association or contrast or anticipation, its particulars are not part of a semiotic system. Hence music cannot subsume its individual meanings under larger abstract systems of meaning, as is possible in intentional language; indeed, this is how totalities are created in intentional language. Instead, music interconnects its particulars into a totality by negating each individual one, creating a configuration, so to speak, of transcended particulars: "With music intentions are broken and scattered out of their own force and reassembled in the configuration of the Name. . . . [Music] realizes itself in opposition to intentions, integrating them by the process of negating each individual, unspecifiable one."[13] Musical content consists of this "summation of such a transcendence of particulars," and musical form is not something externally imposed but "the thought process by which content is defined" ("Music and Language," 6). Thus, Adorno says, music fulfills its potential for resemblance to language not by making the individual parts more like words with specific meanings but by making the totality more meaningful by integrating musical content through musical form.

In "Music and Language," language serves as a foil for music; Adorno is concerned with the intentional or communicative aspect of language rather than its poetic or expressive dimension. But he does note there that "music points to true language as a language in which the substance itself appears, but at the cost of unambiguous meaning, which has migrated to the languages of intentionality" (3). Thus, it would seem that the more language comes to speak for itself, the more it will fulfill its resemblance to music not only in distancing itself from the sensuous, as music does, but precisely by distancing itself from particular meanings and creating form through the way it negates and links content rather than through conceptual subsumption. This seems to be the meaning of Adorno's comment on the way Borchardt's poems approach music while renouncing music-like effects: "Compared with Rilke or Trakl, [the poems] repulse music-like effects in favor of linguistic articulation through the harshness of their jointure. But in return they are all the more musical in their modus operandi, in a way of forming an idiom that provides content for the particular idiom while relegating all others to insignificance" ("Borchardt," 194). It is as though form is created directly through content in its negation of other content. This idea is even more explicit in Adorno's comment on Borchardt's long poems: "The long poems transpose the musical idea of form, the idea of a form immanent in the structure and not derived from anything external to language. Borchardt literally composes, as in music, with language" (196). And in his essay on Hölderlin, Adorno calls great music "aconceptual synthesis" and says it is "the prototype for Hölderlin's late poetry" ("Parataxis," 130). Meaningful form achieved without the mechanism of concepts—"aconceptual synthesis"—is the essence of this potential resemblance between music and language.

Darkness and the Will

If the communicative dimension with its affinity for the logic of domination is what poetic language attempts to elude or otherwise distance itself from, then it is toward the linguistic analogue of musical form that it attempts to move. As we have seen, this is a move away from meaning. Adorno portrays this move away from meaning as a move into a darkness akin to the obscurity peculiar to music. Whereas the absolute always eludes the specificity of intentional language, Adorno tells us in "Music and Language," "music finds the absolute immediately, but at the moment of discovery it becomes obscure, just as too powerful a light dazzles the eyes, preventing them from seeing things which are perfectly visible" (4). We are reminded of Kant's notion that intuitions without concepts are blind, an idea Adorno was fond of citing to explain the work of art's inability to interpret itself. This is the darkness that comes from approaching totality by transcending meaning, the sensory, and the subject. As language too distances itself from self, meaning, and the senses, it seems to speak out of and into a darkness that is felt to be truly other.

In Adorno's comments on Eichendorff's famous poem "Schläft ein Lied in allen Dingen / Die da träumen fort und fort, / Und die Welt hebt an zu singen, / Triffst du nur das Zauberwort" [There is a song sleeping in all things / dreaming there, on and on, / and the world will begin to sing / if you only find the magic word], we see this connection between the movement toward music, the movement into darkness, and the reconciliation of words and things: "The word for which these lines . . . yearn is language itself. What decides whether the world sings is whether the poet manages to hit the mark, to attain the darkness of language as if that were something already existing in itself" ("Eichendorff," 67).

This otherness toward which language moves as it moves toward aconceptual darkness is necessarily indistinct and ungraspable—as indeed *Rauschen* as the sound of murmuring or rustling is. Adorno also characterizes it as vanishing. The fundamental stance of Borchardt's poems, for instance, Adorno describes as "that of speaking into a darkness that makes them dark themselves. Such speech is not, as in traditional rhetoric, directed to others to convince or persuade them. It calls, as if across the abyss, to the Other, who has become indistinct and is in the process of vanishing" ("Borchardt," 200). Similarly, he speaks of the element in Stefan George's work in which "the 'I' imagines itself borne by a collective language which it contains within itself and to which it listens as though to something in the process of disappearing."[14] It is as though this disappearance is evidence of the continuing failure to actually reach across the abyss and become the absolute; it is as though language can listen in that direction, can hear or become *Rauschen,* but cannot wholly free itself from the communicative dimension. Or from the poetic subject; hence the equivocation of listening/becoming and speaking into/speaking out of.

To the extent to which the movement into darkness is a transcendence of the subject, a voluntary self-sacrifice, it is also a
renunciation of violence toward language. This nonviolence allows words to be loosened from the fixity of meanings and to
become illuminated and illuminating in their configurations with
one another, the kind of illumination that characterizes the constellation in the darkness of space. Adorno describes this nonviolent loosening in terms of the flow of water, referring to Brecht's
poem on Lao Tse: "The soft water with its movement, that is the
descending flow of language, the direction it flows of its own
accord, but the poet's power is to be weak, the power not to resist
the descending language rather than the power to control it. . . .
It succeeds in . . . washing words away from their circumscribed
meanings and causing them to light up when they come in
contact with one another" ("Eichendorff," 70). This nonviolence
is a renunciation not only of control over language but also of
the domination of nature. It allows things to be awakened and
words to be reconciled with things, as we have seen in the notion
of the return of an animated nature.

But this renunciation of violence is not and cannot be complete. The movement toward darkness and musical form is a
movement of transcendence via negation. Music creates totality
"not in a system of mutually interdependent meanings, but by
their lethal absorption into a system of interconnections" ("Music
and Language," 5). Language remains divided, and its inevitable
allegorical activity contains an element of death dealing. Eichendorff, Adorno tells us, awakens things, but by rendering them
allegorical. "In freezing things, Eichendorff once more endows
things, which have become reified, with the power to signify, to
point beyond themselves" ("Eichendorff," 67). As we saw earlier
with regard to both *Rauschen* and musical form, configuration is
achieved through a simultaneous negation and interlinking of

particulars. The light of the constellation is a light in a necessary darkness, the light of substance rather than meaning.

If it is the intentionality of language, its specificity of meaning, that is transcended as language moves toward darkness and musical form, the complement of that intentionality is the personal will of the subject. Nonviolence in the poet's stance toward language implies the renunciation, in some sense, of personal will. At the same time, what Adorno calls the "will to language," after Heinrich Schenker's notion of a *Tonwille*, or will to sound, in Beethoven, is almost certainly a prerequisite to that renunciation and provides the motivation for it ("Borchardt," 196). Adorno's essay on Stefan George centers on this dialectic of personal willfulness and the will to self-transcendence. To the extent to which George willed to be remembered, tried to force his own immortality, he damaged his own work and its longevity; "to the force with which George wanted to engrave his image on his contemporaries there responds an equivalent force of forgetting" ("Stefan George," 179). To the extent to which he tried to force naturalness and spontaneity, George damaged even his lyric poetry: "The lack of congruence between willful intervention and the semblance of relaxed spontaneous language is so ubiquitous that it confirms Borchardt's suspicion that there is hardly a poem by George in which violence is not manifested in self-destructive form" (180).

This violence and the horror it inspires even in George himself are most tellingly portrayed in the prose piece that Adorno cites at the end of his essay on George. It is called "The Talking Head":

I had been given a clay mask and hung it on the wall of my room. I invited my friends to see how I had gotten the head to speak, I commanded it audibly to say the name of the person I pointed to and when it was silent I tried to force its lips open with my finger. It made a face and bit my finger. I repeated the command loudly and with the utmost intensity, pointing to a different person. Then it said the name. We all left the room horrified and I knew I would never enter it again. (192)

In both George, as this prose piece indicates, and Borchardt, two early–twentieth-century poets in whom Adorno explicates the dialectic of the will, this willfulness is harnessed to a devotion to language—"for Borchardt devoting oneself to language is the writer's passion" ("Borchardt," 194)—and an attempt to overcome the glaring deficiencies of language in its deteriorated state by a kind of force. Borchardt, Adorno says, "hoped to force the transsubjective objectively binding quality of language, a coherence beyond subjective response . . . through the quixoticness of subjective assertion. The subject transfers its own strength, as it were, to what is naively understood as the medium of subjective expression, in order to then subordinate itself to that medium" ("Borchardt," 195). In Borchardt's emphatic dedication to language, this process manifests itself as philological virtuosity—an engagement both with earlier forms of German and with other languages—that is then used with a certain detachment. In George a similar process takes place, with technical mastery playing a prominent role in his poetry but being linked to a kind of sacrifice for the sake of language as such: "In George's poetry the technical work . . . in an individual poem is almost always work on language as such at the same time. . . . Something to be said for the acts of violence committed in individual poems is that they stem from that work on language; as though George's genius damaged and even sacrificed its own works for the sake of it" ("Stefan George," 187). It is as though the extreme plight of language calls forth this heroic effort, which then makes possible the kind of self-sacrificing nonviolence that allows language itself to speak and to approach music.

This dialectic in which willfulness is subsumed into self-renunciation is the dynamic through which late work comes into being.

As I will have several occasions to note, Adorno presents Beethoven in similar terms. The heroic will that makes Beethoven's middle-period works paradigmatic for the tour de force that is inherent in every work of art is followed in the late-period works by the sacrifice of the will, and we see the appearance of nothingness in the musical work of art (*Aesthetic Theory* 163/156; 276/265). Similarly, as we saw in a passage from his essay on *Faust* cited earlier, Adorno argues that the elements in Goethe's late style that appear forced are actually "the scars poetic language acquired in defending itself against communicative language, and at times they resemble the latter." "For in fact," Adorno continues, "Goethe committed no act of violence against language. . . . Rather, his restitutive nature attempts to awaken that sullied language as a literary language" ("Faust," 112).

It is apparent here that this work on language, this transcendence of the will through the will, is a kind of listening into the Other. It involves a reaching out into what is other, whether it be archaic forms of language or foreign languages or the aconceptual. This is why, as Adorno points out, work on language, the attempt to differentiate a poetic language from a communicative language, displays both backward-looking and forward-looking tendencies ("Borchardt," 198). And the distinction from that disappearing Other will also be maintained on pain of succumbing to a naive illusion of merging with it. Resistance to such merging, Adorno says, is part of what is authentic in George's poetry. In his work, "the glib decorative quality that is so irritating in Rilke, the tendency to surrender to verse and rhyme without resistance, is for the most part restrained by reflection. . . . The power of condensation and concentration is the happy correlate of the anti-artistic element in George's will to art" ("Stefan George," 184). It is the difference between looking into the abyss and throwing oneself into it, between maintaining an awareness of the dual nature of language and deluding oneself that one has achieved an impossible unity.

Particles and Parataxis

Adorno's depiction of the dialectic of will and violence in language points up a hard/soft dimension in the movement toward the "darkness" of language.[15] The dialectic of the "will to language" that is at play in both technique and virtuosity exhibits both the softness of renunciation and the harshness of detachment. At the same time, since language's movement toward authenticity, toward speaking for itself, is both premised on, and constrained by, negativity, both as negation and as the inherent dividedness of language—the division between communicative and poetic language, between concepts and things, words and names—the hard/soft dimension in language is given its meaning by negativity, the same negativity that separates the elements in a constellation. When we find Adorno showing us specific instances of this movement toward authenticity of language in literary works, we find this same prominence of the hard/soft dimension in the forms these instances take: the softness of blank spots, places of looseness and indistinctness, on the one hand, and the hard contours of parataxis or *harte Fügung* [harsh jointure] in larger structures, on the other.

These points at which language comes closest to music—and by their nature they are only points, for they cannot be sustained—are necessarily points of darkness, obscurity, and distance from meaning. They are gaps, breaks, hiatuses. Yet Adorno is drawn to them. If by their nature as gaps or breaks they are inconspicuous and almost imperceptible, at the same time they are in some sense the high points of the work, its points of greatest beauty, the points at which the Other to which language calls vanishes in the darkness. Adorno sometimes refers to them as the work's "seal of permanence," its seal of authenticity. Paradigmatic for such points is Kafka's original name for his novel *Amerika,* which Adorno explicates in "Titles": *Der Verschollene,* the one who was never heard of, or from, again, the "blank space for a name that cannot be found" (7). The name that cannot be found is that of the émigré who disappears into the other land—disappears from the memory, here conceived as the categorizing and dominating function of language as Logos, of those who remain behind on the other side of the ocean.

One of the chief forms that these gaps or breaks take is the illogical particle, the point at which the logical structuring of syntax, for instance, is loosened precisely within the elements that are responsible for insuring its coherence. An analogue for this within music would be notes that drop their function of maintaining rhythm or dramatic structure. Since they serve no quasi-logical function, such notes will be almost unnoticeable. At the same time, this is so unusual a phenomenon—or perhaps, more accurately, it is so unusual for anyone to notice and describe it—that Adorno's description of such notes in Mahler helps to introduce this kind of particle:

Among the idiosyncratic features of Mahler's use of rhythm we find isolated notes . . . in which the flow of the music comes to a halt or rather is suspended in mid-air. . . . These do not represent any build-up of power which then motivates a subsequent discharge. Nor are they simply a pause in which the movement temporarily comes to rest . . . : they are the seal of permanence, of music's inability to fight free of itself.[16]

Such notes, which, like the émigré who is never heard of again, have "no fixed abode," are the equivalent in music to language itself speaking. They are free of the aspect of music that resembles the communicative dimension of language and that can almost assault the music itself (cf. "Music and Language," 4).

Adorno considers such notes the representatives of an "epic" element in Mahler's music, a nonviolent, nonhierarchical, "bottom-up" rather than "top-down" kind of musical form. In the literary epic, such a particle plays an analogous role.[17] Adorno's essay "On Epic Naiveté" turns on the issue of material concreteness *[Gegenständlichkeit]* in the epic, the epic's attempt through narrative to formulate the nonidentical using the material of myth, representative of invariance. The epic's attempt to represent material concreteness as reality within the medium of language is an impossible one, another version of language's attempt to free itself from its communicative dimension:

The attempt to emancipate representation from reflective reason is language's attempt, futile from the outset, to recover from the negativity of its intentionality, the conceptual manipulation of objects, by carrying its defining intention to the extreme and allowing what is real to emerge in pure form, undistorted by the violence of classificatory ordering. . . . It is precisely the material element in the epic poem . . . that drives the narrative to the edge of madness through its apriori impossibility. ("Epic Naiveté," 27)

Adorno gives us an example of what he means. Referring to Odysseus and his son, Homer says, "These two, / after compacting their plot of a foul death for the suitors, / made their way to the glorious town. In fact *[nämlich]* Odysseus / came afterwards; Telemachos led the way." The coordinating particle "nämlich," which Lattimore translates as "in fact," maintains an appearance of cohesion that the purely narrative content of the sentence belies. Adorno goes on to cite other instances: an "or" *[oder]* in Hölderlin, particles in Trakl. It is important that conjunctions and coordinating particles, the instruments of logical coherence, are affected. Language retains the form of logical judgment even though the actual relationships expressed do not conform to it. Both the disjunction between form and content and the persistence of the logical form are important: "In the epic form of linkage, in which the train of thought finally goes slack, language shows a lenience toward judgment while at the same time unquestionably remaining judgment. The flight of ideas, discourse in its sacrificial form, is language's flight from its prison" ("Epic Naiveté," 28).

In another instance, Adorno interprets the loosening of meaningfulness—a blank space where an intention has been—as an erotic transcendence of subjectivity. It is a question of the use of the word "gar," presumably for "ganz und gar" or "completely," in Stefan George's lines "Nun muss ich gar / Um dein aug und haar / Alle tage / In sehnen leben" [Now I must / for your eyes and hair / every day / live in yearning] (the translation has no way to represent the "gar"), from the poem beginning "Im windes-weben." Adorno defends the use of the word "gar" as a Goethean "residue of absurdity," in which language escapes the subjective intention that occasioned the use of the word. The yearning for such an escape transports language beyond the isolated individual and into its intrinsic being: "Language's chimerical yearning for the impossible becomes an expression of the subject's insatiable erotic longing, which finds relief from the self in the other. . . . Only . . . freed from the humiliation of isolation in the particular does lyrical language represent language's intrinsic being as opposed to its service in the realm of ends."[18] Again we see the theme of eros as the renunciation of subjective willfulness and the movement toward the Other within language. Adorno characterizes the results of George's immersion in the French language, as the Other to the German language, similarly: "With this soaring music-like erotic elan, George won for

German poetry a utopian strain that goes beyond his retrospective mentality" ("Stefan George," 186). Music and eros are the utopian Other appearing within the German language in opposition to George's own subjective leanings.

These particles that have lost their function, so to speak, are instances at the micrological level of the phenomenon known as parataxis, in which serial transition replaces logical connection. As Adorno points out in "Parataxis," his essay on Hölderlin's late poetry, parataxis operates, in both poetry and music, on the level of larger structures as well (132). Parataxis, which represents the abandonment of logical coherence in favor of what Adorno calls "aconceptual synthesis," takes a different form in language than in music, because language and music have different relationships to concepts: "By virtue of its significative element, the opposite pole to its mimetic-expressive element, language is chained to the form of judgment and proposition and thereby to the synthetic form of the concept. In poetry, unlike music, aconceptual synthesis turns against its medium; it becomes a constitutive dissociation" (130). In the examples of particles or individual words we saw earlier, in the passage from the *Odyssey* or the poem by George, this dissociation took the form of a dissociation within the individual word, so to speak—the gap between its form and its content, or between the subjective intention and the erotic effect—resulting in a kind of softening or darkening of the word. At the level of the larger structure, the dissociation takes the form of emphatic breaks, of hard contours—what the German calls *harte Fügung*, or harsh jointure. This is why Borchardt's poems do not display what Adorno calls "music-like effects," which are presumably characterized by softness and continuity.

Parataxis, we can now see, is the basis of configuration; the unity of the whole is composed of the dissociations between the

discrete parts as well as of their associations. Adorno's characterization of the paratactic form of Hölderlin's elegies runs along
these lines: "In their fiber the stanzas in the long elegies, not yet
distorted, are already not so much elegaic stanzas and not arbitrary; rather, without in the least aiming at musical effects, as
Lieder texts do, they approach the structuring of the sonata forms
in the music of the same period, an articulation in terms of
movements, of discrete contrasting unities within a unity" (130).
In other words, it is the negation of continuity that marks the
edges of the parts, rendering them discrete. The space between
these larger parts is analogous, on a structural level, to the almost
inconspicuous blank spots filled by the indistinctness of particles
that have lost their logical function.[19]

Foreign Words

Just as these blank spots in a text may seem inconspicuous and
be easily passed over, the topic of foreign words may seem peripheral to a theory of language, and the role of foreign words
in poetic language may seem a negligible one. But foreign words
and foreign languages are in one sense the quintessence of the
Other of and within language. "Foreign words," one might call
the speech of language itself as it moves into the darkness of the
Other. The topic of foreign words is in fact central to Adorno's
implicit theory of language. He wrote two essays on the topic,
both now collected in *Notes to Literature:* the published essay
"Words from Abroad," in which he explicates his own use of
foreign words in his essay on Proust; and the undated and
unpublished but, to judge by its style, quite early essay "On the
Use of Foreign Words."[20] The émigré learning a foreign language
is one of Adorno's primary images of configuration,[21] and as we
have seen, translation plays an important role in the work of

Borchardt and George, two poets Adorno's comments on whom are the locus for much of his theory of language.

The foreign word displays both the harshness of paratactic rupture and the softness of erotic transcendence. Benjamin spoke of the author inserting the "silver rib" of the foreign word into the body of a text,[22] and Adorno speaks of the "hard, contoured quality" of the foreign word as the thing "that makes it stand out from the continuum of language" ("Words from Abroad," 189). At the same time, for Adorno the attraction to foreign words is part of the erotic longing for the Other and thus part of the will to language itself:

> Since language is erotically charged in its words, at least for the kind of person who is capable of expression, love drives us to foreign words. . . . The early craving for foreign words is like the craving for foreign and if possible exotic girls; what lures us is a kind of exogamy of language, which would like to escape from the sphere of what is always the same, the spell of what one is and knows anyway. ("Words from Abroad," 187)

This "exogamy of language" leads someone like Stefan George to immerse himself in another language, in this case French, and the effect of his translations is to extend the German language through its contact with the other language, to help German toward that "erotic elan" mentioned earlier. Hence, while translations might seem to be a lesser or peripheral part of a poet's oeuvre, for Adorno some of George's translations are among his most important work, because they represent work on language as such. They are important "as works in the German language, precisely by virtue of the literal immersion in the other language." If George succeeded in producing with them not so much a faithful imitation as "a German monument, [he did so] only through unlimited self-denial, akin to the erotic" ("Stefan George," 187–88). Eichendorff, too, another poet of *Rauschen,* though not a translator, brings the foreign element into German lyric poetry. He "liberates the lyrical tonal values of foreign words," as in the phrase "phantastische Nacht" [fantastic night] from the poem "Schöne Fremde" [beautiful foreigner] ("Eichendorff," 66). Again, the erotic overtones are striking.

But just as *Rauschen* should not be interpreted as a natural element in language, so foreign words, though expressive of language's erotic longing for the Other and thus potentially lyrical, are also inevitably antinatural and inorganic. This is their harsh aspect. Adorno refers to them as "deaths heads" and comments that Eichendorff discovered the expressive power in "fragments of the *lingua mortua*" (66). As "phantastisch," the example he cites—stage prop rather than sensuous nature—indicates, foreign words belong to the baroque and allegorical tendency in language. Hence Benjamin's reference to the "silver rib of the foreign word"; the foreign word is utterly inorganic. As such it reminds us that language per se is inorganic in that it is socially mediated, a historical rather than a natural phenomenon. This is part of the service that foreign words render us: "The customary ring of naturalness deceives us about language's participation in reification. It creates the illusion that what is said is immediately equivalent to what is meant. By acknowledging itself as a token, the foreign word reminds us bluntly that all real language has something of the token in it. It makes itself language's scapegoat" ("Words from Abroad," 189). In fact, this illusion of naturalness is characteristic of the communicative dimension of language with its "layer of mediocre tacit agreement," and the harsh, inorganic aspect of the foreign word can effect a "beneficial interruption of the conformist moment of language, the muddy stream in which the specific expressive intention drowns" (189). Technical terminology in particular, a primary locus of foreign words, points up the artificial character of language: "Terminology destroys the illusion of naturalness in language, which is historical. . . . [Hence] every foreign word contains the explosive material of enlightenment" (190).

Adorno holds up this historical, antinatural character of language in opposition to both the theory of linguistic purity, which views foreign words as a contaminant in language, and the historicist view that postulates a gradual assimilation of foreign words into the body of language in a quasi-organic process. "Pure creaturely language is hidden from human beings or lost to them," Adorno says, and this is why "the life of language is not lived with the teleological rhythm of creaturely life, with birth, growth, and death" ("On the Use of Foreign Words," 288). The radical historical character of foreign words makes their presence in language a critical one as well as an erotic one. Hence they must be defended "precisely where they are at their worst from the point of view of purism: where they are foreign bodies assailing the body of language" ("On the Use of Foreign Words," 288). In assailing that body, they demonstrate not only that language is not natural but that it can have no ontology: "They confront even concepts that try to pass themselves off as origin itself with their mediatedness, their moment of being subjectively constructed, their arbitrariness" ("Words from Abroad," 189).

The specific historical situation of the German language is relevant here. In Adorno's account, the Latinate, "civilizatory" components of language never fused with the older Germanic layers of the language. Germany did not become a unified bourgeois nation; educated elites and common people remained separate. Similarly, the German language did not achieve the kind of unification, or at least resolution of conflicting linguistic strata, that French or English did. Hence, Adorno says, Benjamin's notion of the foreign word as a silver rib is actually misleading: "What seems inorganic . . . is in actuality only historical evidence, evidence of the failure of that unification" ("Words from

Abroad," 187). This unique situation of the German language not only makes the foreign words—essentially the Latinate element—conspicuous and thus available for use. It also makes the oppressive, dominating quality of the civilizatory element—the barbarism within civilization—more obvious. The kind of unification achieved elsewhere was in fact achieved through coercion and subordination. Accordingly, foreign words also speak to the historical stage of German culture that aimed at what Adorno refers to as *das Humane,* meaning humanity or humaneness, a notion he elaborates with regard to Goethe's *Iphigenie* in the essay "On the Classicism of Goethe's *Iphigenie.*"[23] That culture, which did not prevail any more than the attempt to "civilize" Germany did, stands in for a utopia of the future in which the subordination of language to exchange will have disintegrated. As "the twice-alienated remnants of a culture that once had as its aim *das Humane,*" foreign words "await their resurrection in a better order of things": they represent the potential for a "utopia of language," in which words are used with flexibility, tact, and accuracy in the service of "unselfish expression of the matter at hand rather than in the service of human beings as potential customers" ("Words from Abroad," 192).

Accordingly, while the use of foreign words can be criticized as an exercise of educational privilege—and certainly Adorno himself has been the object of this criticism—Adorno argues that because of its potential for this expression of the matter at hand, the use of foreign words transcends social privilege and has, as we saw, the explosive force of enlightenment. Tact, the ability to make fine distinctions without resorting to rigid definitions, an essential feature of humanness, is the "seal of authenticity" of the utopian as opposed to the oppressive use of foreign words. And when Adorno explicates instances of his own use of foreign words, he continually emphasizes the specific subtle reasons for his choice of words. When he asserts that language is not "creaturely" and not lived with a quasi-organic teleological rhythm, he asserts that it is lived instead "with naming as the enigmatic ur-phenomenon in between grasping thought and manifested truth, with crystallization and disintegration" ("On the Use of Foreign Words," 288). Foreign words as names in this sense are the death heads that signal the movement of language away from its communicative dimension. Perhaps Adorno states this utopian view of their value and role most vividly in the early, unpublished essay, really a manifesto, "On the Use of Foreign Words":

While the writer always thinks that he is quoting from his education and from special knowledge, he is actually quoting from a hidden language that is unknown in the positive sense, a language that overtakes, overshadows, and transfigures the existing one as though it were itself getting ready to be transformed into the language of the future. For the old organic words are like gas lights in a street where the violet light of an oxyacetylene welding apparatus suddenly flames out; they stare into it, inconsolably past, prehistoric and mythological. The power of an unknown, genuine language that is not open to any calculus, a language that arises only in pieces and out of the disintegration of the existing one; this negative, dangerous, and yet assuredly promised power is the true justification of foreign words. (291)

The Language of the Philosopher

To this point I have approached Adorno's implicit theory of language from its dark edge, *Rauschen*, the movement of poetic language away from communication and toward the vanishing Other, the nonidentical object. If we now turn to some of the texts in which Adorno writes about the language of philosophy and criticism, as opposed to poetic or literary language, we will find that the central tenets of this implicit theory and even the themes and the imagery in which they are expressed remain the same.

I have referred to "On the Use of Foreign Words" as a manifesto. Adorno wrote yet another manifesto about language, also unpublished in his lifetime (and as yet untranslated) and probably dating from the same period, the early 1930s—the "Theses on the Language of the Philosopher," referred to earlier. There Adorno defines language in relation to history, truth, and the matter at hand *(die Sache)*—in other words, in relation to the philosopher's aim—and he defines the philosopher's relation to language. Here is Adorno's depiction of the situation in which the contemporary philosopher finds himself: "Today the philosopher is confronted with a deteriorated *[zerfallenen]* language. His material is the ruins of the words to which history binds him: his only freedom is the possibility of configuring them in accordance with the coercion of truth within them. He may no more conceive a word as pregiven than he may invent a word" (368–69). Words, then, are not free-floating, ahistorical givens whose connection with their content is that of arbitrary signs. Rather, words exist within a historical context and as such contain some portion of a historical truth. But in the current historical situation of the deterioration of language, no individual word—and certainly not philosophical terminology—has any full and direct equivalence to truth; rather, the measure to which any word retains some force of truth must be empirically determined. The philosopher cannot naively—and willfully—assume a viability on the part of philosophical terminology that does not exist; nor can he arrogate to himself the capacity to simply create new, viable words. (This is Adorno's critique of Heidegger's "jargon of authenticity"). Hence, a philosopher who wants to express a new truth—a truth appropriate to the current historical moment—can neither express it directly in the old, inadequate words nor explain it by means of those words. Rather, as we saw, his only hope is to "place the words around the new truth in such a way that their configuration alone yields the new truth." And as we saw, this "configurative language" effectively alters the words used, creating a "unity of concept and thing that is dialectically intertwined and cannot be disentangled through explication." The kind of unity created is thus analogous to that in a work of art.

These ideas can be understood in the light of the essays from *Notes to Literature* we looked at earlier. The power of foreign words for a German writer, for instance, derives very specifically from the historical situation of the German language, and they present the writer with certain opportunities (but not guarantees); their power must be tested and harnessed, so to speak, in their tactful use. Similarly, the poets Adorno writes about make use of features or qualities of words that are specific to the historical situation in which they are writing—clichés for the Goethe of *Faust* II, abstractions for Eichendorff, archaisms for Borchardt, technical terminology for Benn—and they liberate the expressive potential in those qualities or features. The precise configuring of words is necessary for that potential to be released, as is particularly evident in the case of the particles and conjunctions that became the seals of authenticity in some of the works Adorno discussed.

Philosophy and art share this practice of linguistic criticism. Hence it is not surprising that when Adorno, writing about Hegel in "Skoteinos, or How to Read Hegel," addresses Hegel's use and conception of language, much of what he says echoes the themes elaborated earlier. The title of the essay itself—the Greek word *skoteinos* means "obscure"—evokes the theme of the darkness of language. Distinguishing between "intelligibility" [*Verständlichkeit*, here used in a positive sense] and the "clarity" he denounced in "The Essay as Form," Adorno presents Hegel's necessarily conceptual language as moving away from the conceptual and toward the mimetic in a way that renders his texts intelligible but not clear in the conventional sense. "Philosophy as a whole," Adorno remarks, echoing his formulations in "Music and Language," "is allied with art in wanting to rescue, in the medium of the concept, the mimesis the concept represses, and here Hegel behaves like Alexander with the Gordian knot. He disempowers individual concepts, uses them as though they were the imageless images of what they mean. Hence the Goethean 'residue of absurdity' in the philosophy of absolute spirit" ("Skoteinos," 123). Accordingly, we see in Hegel's writings the same approximation to music and the same slackening of the logical function of coordinating conjunctions that we saw in literary works: "Hegel's style . . . takes on a musical quality that is absent from the sober style of the romantic Schelling. At times it makes itself felt in such things as a use of antithetical particles like *'aber'* [but] for purposes of mere connection" (122). Hegel attempts a kind of gestural mimesis in language and must be read with the same kind of mimetic approach the work of art requires:

In their presentation his writings attempt a direct resemblance to the substance. Their significative gesture recedes in favor of a mimetic one, a kind of gestural or curvilinear writing strangely at odds with the solemn claims of reason that Hegel inherited from the enlightenment. . . . One must read Hegel by describing along with him the curves of his intellectual movement, by playing his ideas with the speculative ear as though they were musical notes. ("Skoteinos," 122–23)

In these statements, Adorno counterpoints the romantic aspect of Hegel that manifests itself in his use of language with the claims of reason he advances. But his essential criticism of Hegel is based on a deeper, though related contradiction in Hegel's work. Because Hegel fails to engage in the kind of linguistic reflection that philosophy requires, his writing presents itself as though it claimed an absoluteness for reason that contradicts the actual substance of his work. "Hegel's formulations, which neither can be nor are intended to be conclusive, often sound as though they were. Hegel's language has the demeanor of the language of doctrine" (109). Adorno points out Hegel's antilinguistic stance, his indifference to language: "This man who reflected on all reflection did not reflect on language; he moved about in language with a carelessness that is incompatible with what he said" (122). This indifference to language is an indifference to limitation and to historical situatedness that is the correlate of Hegel's overreliance on totality and the absolute objectivity of spirit—a kind of hubris, in other words. The pretension to system in Hegel's work thus amounts to a failure to understand configuration as Adorno conceives it:

The specificity of philosophy as a configuration of moments is qualitatively different from a lack of ambiguity in every particular moment, even within the configuration, because the configuration itself is more, and other, than the quintessence of its moments. Constellation is not system. Everything does not become resolved, everything does not come out even; rather, one moment sheds light on the other, and the figures that the individual moments form together are specific signs and a legible script. This is not yet articulated in Hegel, whose mode of presentation is characterized by a sovereignly indifferent attitude toward language. (109)

While defending the mimetic, the gestural, the equivocal in Hegel's writing, then, Adorno is also pointing out how Hegel failed to reflect on the implications of his own language. This failure with regard to language is the failure of Hegel's philosophy. In this light, it becomes clear that Adorno's theory of language is essential to his own practice of philosophy; it defines the way he differentiates himself from the Hegel who failed to reflect on language. Adorno's negative dialectics is not only a dialectics that renounces pretensions to system and to the absolute, but by the same token a dialectics that operates through linguistic criticism and the configurational method.

The features of Adorno's conception of language just elaborated allow us to articulate what is so strikingly individual—and to some, disconcerting and even objectionable—about his use of language in his own writings. After his earlier period, Adorno's writing is marked by a striking consistency of style as well as by a redundancy of phrases and themes. It would be hard to mistake an essay by Adorno for an essay by anyone else (and in what follows I will use the essays in *Notes to Literature* as paradigmatic for Adorno's writing). At the same time, it is difficult to pinpoint precisely where that consistency is located. It seems, like Odradek, to have "no fixed abode." Further, in contrast to the speechlike and even dialect-like quality that Adorno points out in Hegel's writing,[24] Adorno's use of language has a formal and artificial quality that coexists with the rejection of clarity that he claims for himself as well as for Hegel.

In this context, it will be useful to recall another of Adorno's descriptions of configuration, this one specific to philosophy: his definition of exact imagination, from "The Actuality of Philosophy" (1931). Adorno contrasts "historical images," experimental tools of reason tested in terms of their power to answer questions about reality, with the "organic archetypes" of Klages (and presumably Jung as well). As we have seen, he takes up Bacon's notion of philosophy as *ars inveniendi* and defines the imagination as its organon: "an exact imagination; an imagination that remains strictly within the material which science and scholarship present it and extends beyond them only in the smallest features of their arrangement: features, to be sure, which it must originate of itself" (342). He goes on to emphasize that the validity of this imaginative operation lies in its responding "to the questions specific to a preexisting reality" and "regrouping the elements of the question without going beyond the scope of the elements" in such a way that the question disappears (342). We see here, as I have noted, the germ of what later became the programmatic essay "The Essay as Form." Adorno is attempting to define a function for the imagination that is analogous to rational scientific investigation rather than to artistic creation but that depends not on fixed definitions or rules of procedure but on insightful "arrangement," in other words, configuration. This territory he marks out here as the sphere of philosophy, which, as we have seen, is also the sphere of linguistic criticism.

As we have seen, language in the literary work, unable to attain the direct equivalence of word and thing that would constitute the Name, moves toward the gestural and the mimetic, toward parataxis and configuration. Adorno's own critical writings, works of exact imagination, do so as well. This is the point in which his writings and the literary works he writes about are homologous.[25] The material that his works use, however, their "content," so to speak, consists of what science and scholarship have to offer: the authors' texts, information about biography, the historical context, the critical context, and so on. The philosophical, aesthetic, and literary-critical terminology that form part of the critical context, the context of science and scholarship, becomes part of the material that is subjected to linguistic criticism as it enters the configuration, just as *Aesthetic Theory* is a linguistic-critical reconfiguring of the concepts and terms of previous aesthetic philosophy and criticism. Or, to use Adorno's second formulation regarding the material that is reconfigured by exact imagination, the essays reconfigure the elements of the questions presented by an author's work in its context, in other words, the internal contradictions that form the dynamic aspect of the work: Eichendorff as an allegorist, though usually considered a romantic; the elitist and hermetic pretensions of George's work in relation to the presumably ephemeral and heteronomous work of translating; and so on. Again, as these contradictions, which are not divorced from the social and historical context, become the internal contradictions in the work—a process Adorno describes in "On Lyric Poetry and Society"—they become matters of "work on language" and the "will to language," and thus once again matters of linguistic criticism. As configuration and linguistic criticism, again, Adorno's own essays are homologous to the structure of the literary works he discusses. At the same time, the fact that the "content" of the essays is the "matter-of-fact" stuff of science and scholarship, the philosophical and historical context—and is therefore empirical and contingent—makes the precise location of the homology difficult to pinpoint. Perhaps more accurately, it points up the fact that homology is a matter of form rather than content and thus not localizable.

This imaginative work of "arrangement" in Adorno's essays gives them a paratactic and configurational form, parataxis being a necessary element of configuration, since configuration implies discontinuity and lack of linear or cumulative order. Parataxis, the reader will remember, operates at both the macro- and the microlevels. It is conspicuous as the division of the work into a series of evidently related but not cumulatively sequential blocks and less conspicuous at the microlevel, where it takes the form of a softening of the logical function of language that retains its logical form. Parataxis at the macrolevel is quite obvious and even typographically marked in a number of the essays in *Notes to Literature* that are composed of separate blocks with extra spacing between them rather than anything like paragraphs linked by transitional sentences; see for instance "Titles," "Punctuation Marks," "Short Commentaries on Proust," and "Reading Balzac."

The essay on Stefan George illustrates this paratactic form. It consists of a series of semiautonomous blocks clearly related to a general theme that is stated and restated, though without any one formulation being definitive. It has none of the explicit metacommentary that is customary in academic discourse to mark the sequence of a cumulative argument. There is no overview at the beginning of the essay, no marking of an internal sequence of points in the argument, no explicit internal references that ground a later point in an earlier one, no explicit summary or conclusion. There is nothing, in short, to mark the sequencing that is characteristic of a deductive train of thought. Rather, the various aspects of George's work that Adorno evokes all relate directly to the central theme, and, with one exception (the midpoint of what amounts to a chiasmus), the logic that governs the order of presentation is if anything subtle and implicit. To be specific, the essay revolves around the dialectic of will in relation to literary language, as we saw earlier. The first four blocks deal with the destructiveness of George's willfulness; his will to immortality has provoked oblivion for his work, and his forced spontaneity has wreaked havoc on his lyric poetry. The remainder of the essay, however, deals with what Adorno calls "the reverse": the points at which the work, bearing a slighter weight of willfulness, becomes more authentic, or at which George's will, having become a "will to language," achieves actual work on language as such. We find blocks on the poems that Schoenberg set to music, on points of nonviolent authenticity in other lyric poems, on George's translations from the French, on places in his early work, and on the prose works. The essay concludes with the prose piece on the dream of the talking head cited earlier, in which willfulness and horror at it are both present.

This summary of the contents of the various blocks indicates one source of the sense of formality and artificiality in Adorno's essays: at least in Adorno's case, explicating internal contradictions yields a symmetrical structure, so that we are shown first destruction and then authenticity, with the midpoint where the reversal occurs being explicitly marked. (Hence the sense that chiasmus is characteristic of Adorno's style.) In this arrangement, the initial sentences of the individual blocks resemble the transitional sentences one finds in writing that is not self-consciously paratactic. Here are some examples:

George is flawed where he strives to exercise a power he has usurped as though it were authentic. But this permits almost the reverse. (block #5)

Despite the stigmata, however, a good deal of George's lyric poetry in the narrow sense is as fresh as this poem. (block #6)

The incommensurably new element that George's lyric work gave to German poetry cannot be separated from George's permeation with French poetry. (block #7)

The lack of a cumulative argument that relies on internal grounding in what has come before, however, weakens the connecting function of these sentences, so that they become similar to the nonfunctional particles and conjunctions Adorno explicated in the work of Hölderlin and others. These initial sentences, one might say, provide a mere semblance of logical continuity.

The slackening of the logical function in these initial sentences is one aspect of parataxis at the microlevel of Adorno's writing that shapes his style. Others have been explored elsewhere.[26] Here I will note some additional ways in which linguistic criticism and the renunciation of definition work to create paratactic and configurational form at the level of individual sentences. First of all, Adorno creates what is almost a personal idiom by selecting certain words and phrases as the indefinable, and in that sense empty or blank, yet resonant, positive centers of configurations. *Rauschen* is one example of such a word; name, enigma, *das Humane* are others, and the "speculative ear" is an example of a phrase taken up and elaborated by Adorno as part of his personal lexicon.[27] For the most part, these words and phrases are not part of the traditional public terminology of aesthetics or criticism; rather, they are elevated to the status of aesthetic terms within Adorno's work. The enigmatic, blurred quality of these words makes them in effect the equivalent in Adorno's writing of the allegorical "stage-prop" words in Eichendorff's. Their use contributes to our sense of the individuality and consistency of Adorno's work.

Second, each essay subjects a limited set of words, drawn from the philosophical and critical terminology relevant to the subject at hand, to linguistic criticism. These words appear as sets of oppositions around which series of sentences are structured. The sentences are formulated in such a way as to lay bare the internal contradictions in the terms—the ways in which each term is related to what would seem to be its opposite, perhaps through the mediation of another term that would seem more appropriately linked with its opposite. A portion of the essay on Stefan George, for instance, is organized around the nature/artifact opposition, as in this sentence: "The speeding train and the 'wundersame pflanzenwelt' [flora of a wonder-world] with which the poem closes are the cryptogram of the urge to wrest something completely vegetal from what is completely artificial, to wrest nature from what is absolutely artifactual and distant from it" ("Stefan George," 190). Here, nature rather than artifact is linked with will and intention. Cryptogram, a variant of enigma, serves as the positive void at the center of the configuration.

Issues that are specific to the work being discussed determine the particular set of oppositions Adorno works with, which are generally drawn from the critical literature about the specific author, and the configuring of the oppositions is intertwined with what we might call the empirical material of science and scholarship: biographical data, specific texts, and so on. The sentence from the George essay just quoted, for instance, is one of a number in which the dialectic of ornament and vegetation in *Jugendstil,* a technical term with which the scholarly literature has linked George, is elaborated. (Adorno works similarly with romanticism in the Eichendorff essay and classicism in the Goethe essay.) Elements Adorno introduces into the configuration in the George essay include not only various texts of George's but also Melchior Lechter's book designs for George's works, the German youth movement, Count Stauffenburg, and remarks of Benjamin's and Borchardt's about George. These elements are intertwined with a group of thematically interrelated oppositions: ephemeral/core; early/late; imperial/vulnerable; ornamentation/need; technology/vegetation; vegetal/artificial; nature/artifact. The continual interplay of these oppositions with the empirical material and the blank but positive words from Adorno's personal idiom produces a quality of consistency, because the interplay of opposites remains a constant. It also produces a quality of formality, given the symmetry of opposition, and a sense of redundancy, because the same oppositions and personal idiomatic expressions recur repeatedly in slight variations. At the same time, the combination produces a disquieting and discontinuous quality—the effect of parataxis at the microlevel—because there is no natural resting point in the series of intertwined oppositions and no definitive, substantive, positive statement, because the positive center of the configuration is a void or blank.

Just as, however, the initial sentences provide a semblance of logical continuity, so the final sentences, both of individual sections and especially of whole essays, which are like knots, points of greater density in this structure of intertwining oppositions, provide a semblance of conclusion. Thus they emphasize the hard contours of the separate sections and hence strengthen the sense of larger-scale form within the essay. Often they also emphasize the central thematic opposition in the essay, perhaps in relation to one of the blank positive notions. Here are some examples:

• It is only by abandoning meaning that the epic discourse comes to resemble the image, a figure of objective meaning emerging from the negation of subjectively rational meaning.

• But if Surrealism itself now seems obsolete, it is because human beings are now denying themselves the consciousness of denial that was captured in the photographic negative that was Surrealism.

• The art that has achieved self-awareness as a consequence of Valéry's conception would transcend art itself and fulfill itself in the true life of human beings.[28]

Just as Adorno's essays convey a sense of redundancy—a sense that is not literally accurate—that is more appropriate to music than to writing, so this sense of larger-scale form derives less from logical structure than from a quasi-aesthetic articulation via proportion, weight, and emphasis.

A similarly subtle and refined sense of nondeductive form is at work in Adorno's use of foreign words. Foreign words, as Adorno has told us, destroy the illusion that language is natural and organic, and Adorno's use of them helps to emphasize the formal and artificial quality of his writing (though, as he tells us, his audiences will hallucinate foreign words in his texts even where none are present; cf. "Words from Abroad," 185). He emphasizes that the use of foreign words can be justified only by their greater precision: "Only the foreign word that renders the meaning better, more faithfully, more uncompromisingly than the available German synonyms will allow a spark to flow in the constellation into which it is introduced" ("Words from Abroad," 192). But this greater precision is inseparable from their greater conciseness and their role in adjusting the weight and proportion of the sentences. In this way, too, his use of foreign words strengthens the sense of something other than logic in the form of his writings.

Since for Adorno music stands in for the Other that language yearns for, it is not surprising that at some point in each essay the work in question would be compared in some respect to music. Such a comparison will not be repeated within an individual essay, and it will not occur in the final sentence. It is as though language's movement toward music is a glimpse of its outer limits, an analogue of the positive void at the center of the configuration. Just as Adorno wants to differentiate himself from the method of Hegel's absolute spirit, which produces a "circle of circles" in which each end incorporates its own beginning and forms the basis for the next cycle of reflection, with the result that method becomes an onrushing, all-encompassing system,[29] so, perhaps, he wants to avoid the sense of a cumulative and dramatic movement toward the absolute beyond language that would be suggested if the essays closed with the comparison to music. Instead, these essays, whose subject and medium is language, close with final sentences that are emblems of the limitations, the negativity, and the potential for transcendence that are inextricably contained within language in its capacity for configuration.

3

Configurational Form in the Aesthetic Essay and the Enigma of *Aesthetic Theory*

It thinks in fragments . . . and finds its unity in and through the breaks.
—*Adorno, "The Essay as Form"*

Now newly retranslated and with important recent work devoted to it, *Aesthetic Theory,* this last of Adorno's major works, may be at a pivotal point in its reception.[1] I hope to be of use in what may be a turning from catastrophe to fruitfulness, not so much by explicating or defending *Aesthetic Theory* as by shedding some light on the way its form has helped to make it difficult of access. As we know, the very title of *Aesthetic Theory* highlights Adorno's claim that its form is inseparable from its substance. The book thus poses, even more directly than other of Adorno's works, the question of the relation between philosophy and art, reason and the aesthetic. This makes the peculiar nature of its form particularly relevant. Conversely, it may be that qualities that are particularly appropriate to its form have contributed to the difficulty of its reception.

To inquire into the form of *Aesthetic Theory* is to inquire into how to read Adorno as late work. If the activity of exact imagination produces the configurational form appropriate to it, then reading configurational form conversely requires a mimetic subjective experience of the text appropriate to it. But if subjectivity and objectivity diverge from one another in late works, then late work may require a shift in the mimetic subjective experience it elicits and demands of the reader. Adorno suggests something of the sort, as we have seen, when he says that *Aesthetic Theory* had to be written differently from any of his other works, "concentrically . . . in paratactic parts of equal weight arranged around a central point" (*Aesthetic Theory,* 541/497). Indeed, the initial experience of reading *Aesthetic Theory* is of a field (paratactic parts of equal weight) in which a recurrent, small-scale pattern (the dialectical movement from assertion to negation) plays over an endless surface without depth. In this way, too, *Aesthetic Theory* presents us dramatically with the dilemma of Adorno's work: how to move in reading it beyond, or beneath, a surface we are now infinitely familiar with and which somehow resists further penetration.

In this context, it will be helpful to return to the remarks of Albrecht Wellmer referred to in the introduction to this volume. Wellmer frames the problem of *Aesthetic Theory* in precisely these terms of surface and depth. It is not the book's esoteric character that has hindered its reception, he says, but rather "its systematic aspects: Adorno's aesthetics of negativity has revealed its rigid features: something artificial has become visible in his aporetic constructions." Wellmer, as we have seen, proposes to loosen this rigidity by disentangling the various strands in *Aesthetic Theory,* noting that if the truth content of a work is historical, as Adorno proposes, certain of its moments will fall away in the course of history. He proposes that the reading of *Aesthetic Theory* might take on the function of a magnifying glass: then "the layers of meaning which to the naked eye appear fused" might "separate out and distinguish themselves from one another." Better still, he suggests, would be a "stereoscopic reading," which would produce a "three-dimensional image in which the latent depths of the text became visible."[2] Wellmer's notion of a detailed reading that looks at different strands or layers of the text, with the resulting dimensionality revealing depth, converges with the notion of "layers" that Adorno uses both when talking about late works and when talking about the historicity of the work of art. If we hypothesize that configuration will take a different form in a late work like *Aesthetic Theory,* then the question of precisely how "strands" and "layers" are arranged to produce "depth" may be a useful guide in our investigation.

There are many routes by which one might approach this question of late-style configurational form in *Aesthetic Theory.* Here I will proceed indirectly, through comparison with the configurational form of the more accessible "aesthetic essays,"[3] as I will call them, meaning the essays whose subject matter is itself aesthetic: works of literature, art, or music. Adorno himself has given us, of course, in "The Essay as Form," a characterization of the textual form of his essays and the relationship of reason and the aesthetic in that form. I will take that programmatic statement as my starting point.

The Essay as Form

"The Essay as Form" comes closer than anything else we have to a statement from Adorno about his own writing.[4] Here he takes pains to describe the kind of form that would be the product of an open but fallible intellectual experience of a specific culturally formed object. It is here, too, that many of the familiar terms in which he characterizes his work and which have formed the mainstay of discussions of his mode of thought are gathered together. This material is thus very familiar to most scholars of

Adorno. I beg the reader's indulgence while I bring these terms forward briefly so that I can then use them to examine Adorno's own practice in one of his aesthetic essays.

In "The Essay as Form," Adorno is concerned primarily to differentiate the essay and the thought it presents from systematic, discursive thought. In the process, he draws repeatedly on comparisons between the essay form and the aesthetic, at the same time emphasizing that the essay, which works with concepts, is not and cannot be art. My primary concern here is to highlight the terms in which Adorno characterizes the similarity and difference between the essay and the aesthetic and to link them to the terms in which he characterizes the formal qualities of the essay as text, in particular the notions of "aconceptual transition" and "equivocation."

As Adorno emphasizes, the essay's medium is concepts. But it is the primacy of the object that determines the use of concepts in the essay. That is to say, in contrast to systematic, discursive presentation, the essay provides neither definition of its concepts, exhaustive treatment of its object, nor a chain of deductive logic that proceeds from first principles. All of that would subsume the particular under the general and presuppose a fixed correlation between the order of things and the order of ideas. Conversely, all of that would preclude open and genuine intellectual experience—freedom.

The relationship between subject and object here is analogous to that in aesthetic experience. As Adorno puts it, "in order to be disclosed . . . , the objective wealth of meanings encapsulated in every intellectual phenomenon demands of the recipient the same spontaneity of subjective fantasy that is castigated in the name of objective discipline" ("Essay as Form," 4). As we saw with regard to subjective aesthetic experience, adequate experience imitates the aesthetic object; "it is scarcely possible to speak of the aesthetic unaesthetically."[5] In the essay, this mimesis takes the form of the construction of "a complex of concepts interconnected in the same way [the essay] imagines them to be interconnected in the object" (23). This mimetic adequation of subject and object gives the essay a kind of aesthetic autonomy. At the same time, again, Adorno reminds us that the essay is distinguished from art "by its medium, concepts, and its claim to a truth devoid of aesthetic semblance" (95). Because the medium of the essay is so different from that of the artworks that are its subject matter, the mimetic activity takes place through the mode of presentation. The same thing, however, is true of art; hence, in this way too the aesthetic is analogous to art: "Consciousness of the nonidentity of presentation and subject matter forces presentation to unremitting efforts. In this alone the essay resembles art" (18).

Adorno's formulations tell us that in the essay, "presentation"—that is, form—and the "complex of interconnected concepts" that imitates the internal logic of the subject matter are one and the same. Configuration is both form and substance. To put this another way, form in the essay is defined by the way concepts are used; essentially, by the way they are set in relation to one another. Adorno characterizes this relationship in such terms as "configuration," "reciprocal interaction," and "tension in stasis," as in the following typical formulations: "All the essay's concepts are to be presented in such a way that they support one another, that each becomes articulated through its configuration with the others" (13); "in the essay discrete elements set off against one another come together to form a readable context" (13); "the elements crystallize as a configuration through their motion" (13); concepts "are made more precise only through their relationship to one another" (12); "the essay presses for the reciprocal interaction of its concepts" (13); the subject matter of the essay is "always a conflict brought to a standstill" (16); "the essay's transitions repudiate conclusive deduction in favor of crossconnections between elements" (22); "the moments are interwoven as in a carpet" (13). And finally, the essay's insights "multiply, confirm, and qualify themselves, whether in the further course of the essay itself or in a mosaiclike relationship to other essays" (17). Indeed, this list itself shows us how Adorno's formulations "multiply, confirm, and qualify themselves."

In "The Essay as Form," the structure of subjective aesthetic experience we investigated earlier is reformulated in terms of the relationships among word, concept, and object. It is in this context, in connection with the role of language in this grouping, that the less familiar notions of "aconceptual transition" and "equivocation," which Adorno presents as derived from the sphere of rhetoric, enter his formulations. Just as Adorno emphatically rejected the notion that art and *Wissenschaft,* or science and scholarship, could be or become identical, so he emphatically rejects the notion that word and image could be identical ("Language's ambitious transcendence of meaning ends up in . . . meaninglessness," p. 7). But just as he also rejects a rigid division between art and science/scholarship, positing individual experience as the mediating factor, so he rejects the rigid distinction between logic and rhetoric. The mediating factor in this case is a reformulation of rhetoric's communicative function in the essay. Whereas rhetoric in its customary sense, which, Adorno says, "was probably never anything but thought in its adaptation to communicative language," aimed at the gratification of the listener, in the essay the rhetorical moment becomes "sublimated into the idea of a happiness in freedom vis-à-vis the object" (20–21). In these formulations Adorno captures communication for a Kantian notion of the aesthetic. He again formulates the relationship of the essay's truth to logic: the essay "is not unlogical; it obeys logical criteria insofar as the totality of its propositions must fit together coherently" (22). But the mode of development, as opposed to the ensemble, is not discursive. It lacks the tightness of deductive logic. The transitions are looser and are not based on deductive relationships between concepts. Instead, the transitions have the function of helping to create a configuration, and in this sense they are closer to image than to concept: "the essay is more dynamic than traditional thought by virtue of the tension between the presentation and the matter presented. But at the same time, as a constructed juxtaposition of elements it is more static. Its affinity with the image lies solely in this, except that the staticness of the essay is one in which relationships of tension have been brought, as it were, to a standstill" (22). In this combination of loose movement and static, imagelike quality, the essay's mode of development is more akin to rhetoric—and more in tune with the free play of the subjective faculties—than to logic with its strict forward progression.

In orienting itself toward the free play of the subject's faculties in the perception of the internal dynamics of the object, the essay redirects both logic and rhetoric away from power and domination. This redirection occurs through the loose connections the essay employs. Whereas in rhetoric such transitions customarily serve the power relationship between speaker and listener, in the essay they are absorbed into the configurational form. The loose logic becomes nonsubsumptive interaction, aconceptual transition: "The offensive transitions in rhetoric, in which association, verbal ambiguity, and a relaxation of logical synthesis made it easy for the listener and subjugated him, enfeebled, to the orator's will, are fused in the essay with the truth content. Its transitions repudiate conclusive relationships in favor of crossconnections between elements" (21–22). Similarly, individual words are used equivocally, in keeping with the fact that the object is not a single thing but a constellation of dynamic moments: "The essay uses equivocations not out of sloppiness . . . but to make it clear . . . that when a word covers different things they are not completely different; the unity of the word calls to mind a unity, however, hidden, in the object itself" (22). There is a kind of cunning at work here, whereby the essay appropriates the aesthetic while retaining its own conceptual character: "Here too the essay approaches the logic of music, that stringent and yet aconceptual art of transition, in order to appropriate for verbal language something it forfeited under the domination of discursive logic" (22). These aconceptual transitions, then, are both the locus of the essay's affinity with art and the means by which the configurations that constitute the essay's truth content are established.

The configuration, then, is formed from the crossconnections of interrelated equivocal terms with their penumbrae of associations, brought to them in the subjective experience of the thinker who becomes an arena for the intellectual experience of this very specific, contingently chosen object. The aconceptual linking of particulars creates a unique amalgam of subject and object, the conceptual and the aconceptual, which resembles the artwork in its autonomy but nevertheless puts forth a claim to truth through its use of the medium of concepts.

Configurational Form in the Aesthetic Essay "Titles"

An examination of one of Adorno's aesthetic essays will show us this art of aconceptual transition in practice and provide the basis for comparison with the late version of configurational form we expect to find in *Aesthetic Theory*. "Titles," the essay I have chosen, is composed of a number of segments, separated by spaces (or asterisks, depending on the edition). These segments have the appearance of paragraphs (there are no paragraph breaks within them), but, as we will see, though they are self-contained in certain ways they do not have the kind of logical or rhetorical structure that characterizes the familiar paragraph form in discursive presentation. Instead, on the basis of what Adorno says in "The Essay as Form," we can expect both the essay as a whole and each segment to be characterized by configurational form. Let me begin by providing a sketch of the configurational form of "Titles" as a whole.

The element of contingency and subjective experience inherent in the essay form as Adorno describes it is much in evidence in "Titles." Adorno's mind seems to move from one idea or one reminiscence of a work's title to another as he writes what seems to be a series of random reflections on titles, including both comments on the titles of specific books and comments on the process of finding a title for a book. He begins with comments on Lessing's remarks on titles; moves to the difficulties an author experiences in titling his own book; then to reminiscences of his own publisher, Peter Suhrkamp; to anecdotes about how some of his own books got their titles; to comments on the titles of Kafka's novels; and so on. Only very occasionally is there any explicit transition from one segment to the next. The coherence across individual segments, then, must emerge from something other than an explicit, discursive presentation with its familiar forms of transition, and the configurational form of the essay as a whole, presumably, will result from relationships between the forces keeping the segments separate and the forces linking them together.

In some cases, associations provide links between one segment and the next. Peter Suhrkamp's aversion to titles with the word "and" in them, for instance, provides the link to the segment that follows, which explains how Adorno's book *Prisms* got its name:

Suhrkamp rejected Adorno's original title, *Cultural Criticism and Society*, because it contained the word "and." Primarily, however, the segments are linked, though not in any clear sequential order, through the fact that each of them is connected in some way with an aspect of the link between titles and names and naming. The manifold meanings and conceptual ramifications of the word or concept "name" make for a whole spectrum of links between titles and names. The first segment of "Titles," for instance, begins with a proper name used as a title for a play (*Nanine*), mentioned in a passage from Lessing, and ends with the essential impossibility of naming, that is, titling, contemporary works of art, with Adorno citing Beckett's title *L'innomable* (*The Unnamable*) as correctly indicating this aporia. No synthetic statement of the complex of ideas generated by or constituting the name/title link is provided in "Titles," although the individual segments do have recognizable endings, as they have recognizable beginnings, and the first and last segments are clearly linked through their reference to Lessing.[6]

In many cases, the connections between the various aspects of titling and naming are made through "things"—what I will call the "concrete," that is, empirical or aconceptual, elements that appear in the essay: the specific contingent events, titles, persons, and so on.[7] There is, however, no stable distinction of levels of abstractness that divides these concrete elements from abstractions or concepts. The concrete elements include, for instance, the names of a group of modern authors—Beckett, Kafka, Kraus, Proust, Adorno himself—whose work is not merely an occasion for Adorno's reflection but itself already reflects on this link. (Adorno's essay on Kafka in *Prisms*, for instance, has as its motto a quotation from Proust: "If God the Father created things by naming them, it is by taking away their names or giving them others that the artist recreates them.") They also include a group of titles—*The Unnamable, The One Who Was Never Heard of Again,* and so on—that in turn refer to conceptual issues around naming and titling.

At this point, then, we can formulate configurational form in this essay as a grouping, in the form of a series partially linked by association, of (for the most part) concrete elements, each of which illuminates one or more aspects of what is essentially a conceptual issue, with the various interrelated but not identical aspects providing linkages between the presentations that go beyond mere juxtaposition in a series. At the same time, however, the terms in which the conceptual issues appear can refer variously to concrete elements in the presentations or to concepts; conversely, the concrete elements in the presentations can themselves contain or embody reflections on aspects of the conceptual issue. This formulation, which I will exemplify in what follows, points up an aspect of configurational form that does not stand out clearly in Adorno's own comments in "The Essay as Form," namely, the fact that both the "conceptual" and the "concrete" (or "aconceptual") elements in the essay are equivocal, in Adorno's term, that is, possessed of multiple, interrelated meanings. Equivocation thus crosses the boundary between the conceptual and the aconceptual, so that the configuration is full of linkages or movements between the conceptual and the concrete, linkages as various as the various aspects of the central issue itself. This complex structuring of the relationship between the conceptual and the concrete is, I believe, the key to the aesthetic dimension of Adorno's aesthetic essays.

A detailed analysis of one of the individual segments from "Titles" will shed further light on this crucial feature of configurational form. The segment I have chosen is the second of two segments on Kafka's titles. It is six sentences long and reads as follows:

For Kafka's America novel, the title he used in his diary, *The One Who Was Never Heard of Again [Der Verschollene]*, would have been better than the title under which the book went down in history. That too is a fine title; for the work has as much to do with America as the prehistoric photograph "In New York Harbor" that is included as a loose page in my edition of the *Stoker* fragment of 1913. The novel takes place in an America that moved while the picture was being taken, the same and yet not the same America on which the emigrant seeks to rest his eye after a long, barren crossing. —But nothing would fit that better than *The One Who Was Never Heard of Again*, a blank space for a name that cannot be found. The perfect passive participle *verschollen*, "never heard of again," has lost its verb the way the family's memory loses the emigrant who goes to ruin and dies. Far beyond its actual meaning, the expression of the word *verschollen* is the expression of the novel itself. (7)[8]

Since discursive logic works at the level of sentences and sequences of sentences, that is the level, or one of the levels, at which equivocation in the sense I have just discussed—reference to a variety of interrelated aspects of something, those aspects ranging across the conceptual/aconceptual boundary—is practiced. In other words, if the rhetorical dimension in the essay is to outwit, as Adorno suggests, the discursive logical form of expository writing, which cannot be circumvented, then the configurational process must operate in the fine texture of the writing—within, between, and across sentences. According, I will use a sentence-by-sentence analysis here to show equivocation and the creation of configurational form at work.

Sentence 1: For Kafka's America novel, the title he used in his diary, *The One Who Was Never Heard of Again [Der Verschollene]* would have been better than the title under which the book went down in history.

This sentence presents an aesthetic judgment: the "working title" of Kafka's book *Amerika* would have been better than its final title. By the conventions of discursive presentation, the rest of the segment should present the grounds for this judgment; we shall see whether, and how, it does. This first sentence also presents us with two concrete elements in the form of two specific names for an existing book. (The reader also reflects, perhaps, that one name is ostensibly that of a real place, America, in which the book is presumably set, whereas the other title presumably refers to a character in the book.) The sentence also refers in two different places to the thematic content of the essay "Titles" as a whole. Fairly obviously, it links up with the discussion, in the preceding segment, of Kafka's use of provisional titles and his unwillingness to give definitive titles to his own works. The other reference is more puzzling and less conspicuous: *Amerika* is the title under which Kafka's book "went down in," literally "entered into" history. One of the themes of the essay "Titles" is the relationship of the title to the book's afterlife, its fame; Adorno's phrase alludes to this theme and to the issue of Kafka's fame and the afterlife of his work. Further, although the reader probably assumes that the title *The One Who Was Never Heard of Again* refers to the novel's protagonist and that the phrase "went down in history" refers to the subsequent history of the book's reception, still the copresence of these phrases in the same sentence raises the question of the relationship between fame and oblivion. And since the sentence seems to suggest these relationships, the reader easily makes the association to Adorno the emigrant in America and the relationship of Adorno the emigrant to Adorno the author.

Sentence 2: That too is a fine title; for the work has as much to do with America as the prehistoric photograph "In New York Harbor" that is included as a loose page in my edition of the *Stoker* fragment of 1913.

In terms of discursive logic, this sentence is a digression, or a qualification. Rather than immediately giving the grounds for the aesthetic judgment announced in the first sentence, it offers a second, subordinate judgment: the title *Amerika* is also a good title. And the semicolon leads the reader to expect that the grounds for that second judgment will be offered in the second part of the sentence. Indeed, the second part of the sentence does begin with the word "for," indicating that reasons, or grounds, are to follow. But what is then provided is a complex and ambiguous analogy that introduces two new, though related, concrete elements. To paraphrase Adorno's analogy: Kafka's book is related to the land or nation America as a certain real photograph is related to it; the degree of relationship in each case is that befitting a good title. This sentence blocks the operation of discursive thought by leaving two crucial matters unspecified: what *is* the relationship, and what degree of relationship *is* fitting for a title? Certainly the comparison of a photograph and a book raises (though in a dubious context) the idea of "photographic realism." But because the statement is so unspecified, other aspects of the sentence come to the fore and enter into relationships with the previous sentence: the word "prehistoric" enters into relationship with "went down in history" of the previous sentence, and the presence of Adorno's personal copy of the *Stoker* fragment of 1913 (an early portion of Kafka's novel published before the novel as a whole) seems to echo the earlier title of the novel, while the conjunction of the word "prehistoric" and a specific date, 1913, echoes the question of the relationship between history and oblivion raised in the first sentence.

The disproportion between the length of the preceding commentary on these connections and their object—two sentences, approximately six printed lines, of Adorno's writing—is only partially due to the fact that some of the elements in the sentences refer beyond themselves to the context of the essay "Titles" as a whole. In these two sentences, Adorno has introduced two judgments, the incompletely specified criterion for one of the judgments, along with the incompletely specified reasons for the judgment, and approximately six of what I have been calling concrete elements: one book with two (or three) titles, a country with a harbor, a photograph, and a copy of an earlier version of the book. All of these concrete elements are linked through their relationship either to the book or to its presumed subject matter. Adorno has encouraged the reader, shall we say, to envision many linkages among these various elements, and between them and the rest of the essay, but he himself has specified or defined no relationships (although he has alluded or referred to certain matters of fact, such as that the *Stoker* fragment was published in 1913).

Sentence 3: The novel takes place in an America that moved while the picture was being taken, the same and yet not the same America on which the emigrant seeks to rest his eye after a long, barren crossing.

In terms of discursive logic, here we recognize the explanation for Adorno's comparison of the novel and the photograph in the previous sentence. But the third thing to which both are being referred, America, is unstable in various senses, as Adorno indicates quite explicitly. While it is tempting to recast this sentence in commonsense terms to mean that a photograph of America taken by an arriving emigrant from on board will be blurred because the ship is moving, and while it is virtually inevitable that this resolution of the relationship among the terms in the sentence (novel, photograph, America, emigrant) will occur to the reader, still this meaning of the sentence is only an initial and partial resolution. To take it as the final meaning of the sentence would be to obscure Adorno's allusive structure and to destroy the generative power of the sentence,[9] which is contained in the relationship between the sentence's logical form and the elements that form employs. Here we are in fact told, syntactically speaking, only that the novel takes place (*spielt*, plays) in America, an America qualified in a variety of ways, which are the same and yet not the same as each other—the America of the novel, which encompasses more than the fictional New York Harbor with which the novel begins; a moving America in a picture, which is both the blurred shipboard snapshot taken by the immigrant and the distorted image of America captured on film or in motion pictures; and the emigrant's wishful image of America, also in motion in some sense, though he wishes his relation to it to be one of rest. Each of these ambiguously equated elements of the sentence is itself in motion in relation to the others. Although logically the sentence seems to do no more than name a place in several ways, in fact it evokes movement and instability across its referents; one is reminded of Adorno's evocation of Ravel's title "Une barque sur l'océan" to express the fragmentation inherent in modern music.[10] The sentence permits no resolution of its elements. Certainly, it demolishes any notion of the novel as photographic realism that may have been aroused by the previous sentence. At no level do Adorno's terms "hold still."

Sentence 4: But nothing would fit that better than *The One Who Was Never Heard of Again,* a blank space for a name that cannot be found.

In terms of discursive logic, this sentence marks a return to the aesthetic judgment presented in the first sentence. It seems to tell us why Kafka's working title was in fact better, and in doing so it incorporates what we have been told about why the eventual title was also good: Kafka's working title is better because it fits "that" better, and the appositive Adorno provides for it—"a blank space for a name that cannot be found"—presumably indicates *how* it fits better. We have the form of discursive argumentation, then, but we do not have its conclusiveness. Far from explaining the reasons for the judgment, the sentence sets up still another complex comparison that gives rise to unresolved speculation on the reader's part and thus functions as a question rather than a statement. The question might be formulated to read: how does a blank space for a name that cannot be found fit an America that moves while having its picture taken better than a prehistoric photograph that is and is not like the arriving emigrant's image of America? Even this formulation gives more specification to the terms of the comparison than Adorno does.

Here it is particularly evident that it is the use of a whole series of interrelated, concrete elements (for a "blank space for a name that cannot be found" is also a concrete element in that it names something that appears within everyday reality) that turns the comparisons into picture puzzles, giving rise to a process of speculation on the reader's part in an attempt to solve them. The discursive movement from sentence to sentence is thus accompanied by a movement from one concrete element to another, the presences being linked both through syntactic or semantic indications of relationship (similes, appositions, comparisons, etc.) and through intrinsic or "objective" relationships (New York Harbor is part of America, a book's title is related to the book, etc.). At the same time, we see that negativity, or emptiness, is built into what I have been calling concrete elements: a blank space can be found in reality, but it is blank, a name that cannot be found is a familiar absence, and so on.

Sentence 5: The perfect passive participle *verschollen,* "never heard of again," has lost its verb the way the family's memory loses the emigrant who goes to ruin and dies.

Discursively, this sentence would seem to provide an explanation for what was so puzzling in the previous sentence. It provides an explicit analogy and links the emigrant with the working title being discussed. It is easy to fill in the comparison by assuming that it is the emigrant's name that has been lost and therefore cannot be entered in the blank space that is the title. But Adorno's apparently explanatory analogy uses as its terms new concrete elements related to, but not identical with, the previous ones. The title *Der Verschollene* is now considered in its grammatical form (the German word *verschollen* is a past participle to which there is no longer a corresponding main verb or infinitive), and the emigrant is now considered from the point of view of his family's memory. Once again, rather than settling matters, these new terms provoke reflection: the perspective has been shifted from the emigrant's view of America to the memory of his family in the country he left behind, and, instead of thinking of America as the land of the future, we are reminded of the way things disappear into the past as history moves forward, like the lost main verb of which *verschollen* is the remnant. We are returned, then, to the complex of speculations concerning history and prehistory, fame and oblivion, that were aroused several sentences earlier. Kafka's title *The One Who Was Never Heard of Again* is the complement of Beckett's title *The Unnamable*, presented earlier in Adorno's essay: there are blank spaces where names (or titles) once were, not only because it becomes impossible to name things in modern times but also because names have sunk into an archaic prehistory and have gone to ruin there. We begin to see how a configuration formed of these concrete elements can be enigmatic or mutilated, a picture puzzle that cannot be solved.

Sentence 6: Far beyond its actual meaning, the expression of the word *verschollen* is the expression of the novel itself.

This is the concluding sentence of the segment, and we read it as finally explaining the basis for the aesthetic judgment announced in the first sentence. It does in fact differ from the previous sentences. It introduces no new concrete elements but instead a contrasting pair of concepts: expression (*Ausdruck*) and meaning (*Bedeutung*). Using these concepts, it makes a statement that requires relatively little paraphrase or interpolation. It says that Kafka's working title *Der Verschollene* is better than the title *Amerika* because its expression—as opposed to its meaning—is the same as the expression of the novel itself. We are asked, then, to consider all that has gone before—the whole complex of associations and comparisons and analogies—as constituting the *expression* both of the title and of the novel. Meaning, in contrast, is the literal significance or reference of the word. Expression, however, includes the moments of blankness or negativity we have seen; it is other than meaning both in extending beyond meaning and in being incapable of resolution into a determinate meaning.

In this final sentence, Adorno's presentation moves from concrete elements to concepts and thus to the level of aesthetic theory; the terms "expression" and "meaning" are terms in the philosophical discussion of the aesthetic. In terms of theory, this sentence fairly straightforwardly indicates Adorno's criterion of a good title: one whose expression fits that of its work. While not defining the term "expression," the sentence indicates that it consists of the kind of thing we saw in the previous sentences. But what we saw in those sentences consisted precisely of interrelations among concrete elements that provoked but did not resolve speculation on the reader's part. One might be tempted to say that the concrete elements themselves are the bearers of the expression peculiar to Kafka's novel, whereas the kinds of unresolvable interrelationships set up between them are the work of Adorno rather than Kafka. But that would not be accurate.

"Expression" refers here both to the substance of Kafka's novel and to the substance of Adorno's discussion of it, because both relationships (such as instability of reference or disappearance in prehistorical oblivion) and concrete elements (such as names and images) refer as much to terms in Adorno's discussion as to elements in Kafka's book. Here, in other words, we see a vivid illustration of the continuity between the essay and its object.

If we are tempted to discount the intimacy between the concrete elements in Kafka's content and the expressive logic of Adorno's writing, we need only refer to Adorno's comment earlier in "Titles": "Decent titles are the ones into which ideas immigrate and then disappear, having become unrecognizable" (6). Just as Kafka's title expresses the novel, so the figure in the novel, as well as its title, serves as a figure for titles as such. In other words, the expressiveness that is specific to Kafka's work is the same expressiveness that characterizes Adorno's writing here. The difference is simply that in the essay segment we follow the riddlelike configurations of concrete elements within a sequential discursive pattern, and the riddlelike configurations and configurational process can eventually be named in conceptual terms like "expression." The aesthetic essay demonstrates and names interreferences among work, title, and aesthetic theory by rearranging concrete elements in unresolved relationships within a sentence logic that conforms to a discursive pattern.

To formulate this in more general terms, in the essay's configurational form, a number of concrete elements from the aesthetic domain in general and the domain of the work discussed, which extends into the domain of everyday reality, are brought into the essay and placed in relationship with one another. The relationships produced may be of reference, resemblance, or kinship, and they may be invoked explicitly or created by the reader in his search for resolutions of the relationships explicitly mentioned. At the same time, something resembling the form of discursive argumentation is maintained throughout each segment of the essay, with sentences ostensibly fitting established functions of explanation, support, distinction, and so forth. For the most part, however, the actual substance of the sentences, the terms of the implied logical structure, is filled not with conceptual specification but with concrete elements, so that the relationships evoked by the apparent logical form of the sentences remain unspecified and provoke reflection on the reader's part. The sentences can thus be said to have what Adorno calls "logicity" rather than logic as such. Their lack of specification or resolution provokes reflection that extends beyond the immediate context and freely draws concrete elements from elsewhere into the process of creating and reflecting on relationships. There is a freedom and lack of restriction in this reflective process that resembles the free play of the subject's faculties in Kant's definition of aesthetic experience.

This mass of reflection-provoking configurations of concrete elements is ultimately drawn back within the discursive form as a conceptual conclusion is drawn on the basis of it. This conclusion, however, is not grounded through explicit argument using discursive logic; rather, its grounds are embodied in the configurational mass, the whole of which forms a presentation or demonstration of the conclusion rather than an argument for it—a demonstration in which the concepts and conclusions involved are terms in aesthetic theory and have concrete elements, such as titles, as their referents.

While nothing in these formulations contradicts what Adorno says about the essay and its relationship to discursive logic in "The Essay as Form," this analysis highlights the importance of the concrete elements in the text, of the reader's continued configurational reflections, and of the discursive pattern or shell in relation to which the reflective process takes place. The configurational form we have just examined in "Titles" is aesthetic in its use of an aconceptual "logicity" that provokes but does not resolve reflection. In tying that reflection to a discursive pattern and a conceptual conclusion, the configurational form sustains a movement between the aesthetic and the philosophical dimensions of the writing. The reader's experience is one of expansive reflection that returns to the concrete and eventually to the conceptual conclusion as well. The reflection extends outward but is nevertheless contained. What is achieved is a sense of aesthetic richness—the pleasurable free play of subjective faculties—with conceptual import, in the space, perhaps, of six sentences.

Subjective Experience and *Aesthetic Theory*'s Late Configurational Form

To what extent can the form of *Aesthetic Theory*—certainly not an essay in the literal sense—be described in the terms in which Adorno characterized configurational form in "The Essay as Form" and in which I articulated it in "Titles"? For Wellmer, *Aesthetic Theory* merely made more conspicuous (his word is *hervorkehren*) a rigidity and artificiality that presumably characterized the essays as well. Adorno, in contrast, was surprised by how the content of *Aesthetic Theory* forced differences of form on him. "From my theorem that there is nothing that has 'primacy' philosophically," he writes in a letter composed during work on the book, "it now follows as well that one cannot construct an argumentative context in the customary sequence of stages; instead, one must assemble the whole from a series of part-complexes that are of equal weight, so to speak, and arranged concentrically, on the same level" (*Aesthetic Theory* 541/496). Certainly these formulations at least resemble those in "The Essay as Form"; "the idea must result from their constellation, not their sequence," Adorno continues. But his description of the form of *Aesthetic Theory* also introduces new terms: weight, level, concentricity, "part-complexes." While we are no doubt dealing with differences of degree here, it may also be that these new terms point to some subtle differences in the nature of the form as well. Without going into the kind of detailed sentence-by-sentence analysis I undertook with "Titles," I will begin to explore this possibility by examining a portion of one of the many very long segments that make up, in groups, the "part-complexes" of *Aesthetic Theory*. Here is the beginning of a segment that initiates a group of segments on the concept of natural beauty *(das Naturschöne)*:

Since Schelling, whose aesthetics is called philosophy of art, aesthetic interest has concentrated on works of art. Natural beauty, to which the most penetrating definitions of the *Critique of Judgment* were directed, is hardly thematic for theory any more. Scarcely, however, because, as Hegel would have it, it has actually been sublated to something higher; it was repressed. The concept of natural beauty touches a wound, and one comes close to thinking of it in connection with the violence that the work of art, pure artifact, does to the quasi-natural. Completely and wholly made by man, it [the work of art as artifact] is opposed to what has seemingly not been made: nature. But as the pure antithesis of one another, they are dependent on one another: nature is dependent on the experience of a mediated, objectified world, and the work of art is dependent on nature, the mediated representation of immediacy. This is why it is incumbent upon the theory of art to reflect on natural beauty. (*Aesthetic Theory* 97–98/91)

We recognize in this passage certain features that characterized the passage from "Titles" examined earlier. First, there is a discursive pattern in which each sentence can be construed as fulfilling a function in an expository argumentative sequence, but in which the links are never fully spelled out. Here, the first two sentences attest to the transition through which the concept of natural beauty disappears from the philosophy of art, and the third suggests the reason: that concept was repressed. The fourth seems to explicate the reason for the repression, and the fifth and sixth to explicate the notion of violence. The seventh sentence then makes an assertion whose grounds are seen to consist in what has gone before. Second, there is the pattern of adding new elements through opposition and comparison or contrast. Thus, in the first three sentences, it is not only asserted that the concept of natural beauty has been suppressed in aesthetics, but a complex relationship between the three figures Kant, Schelling, and Hegel is also set up. The concept of the work of art as artifact *[Artefakt]* is introduced in sentence four, and in sentence five this concept, in a different verbal form (*Gemachtes,* something made) appears in the main statement. In sentence six, a new conceptual pair, mediatedness and immediacy, is introduced through linkage to the previous opposition of nature and artifact.

To some extent, then, we see a pattern similar to the one in "Titles": a discursive movement that is not fully resolved as it proceeds, and an interlocking series of elements introduced in the course of that movement. At the same time, there are striking differences between this text from *Aesthetic Theory* and the segment from "Titles." The concrete elements here are fewer and less diverse in kind, and the interreference of concrete and abstract lacks the richness and complexity we saw in the segment from "Titles." (The reader who objects that the segment from "Titles" is particularly rich in concrete elements and that there is much in the aesthetic essays that resembles the writing in *Aesthetic Theory* will nevertheless agree, I am sure, that the segment from "Titles" could not appear in *Aesthetic Theory.*) To be specific, as concrete elements here we have the names Kant,

Schelling, and Hegel, but the reference is immediately to the conceptual terms of their theories. We have the connection of "wound" and "violence," something closer to the sort of thing we saw in "Titles," but although, as we shall see, Adorno does play on this theme, it finds too little resonance in the immediate context to bring a rich concrete dimension into play. The reflections engendered in the reader by the sentences in his effort to fit the content of the sentences with the discursive function allotted to them largely fail to span different kinds of concreteness or to connect the concrete with the abstract.

In this sense, Adorno's statement that the part complexes in *Aesthetic Theory* are of equal weight and on the same level holds at the level of individual sentences in sequence as well. The elements within the segment and the individual sentence are (largely, again) of equal weight and on the same level in that they do not move from one type of concreteness to another and do not utilize the equivocation between the conceptual and the aconceptual. In this way, the mass of concepts presented is not subjected to the same kind of aesthetic demonstration as were those in the aesthetic essays. In particular, allusion to other texts can no longer bring concrete elements, and through them the aesthetic dimension, into the writing. There is, to be sure, a pattern of commentary on other philosophical works, especially those of Kant and Hegel, and there are numerous references to individual artists, artworks, and art movements. But the references to philosophical works remain conceptual, and the individual works of art mentioned function more as examples than as cultural objects to be opened up in the essay mode. With this absence of concrete elements and of an interplay across levels of abstraction, the reader lacks that sense of expansive, pleasurable free play contained within the experience of the aesthetic autonomy of the text.

Given that the subject matter of *Aesthetic Theory* is not individual cultural artifacts but aesthetic theory itself, it may not be surprising that the interplay of the concrete and the abstract does not function the way it does in the essay form. *Aesthetic Theory*'s subject matter is previous aesthetic theories, which it criticizes. Its material is concepts—individual concepts rather than lines of argument—from other theories, Kant's and Hegel's chief among them. But what of the reciprocal interaction and cross-referencing of concepts through the use of equivocal terms in shifting contexts that is so crucial to configurational form as Adorno presents it in "The Essay as Form"? Does that too undergo modification in the form of *Aesthetic Theory*?

Certainly *Aesthetic Theory* operates configurationally. The configurations are composed of concepts: classicism, modernity, the whole and the parts, natural beauty, aesthetic contemplation, and so on. Concepts figure first in one conceptual opposition and then in another. No concept is relately solely to one opposing concept, and no complex of interrelated concepts stands alone. Adorno's image of concepts as being "interwoven as in a carpet," with their fruitfulness depending on "the density of the texture" ("The Essay as Form," 13), holds true both within and across passages in *Aesthetic Theory*.[11] The notion of the work of art as artifact, for instance, with which the passage on natural beauty was concerned, is also implicit in the notion of the work as a tour de force: "Every artifact works against itself. Works that are designed as tours de force, balancing acts, reveal something that goes beyond all artifice: the realization of the impossible. In actuality, the impossibility of any and every work of art makes even the simplest work of art a tour de force" (*Aesthetic Theory* 162/156). In the tour de force, the violence necessary to produce an illusion of wholeness, simplicity, or unity in the diverse parts becomes evident. The issue of the relationship of parts to whole also figures, for instance, in a passage in which the emphasis shifts to the historical mortality of works of art (and thus also to their ambiguous relation to natural beauty): "It is essentially in the relationship between the whole and the parts that the work of art is processual. . . . Even in its objectivated form, the work of art remains, by virtue of the tendencies at work within it, something in the process of producing itself. . . . If, by virtue of the processual character peculiar to them, works of art live within history, then they can also perish within history" (*Aesthetic Theory* 266/255). If at one point we saw the work as tour de force, here we see works aging and dying through the activity of forces at work within them. Each conception is startling in itself; the configuration puts them in conjunction with each other.

Although this structure of overlapping conceptual contexts is similar to that described in "The Essay as Form," here too there are differences in the kind of experience elicited from, and demanded of, the reader. The form of *Aesthetic Theory* and the effect of the overlapping conceptual contexts within it have become still more unbounded than that of the essay. In a letter on *Aesthetic Theory*'s "presentational difficulties," worded much like the one we just saw, Adorno ascribes those difficulties to "the fact that the sequence of first and afterwards which is almost indispensable to a book proves to be so incompatible with the matter itself that an arrangement *(dispositio)* in the traditional sense"—something Adorno here asserts that he has followed until now, even in *Negative Dialectics*—has proved impracticable (*Aesthetic Theory* 541/496). Again, it is a matter of degree, but Adorno's letter suggests a less binding sense of sequence in *Aesthetic Theory* even than in the aesthetic essays. Whereas individual segments in *Aesthetic Theory* seem to have beginnings and endings, the book as a whole (even given that it is unfinished) has neither beginning nor ending, nor do the larger part complexes within it. Although the aesthetic experience engendered by Adorno's aesthetic essays is disorienting in that issues raised do not reach definitive resolution, still the reader of the essays enjoys a limited measure of orientation or boundedness: the essay begins and ends and has its own aesthetic autonomy. And although the authority of the texts and artifacts discussed is in some sense illusory ("The essay cunningly anchors itself in texts, as though they were simply there and had authority" ["The Essay as Form," 20]), still the texts discussed present a kind of finite basis for the essay, as do the concepts to which the mass of concrete aesthetic demonstration is ultimately tied. Where larger-scale structures are concerned, these sources of orientation are largely absent in *Aesthetic Theory*. Without boundaries or groundings, the "center" that the textual configuration "expresses," as Adorno says in the letter just quoted, becomes the only source of orientation. If "adequate" experience—to use Adorno's word—on the reader's part requires an imitation of the work's structure, then the reader must create this unexpressed center by configuring the shifting conceptual contexts encountered.

In "The Essay as Form," Adorno notes that the essay has to "pay for its affinity with open intellectual experience with a lack of security" (13). That lack of security is further intensified in *Aesthetic Theory* by the lack of any fixed theoretical standpoints. In "The Essay as Form," Adorno has sharp criticisms of "perspectival" or "standpoint" thinking. Still, as I have just noted, the essay's object—which is generally not theory but a work of art—retains a degree of privilege or authority. Despite Adorno's affinities with both Kant and Hegel, there is in *Aesthetic Theory* no theoretical standpoint the reader can adopt to maintain a point of reference within the various theoretical standpoints that appear in the conceptual contexts encountered. Again, rather than the expansive but contained aesthetic-reflective experience elicited by the essay, the reader must cope with a demanding and unsettling experience. There is no fixed ground whatsoever, and the reader must continually maintain or reestablish a sense of relation to the unexpressed center of the book's overarching constellation. Put in other terms, the reader's sense of experiential authority must become shifting, mobile, and decentered.[12]

The kind of radically decentered and mobile experience required of the reader of *Aesthetic Theory* suggests, and is appropriate to, the fieldlike structures toward which late works, and art in late capitalism, move. The text itself tells us that the kind of experience required of readers of *Aesthetic Theory* is both historically determined and characteristically demanded by late works. For implicit in *Aesthetic Theory* is the requirement of artistic experience *(künstlerische Erfahrung)*. Neither traditional concepts nor immediate subjective experience, Adorno tells us, is an unmediated and definitive source of aesthetic understanding; knowledge results from their confrontation, which occurs in historical context: "Art awaits its own explication. Methodologically, this is accomplished through the confrontation of historically transmitted categories and moments of aesthetic theory with artistic experience; they reciprocally correct one another" (*Aesthetic Theory* 524/484). The term "artistic experience," even more than "aesthetic experience," indicates that experience with individual works of art has been mediated through reflection on the historical development of art to the present, including reflection on the self-understanding of the arts; it highlights the realm of artistic practice. The concepts *Aesthetic Theory* is concerned with, that is, are drawn not only from aesthetics or the philosophy of art but also from artistic practice as it has entered historical experience. The passage on the work of art as tour de force, for instance, continues as follows: "Hegel's denunciation of the virtuoso element—although he was enchanted with Rossini, a denigration that lives on in the resentment directed against Picasso, is in secret complicity with the affirmative ideology that glosses over the antinomic character of art and all its products" (*Aesthetic Theory* 162/156). The work of art, in other words, is attempting the impossible in attempting to achieve a pacified unity of conflicting elements. This impossibility, which is openly displayed in the risk, daring, and exertion inherent in virtuoso pieces, reveals the falseness of the idea that art should be simple (and spontaneous). But the tour de force and its associated concept of virtuosity derive from the realm of artistic practice rather than from the realm of philosophical aesthetics. It is only from a historical standpoint that has seen the dialectic of virtuosity and open form in the works of individual artists and art movements that the notion of the tour de force can be mediated with the aesthetic-philosophical concept of simplicity.[13]

The experientially mediated aesthetic analysis necessary to such historical reflection is represented only tangentially in *Aesthetic Theory*, as when Adorno compares the work of Beethoven, master of the tour de force, with Hegel's logic: "One could demonstrate the paradoxical nature of the tour de force with equal stringency in the work of Beethoven: out of nothing comes something; the aesthetic-bodily proving of the first steps of Hegel's *Logic*" (*Aesthetic Theory* 163/156). This reference to Beethoven's work is not itself a substantiation of Adorno's idea but only a hint, an appeal to a possible demonstration outside *Aesthetic Theory* itself. *Aesthetic Theory*, that is, does not promote or enable aesthetic experience on the part of its reader so much as require that the reader bring that experience to it in order to make sense of the book's assertions. For while there is indeed a sense in which Beethoven's music—the variation movements in the late piano sonatas, in particular[14]—can be experienced as creating something out of nothing, Adorno's statement to that effect makes sense only in the light of specific prior experience on the reader's part.

This confrontation between theory and historical artistic experience functions to create a play in the text not of levels but of contingency and absence. This takes the place of the interplay between abstract and concrete that characterizes the aesthetic essays. In the passages from *Aesthetic Theory* presented earlier, for instance, Hegel appears at one point as a proponent of the philosophical notion of semblance, at another as an individual whose musical preferences contradict his statements on virtuosity, and at a third as a thinker who performs a tour de force in the theoretical realm that is analogous to Beethoven's in music. But "Hegel" does not function as a concrete element in *Aesthetic Theory* the way the emigrant does in the section from "Titles." Rather, these empirical facets of Hegel's life and thought in the text point to the role of the absent reader's historically mediated reflection on artistic experience.

Because *Aesthetic Theory* does not contain the aesthetic dimension but rather presupposes it in historically mediated form and neither reflects nor enables contingent, individual aesthetic experience, then, it implies a certain historical situatedness or perspective, an accumulation of historical experience rather than an immediate subjectivity. The decentered and mobile form of experience that the book requires is thus simultaneously an impersonal and a historically saturated form of experience. This form of experience and its relation to the text of *Aesthetic Theory* are well described by some of Adorno's comments on late style. Subjectivity and objectivity grow farther apart in late works, Adorno says. As subjectivity withdraws from the works themselves, leaving them fragments, it remains the light that illuminates them.[15] In *Aesthetic Theory*, the subjectivity that has withdrawn is that of direct aesthetic experience, the kind of genuine aesthetic experience Adorno describes and tries to foster elsewhere. Insofar as that kind of experience is necessary to the ability to continually reestablish equilibrium in the shifting contexts of *Aesthetic Theory*, it is crucial not only in establishing the absent center of *Aesthetic Theory*'s constellation but also—to return to Wellmer's suggestion—in experiencing a depth below its surface. The reader needs to be able not only to reweave the surface of the text across its passages but also to dis-integrate the text and test its assertions in the depth light of accumulated aesthetic experience. To use another analogy to connect Adorno's image of a constellation with this image of surface and depth, the difference between the aesthetic essays and *Aesthetic Theory* is like the evolution from Impressionism, where local fragmentation of color coexists with a depth perspective; past pointillism; to Monet's late paintings, the water-lily series, where both water and sky are presented in a repetitive but variegated surface, which is experienced in its expansiveness and its depth only through the work of the viewer's own dis-integrated or decentered but expanded subjectivity.

My efforts here to fathom the nature of *Aesthetic Theory*'s difficulties have led to a formulation of the difference in the nature of the reader's experience in the aesthetic essay as opposed to *Aesthetic Theory*. Appropriate to a late work, subjective aesthetic experience seems to lie outside the text of *Aesthetic Theory*, while the actual reading seems to demand an even more agile shifting equilibrium within overlapping contexts than is the case with the aesthetic essay. Chapter four, "*Aesthetic Theory*'s Mimesis of Walter Benjamin," addresses the same issue—the problem of form in *Aesthetic Theory*—by a different route. It examines mimesis, an activity we know to be central to aesthetic experience, in Adorno's relation to Benjamin and as a concept, undefined and equivocally used, in *Aesthetic Theory* itself. In that essay, then, Benjamin's texts on mimesis and Adorno's relation to them become the external experiential referent that is only obscurely named within the text itself.

4

Aesthetic Theory's Mimesis of Walter Benjamin

... to grasp Benjamin's 'influence' on Adorno as a liberation by mimesis and as the practical demonstration of the possibility of another kind of writing—which is to say another kind of thinking.
—*Fredric Jameson,* Late Marxism

It was Walter Benjamin who, as we know, introduced the notion of constellational form, and I have elsewhere alluded to Benjamin's exemplary status for Adorno and discussed the continuities between Adorno's work and Benjamin's.[1] In *Late Marxism,* his book on Adorno, Fredric Jameson makes two provocative suggestions that link the question of how we are to understand Adorno's relationship to Benjamin with the question of configurational form in *Aesthetic Theory.* First, Jameson suggests that we conceive Adorno's relation to Benjamin not in historicist terms, as an "influence" of the kind intellectual historians might be concerned with, but rather as a mimetic one. Second, Jameson suggests that mimesis is itself a foundational, but strikingly undefined concept in *Aesthetic Theory,* occupying much the same status as the notion of the aura for Benjamin.[2] Mimesis has until recently been out of fashion with us; we have associated it with premodernist representational art, and we have been preoccu-

pied with deconstructing representations. But Jameson's suggestion resonates with renewed critical interest in mimesis and with
greater acknowledgment in the past few years of its crucial role
in Adorno's work.[3] I proceed here on the assumption that
Jameson's two suggestions are related, although he himself does
not say this. Namely, the exploration of mimesis as a foundational
concept in *Aesthetic Theory* will help us to understand not only
Adorno's relation to Benjamin but also configurational form,
which is, in a manner of speaking, the basis of that relationship.
Jameson's suggestions prove even more fruitful than he might
have realized. As I try to show here, mimesis in *Aesthetic Theory* is
in fact the hidden face of a figure whose explicit face is sometimes
enigma, sometimes language, a figure in which subject and object, psyche and matter are both continuous and discontinuous;
to pursue the elusive mimesis is to begin to illuminate the whole
conceptual design and form of *Aesthetic Theory*.

Mimesis plays a crucial role in Benjamin's work as well, although Jameson does not acknowledge this. In fact, it figures
more conspicuously in Benjamin's work than in Adorno's. It is
explicitly tied to Benjamin's theories of language in their theo-
logical or mystical aspect as well as to his interest in the occult,
not to mention his physiognomic approach to the reading of
historical phenomena. Benjamin deals explicitly with mimesis in
an important text, "On the Mimetic Faculty," and its earlier
version, "Doctrine of the Similar," both of which date from the
early 1930s and are linked in their content with other important
works of his from that period.[4] It is in language, Benjamin claims,
that the mimetic faculty has come to be housed over the course
of history. Here I will use Benjamin's work on mimesis as a guide
both in explicating the nature and function of mimesis in *Aesthetic
Theory* and in examining Adorno's relation to Benjamin. Since I
will try to show that the very notion of philosophical form in the

two thinkers emerges from their conception of mimesis, Jameson's provocative suggestion that Benjamin's influence on Adorno should be seen as a "liberation by mimesis," opening the possibility of another kind of thinking and writing, will prove doubly to the point.

Approaching Mimesis: Benjamin's "On the Mimetic Faculty" and "Doctrine of the Similar"

[Benjamin's] idiosyncratic notion of language as 'non-representational mimesis' . . .

—*Jameson*, Late Marxism

Let me set the stage for Benjamin's texts by pointing out some dimensions of the question of mimesis. If we think of mimesis as imitation or representation, we may easily proceed to think about copies and replicas, and more generally about visual representations and likenesses. Although, in the case of copies, we may speak dismissively of "mere imitation," the question is not so simple. We may ask, for instance, what kind of "things" can be represented and in what form? Must a visual representation, for instance, be an imitation of a visual phenomenon? And what is the nature of the sameness or similarity or resemblance of the imitation to what it imitates? By what process is that similarity grasped and embodied? In the most general form of the question, what is the nature of the link with otherness that is both presupposed and created by imitation? Alternatively, we may ask about the purpose or function of imitation. This question can lead to considerations of power and to notions of magic and ritual. We might understand imitation as a means of connecting with and controlling, or being transformed by, the power and the order inherent in the other. As several writers have recently noted, this kind of magical imitation, as opposed to "mere" imitation, might take the form of sympathetic magic, based on similarity and akin to Roman Jakobson's notion of the paradigmatic or metaphorical axis of language, or of contagious magic, based on combination and contiguity and akin to the syntagmatic or metonymic axis of language.[5] Indeed, it is from the direction of such considerations that Benjamin approaches mimesis in "On the Mimetic Faculty" and "Doctrine of the Similar."

In those texts, Benjamin's remarks on mimesis focus not on works of art but on the human mimetic faculty, the capacity to both produce and perceive resemblances. Indeed, for Benjamin, the crucial arena within which the mimetic faculty is exercised is the human being and human experience itself; the human being's "gift of seeing resemblances is nothing other than a rudiment of the powerful compulsion in former times to become and behave like something else" ("Mimetic Faculty," 333). This perspective on mimesis is linked with his interest in occult experience, which signifies for him an identification of perception with its objects, a kind of continuity or affinity between subject and object, psyche and matter, macrocosm and microcosm. Benjamin notes that it is the process of producing similarities, rather than the similarities themselves, that will best help us understand this dimension of experience ("Doctrine of the Similar," 65). He sees this mimetic capacity at work in an archaic period in which cosmic order was perceived, through forms of divination that were forms of "reading," as a system of correspondences, in which—as astrology tells us—the human being participated fully, both embodying and perceiving these correspondences.

Benjamin sets his remarks on the mimetic faculty in a historical framework. He argues that the mimetic faculty has not withered in the course of history, as one might suppose from the disappearance of magic, ritual, and forms of divination, but rather has migrated from a more direct perception and reading of correspondences into language: "It is now language which represents the medium in which objects meet and enter into relationship with each other, no longer directly, as once in the mind of the augur or priest, but in their essences, in their most volatile and delicate substance, even in their aromata. In other words: it is to writing and language that clairvoyance has, over the course of history, yielded its old powers" ("Doctrine of the Similar," 68). Language, he says in a striking phrase from "On the Mimetic Faculty," is an "archive of nonsensuous similarity" (336).

The question of what Benjamin might mean by the phrase "nonsensuous similarity" and the implications of the notion that the mimetic faculty has migrated into language will be central to my inquiry. For the moment, let me simply note some of the phrases and images with which he begins to elaborate this idea in "On the Mimetic Faculty." First, he makes it clear that he means something beyond onomatopoeia, which would represent a sensuous rather than a nonsensuous similarity. To suggest what this further something might be, he presents the image of a set of words in various languages arrayed around the thing they all mean—a configuration, in short. Further, he proposes that language incorporates nonsensuous similarities in written script as well as in the spoken language, and that this is the basis for the graphologist's reading of handwriting. Finally, in an extremely evocative phrase that has resonances in the "Theses on the Philosophy of History" and elsewhere, Benjamin compares the mimetic element in language to a flame that manifests itself through a bearer, the "semiotic," or communicative, aspect of language, and that "flashes up briefly and flits by" ("Mimetic Faculty," 335).[6]

The child and childhood experience play an important and explicit role in Benjamin's discussion of the mimetic faculty. Ontogeny recapitulates phylogeny, and in the child's imitative play we see the mimetic faculty at work. Further, this play shows us how mimesis builds on similarities between the human and the nonhuman, between consciousness and matter or the order of nature. As Benjamin points out, children by no means confine their imitations to other human beings: "The child plays at being not only a shopkeeper or teacher but also a windmill and a train" ("Mimetic Faculty," 333). In fact, it is in connection with the astrological view of the child that Benjamin introduces the notion of nonsensuous similarity. If the ancients considered the cosmic processes capable of being imitated, "it is not difficult to imagine that the newborn child was thought to be in full possession of [the mimetic] gift, and in particular to be perfectly molded on the structure of cosmic being" (334). The similarity between child and cosmos, in other words, is the initial exemplar of nonsensuous similarity.

"On the Mimetic Faculty" and "Doctrine of the Similar" are wild texts, exciting and suggestive but difficult to pin down. The centrality of the figure of the child in them, however, points us to another of Benjamin's texts from the same period, one that gives body to some of these notions about mimesis. The text I am referring to is *A Berlin Childhood ca. 1900,* a set of miniatures that depict childhood experience, some of which read like glosses on Benjamin's remarks on mimesis. Indeed, as we will see, even the textual form of some of these miniatures serves to demonstrate the way language can embody nonsensuous similarity and the way a notion of constellational form emerges from Benjamin's conception of mimesis in language. While I cannot do justice here to all that this rich and complex text could do to illustrate Benjamin's concept of mimesis, I will note some of the most relevant miniatures and the themes they develop about mimesis.

"Hiding Places" shows the child's "compulsion to become and behave like something else" (*Berlin Childhoo*d, 418). It manifests itself as a compulsion to imitate the objects around him, and it is intertwined with archaic forces: "The child who stands behind the door-curtain becomes something fluttering and white, a ghost. The dining room table under which the child crouches turns him into a wooden idol in a temple whose four columns are the carved legs of the table. And behind a door the child is a door himself, is clad in the door as in a heavy mask" (418). "Hiding Places" highlights the way the self jeopardizes its autonomous existence by assimilating itself to the other. The self identified with the object, with the world of matter, is in danger of falling prey to archaic powers and being irretrievably lost: "I was enclosed in the world of matter. It approached me without words. In the same way one who is hanged becomes aware only then of what rope and wood are" (418). The child hiding under a wooden table becomes a wooden idol in a temple; if discovered, he could be frozen there forever. He frees himself with a "shriek of self-liberation" just as he is about to be discovered (418).

"The Mummerehlen" implicates language in this dialectic of disguise and entrapment. Echoing the language of "On the Mimetic Faculty," a passage in this miniature reads, "In time I learned to disguise myself in words, which were actually clouds. For the gift of seeing likeness is nothing but a weak vestige of the old compulsion to become and act like something else. But words exercised this coercion on me. Not those that made me resemble models of good behavior but those that made me like dwellings, furniture, clothing" (417). Language, in short, can mediate the mimetic assimilation of self to other. Words mediate the loss of self as a loss of one's own image, figure, or face. Words could make him like things, Benjamin says, but "never like my own image"; the child is "disfigured by likeness" to everything that surrounds him (417). The face, the image or figure of the self, cannot appear amidst the things that hold the self hostage.

A Berlin Childhood also links childhood mimesis to Benjamin's *Passagen-Werk,* or *Arcades Project,* his project of "reading" the nineteenth century in cultural artifacts. The miniature "Loggias," which Benjamin intended as the signature piece for the work, shows the newborn child, the "new citizen of Berlin," molded not so much by cosmic, astrological forces as by historical and cultural forces: "The rhythm of streetcars and carpet-beating rocked me in my sleep. It was the mold in which my dreams took shape. . . . And when a dusty cover of foliage brushed against the wall of the building a thousand times a day later in the year, the scratching of the branches received me into a teaching for which I was unprepared. For in the courtyard everything became a sign for me" (386). The objects and settings to which we see the child here being involuntarily assimilated are those from which the fate of generations is to be read in the *Passagen-Werk.* Like the child's assimilation to matter in "Hiding Places," this historical molding, too, is a kind of entrapment: "The Berliner's dwelling reaches its endpoint in the loggias. Berlin—the city god himself—begins in them. He remains so present there that nothing can survive in his proximity. Under his protection time and place find themselves and one another. Both repose there at his feet. The child, however, who was once part of this alliance, remains in his loggia, enclosed by this group as in a mausoleum long intended for him" (388).

If these miniatures show us the dark side of childhood mimesis, this helps us to understand why Benjamin saw the *Passagen-Werk* as an attempt to awaken from the nineteenth century. It was to be, in effect, a "shriek of self-liberation." A similar project is implicit in the *Berlin Childhood.* The text of "The Mummerehlen" continues, "As a mollusk lives in its shell, I lived in the nineteenth century, which now lies before me like an empty shell. I hold it to my ear" (417).

A Berlin Childhood gives body to some of the enigmatic phrasings of Benjamin's texts on mimesis. Configured quite differently, the lines of thought he introduces have an important presence in Adorno's *Aesthetic Theory,* as we will now see.

Mimesis in Adorno's *Aesthetic Theory:* Experience and Enigma

. . . the peculiar status of *mimesis* in Adorno—a foundational concept never defined nor argued but always alluded to, by name, as though it had preexisted all the texts.

—*Jameson,* Late Marxism

Initially, it is not so obvious that Adorno's use of mimesis can be understood via Benjamin's. With Adorno we find ourselves in a different context—aesthetic theory, as opposed to the theory of mimesis as such, or the philosophy of language, or narratives of experience. Even Jameson, who draws attention to the importance of mimesis in Adorno, considers that Adorno's use of the concept "has very little in common with Benjamin's." He compares the status of mimesis in Adorno's work instead with that of the aura in Benjamin's work, adding that Benjamin's notion of the aura "otherwise has nothing to do with" mimesis in Adorno.[7] In fact, though, as we will see, not only is Adorno's notion of mimesis closely related to Benjamin's, the concept of the aura is implicated in that of mimesis.

Mimesis does indeed have a peculiar status in *Aesthetic Theory.* It becomes articulated only by appearing in contexts in which other aesthetic concepts are more explicitly thematized. Even a small selection of the contexts in which the term "mimesis" appears in *Aesthetic Theory* demonstrates the great diversity of those contexts. But this very diversity offers us a configuration in which we can begin to see the dimensions of Adorno's notion of mimesis and the ways in which it is indeed illuminated by Benjamin's interpretation of the concept. I begin, then, with a display of some of the contexts in which the term "mimesis" appears in *Aesthetic Theory:*

Art is a refuge for mimetic behavior. (86/79)

Mimetic behavior does not imitate something but assimilates itself to *[sich selbst gleichmacht]* that something. (169/162)

The idea that only like can know like . . . distinguishes the knowledge that is art from conceptual knowledge: what is essentially mimetic calls for mimetic behavior. (190/183)

The most drastic form in which the mimetic faculty manifests itself in the practice of artistic representation is as an imitation of the dynamic curve of the work being performed. (189/192)

The mimesis of works of art is their resemblance to themselves. (159/153)

The mimetic moment that is indispensable to art may well be universal in its substance, but it can be attained only by way of the irreducible particularity of individual subjects. (68/61)

Expression in art is mimetic, just as the expression of living creatures is the expression of pain. (169/162)

Construction is not a corrective to expression, or a way of securing it through objectification; rather it has to emerge unplanned, as it were, from mimetic impulses. (72/65)

There is something of the dowser in art's immanent process. Following the hand in the direction in which it is being pulled: this is mimesis as the full execution of objectivity. (175/168)

The process that every work of art is, is dug to its depths by the irreconcilability of two moments: regression to literal magic on the one hand, and cession of the mimetic impulse to a thinglike rationality on the other. (87/81)

Through spiritualization, works of art attain the mimetic features that the primary tendency of their spirit is to suppress. (275/264)

The continued existence of mimesis, the nonconceptual affinity of a subjective creation to its non-posited other, defines art as a form of cognition and to that extent as 'rational.' (86–87/80)

Mimesis . . . is called forth by the complexity of the technical procedure, whose immanent rationality seems, however, to work against expression. (174/167)

The tension between an objectifying technique and the mimetic nature of artworks is played out in an effort to salvage permanently what is fleeting and transitory, as something immune from reification and paired with it. (325–26/312)

Works of modern art abandon themselves mimetically to reification, which for them is the principle of death. (201/193)

The mimetic impulses that move the work of art, that are integrated within it and disintegrate it in turn, represent non-linguistic expression. (274/263)

In non-intentional language, mimetic impulses are passed on to the whole, which synthesizes them. (274/263)

The efforts of prose writers since Joyce . . . might be explained as attempts to transform communicative language into a mimetic language. (171/164)

This display renders visible the main contours of Adorno's notion of mimesis. First, like Benjamin, Adorno thinks of mimesis as an assimilation of the self to the other, thus a kind of enactment—mimetic behavior. Second, like Benjamin, Adorno posits a historical trajectory in which mimetic behavior migrates out of an archaic context, although in *Aesthetic Theory* he takes art rather than language to be its refuge. Third, in the sphere of art and aesthetics, Adorno conceives mimesis both as the activity of assimilating the self to the other—this is the link with expression—and as the affinity of the creation, the work of art, with objectivity. He is interested in the work as well as in the subject's mimetic activity. Fourth, mimesis in art is inherently engaged in a dialectic with reason in its various aspects: as cognition, as construction, as technique, as spiritualization, as objectification, and so on. Finally, the mimetic impulse finds expression in the "language-like" character of art.

In what follows, I will not set out to explore all these diverse faces of Adorno's conception of mimesis. Indeed, I suspect that in pursuing any of these paths we will cross the others, and that all roads lead from mimesis to language, as in Benjamin's "On the Mimetic Faculty." Here, however, I will follow the path indicated by Benjamin and begin with the subject's mimetic behavior as exercised in both perceiving and producing resemblances, and specifically with Adorno's conception of the part mimesis plays in understanding the work of art, for it is there that we see most vividly Adorno's notion of mimesis as enactment.

"Only like can know like . . . : what is essentially mimetic calls for mimetic behavior" (*Aesthetic Theory*, 190/183). As I indicated earlier, Adorno follows Benjamin in locating mimesis within the subject's experience, both the experience of producing and that of perceiving resemblances—experience as evidenced in behavior. This experience, Adorno indicates, is necessarily that of a specific individual, but, as he rightly insists, this does not mean that his theory is psychologistic. Rather, Adorno is interested in the objective aspects of that subjective experience. Indeed, as we have seen, the mimetic experience is precisely one of assimilating the self to the other through mimetic behavior.

It is in Adorno's description of aesthetic receptivity, or under-standing, that we can best see this notion at work.[8] For Adorno, understanding a work of art is not a matter of conceptual analy-sis. Rather, the prototype for aesthetic understanding is the per-formance of a dramatic script or, by analogy, a musical composition. The performer's activity is a mimetic one: the per-former actually creates an imitation of the work that is noted in the score by recreating its every detail (no matter that there is no "original" work but only a score and its many imitations or reproductions). Hence, as Adorno says, "imitation of the dynamic curve of the work being performed" is the "most drastic" mani-festation of the mimetic faculty in the practice of artistic repre-sentation (189/192). This does not apply to music or drama alone, however; every work of art can be seen as a dynamic totality that requires a kind of performance or reenactment by the listener or viewer. The work itself is analogous to a musical score. The recipient—listener, viewer, reader—follows along or mimes the internal trajectories of the work at hand, tracing its internal articulations down to the finest nuance, just as, more crudely, the mimicking child mimes various aspects of a train or a windmill. A work is certainly different from a person, and yet the act of aesthetic understanding is an act whereby the self is assimilated to the other; the subject virtually embodies, in a quasi-sensuous mode, the work, which is the other. This is the case whether the mimicking takes the form of an audible performance or is a silent internal tracing of the work's articulations.

This notion of an active, experiential reproduction of the work by its receiver is expounded in many places in Adorno's aesthetic writings. But in *Aesthetic Theory,* Adorno lays equal weight on the respects in which this kind of nonconceptual mimetic reen-actment is not adequate for an understanding of art as such—or indeed, for an understanding of any single work of art, for each

work seems also to say something about art as such. Mimetic
aesthetic experience must be supplemented by philosophical
reflection; in a different tonality, this is the need for the shriek
of self-liberation that we saw in the *Berlin Childhood,* a response
to the limiting and entrapping potential of mimesis.

It is the enigmatic face of the work of art, the enigmatic gaze
it directs at us, that incites this philosophical reflection. The
notion of art's enigmatic quality—or its picture-puzzle or rebus-
like quality, in an image more familiar from Benjamin's work
than Adorno's—is crucial to Adorno's concept of art and is inseparable from the notion of the work of art as mimetic and
requiring or inciting mimetic behavior in the viewer or listener.
First of all, the work is enigmatic because it is mimetic rather than
conceptual. Being nonconceptual, it cannot be unenigmatic, because it cannot have a discursive meaning. Further, it is enigmatic
because it lost its purpose when the mimetic migrated from ritual
into art; art has become, in Kant's phrase, purposive but without
purpose. As Adorno says, art cannot answer the question, "What
are you for?"

Full understanding of art would not mean dissolving the enigmatic quality, which is intrinsic to it, but rather understanding
that art is enigmatic and reflecting on the meaning of its enigmatic quality. But this cannot be done through the mimetic
experiencing of the work of art. The enigmatic quality implies
otherness as well as affinity. It requires distance if it is to be
perceived. The experiential understanding of art that is gained
through mimetic assimilation to the work does not have this kind
of distance. It is trapped inside the work, so to speak, and accordingly cannot do full justice to it: "When one is inside works
of art, reenacting them, the enigmatic quality makes itself invisible" (183/176). Or, in an even blunter formulation, "The musician who understands his score follows the most minute

movements in it, but in a certain sense he does not know what he is playing" (189/182).

If the skilled interpreter is likely to miss the enigmatic quality, what enables us to perceive it? Adorno suggests that we can begin to get a sense of this enigmatic quality by thinking of the person without aesthetic sensibility, to whom the work may seem simply unintelligible, offering no point of access: "The enigmatic quality of art can be given direct confirmation by the so-called unmusical person who does not understand 'the language of music,' hears only galimatias, and asks himself what all these noises are supposed to mean" (183/177). He ends by defining the enigmatic quality as the difference between what such a person hears and what a knowledgeable listener hears. Enigma is, as it were, the difference between what is experienced from completely outside the work of art and what is experienced from completely inside it. Thus, when Adorno says that artworks' demand to be understood in terms of their substance "is tied to specific experience of the works but can be fulfilled only in and through theory that actively reflects experience" (185/179), he is not talking about two separate mental activities, experience and theoretical reflection. Rather, he is attempting to specify a reflection that takes place on and perhaps within that enigmatic zone of difference, a zone of experience in which the enactment and assimilation of the other that constitute mimesis are inseparable from—but also distinct from—the rationality of philosophical reflection. This is not a zone or a kind of reflection in which "subject" (the one reflecting) knows "object" (the work of art, or the mimetic experience of it). Rather, the enigmatic quality, too, and the experience of it, seem to be characterized by the kind of resemblance that is the hallmark of mimesis, a resemblance that implies continuity and affinity, as well as discontinuity, between subject and object.

For Adorno as for Benjamin, rationality is inseparable from language. In order to investigate further the dialectic of mimesis and rationality that is so apparent in the passages from *Aesthetic Theory* displayed earlier, as well as the question of the kind of reflection the enigmatic quality incites, we will need to explore the relationship between mimesis and language.[9] The enigmatic or rebus-like face of art, which is nonconceptual but languagelike, can serve as our point of departure for this next step, and here again Benjamin can serve as our guide. Our path will lead us to language by way of his conception of the aura. The questions of resemblance as both similarity and difference and of the continuity and affinity between subject and object will continue to be central to our inquiry.

Enigma and Aura: Matter in a State of Resemblance

The beautiful may require the servile imitation of what is indefinable in things.

—*Paul Valéry, quoted in Benjamin's "On Some Motifs in Baudelaire"*

Enigma, especially in the form of the picture puzzle or rebus (*Rätselbild, Vexierbild*), is a familiar notion in Benjamin's work, and in his work as in Adorno's it is associated with the complex of ideas clustered around mimesis. In "Doctrine of the Similar," Benjamin mentions the "images, or more precisely, picture puzzles" in handwriting as one of the places in language to which mimesis has emigrated (67–68). The enigma or picture puzzle, then, appears to be one of the forms in which nonsensuous similarity appears.

How can we elucidate this notion of a "picture puzzle" in its relevance for Benjamin's conception of mimesis? Once again, one of the miniatures from the *Berlin Childhood* affords us a starting point. This one is entitled "The Stocking" ["Der Strumpf"]. It describes a childhood game in which the child unrolls a rolled-up pair of socks:

> The first cabinet that opened when I wanted it to was the bureau. I had only to pull on the knob and the door clicked open for me. Among the underclothing stored there was the thing that made the bureau an adventure. I had to make a path to the farthest corner; there I found my stockings piled, rolled up in the old-fashioned way. Each pair looked like a small pouch. Nothing gave me more pleasure than plunging my hand as deep as possible into the inside of that pouch. I did not do so for the sake of warmth. It was "the Dowry" [*das Mitgebrachte*], which I held in my hand in the rolled-up interior, that drew me into its depths. When I had got my hand around it and confirmed my possession of the soft woolen mass to the best of my ability, the second part of the game, which brought the revelation, began. For now I began working "the Dowry" out of its woolen pouch. I drew it closer and closer to me until the amazing event occurred: I had extracted "the Dowry," but "the Pouch" in which it had lain no longer existed. I could not test this process often enough. It taught me that form and content, the veil and what it hides, are one and the same. It led me to extricate the truth from literature as cautiously as the child's hand brought the stocking out of "the Pouch." (416–17)

This miniature seems to consist of a narrative followed by an interpretation of its meaning ("It taught me . . ."), its message. The message seems to concern the enigmatic quality of art and to offer a very clear statement: the pouch, which seemed to hide, veil, or contain the precious internal gift, or "dowry," was in fact one and the same with it; in other words, one cannot extract a "truth" from literature without at the same time destroying the literary covering. But of course this clear division into narrative and message is inconsistent with the purported message itself, which says that the one cannot be extracted from the other. A puzzling picture indeed! The text in fact poses a riddle that is not capable of this kind of solution, for the "amazing event," the moment in which dowry and pouch fuse into one and the same third thing, the stocking, occurs in a flash that is absent from the narrative itself, a flash that no doubt is the moment of continuity and discontinuity between the narrative and the message, the moment that both confirms and explodes the illusions of possession and revelation. And the child must repeat the process over and over again, beginning with an excursion into the depths and the interior, and ending with a purported message that fails to capture the mysterious combination of continuity and discontinuity that is the essence of the picture puzzle, which both is and is about enigma. Similarly, the reader will recall, for Adorno enigma marked the point of continuity and discontinuity between the subject's experience of the work and its nonconceptual or mimetic aspect.

This enigmatic mixture of continuity and discontinuity is at the heart of Benjamin's notion of mimesis. For what are similarity and resemblance—which for Benjamin are the essence of mimesis—but that mixture, "the same and yet not the same"? Another of his central texts from this period, the essay "The Image of Proust," sheds further light on this connection and demonstrates the relationship in his work between the mimetic and the aesthetic. Benjamin tells us that Proust's "impassioned cult of similarity" and his homesickness for "the world distorted in a state of resemblance," to which the *mémoire involontaire* provides access, are indicators of the hegemony of the dreamworld, in which "everything that happens appears not in identical but in similar guise, opaquely similar one to another."[10] "The world distorted in a state of resemblance": this is not a matter of individual acts of imitation but rather a tissue of reality in which the glue of coherence is resemblance. But it is a world in which enigma and distortion are pervasive, for the resemblances are always opaque. Like the "third thing" in the stocking game, they can never be separated and laid bare. It is a pervasive mimesis, in other words, that constitutes this world of the special images of Proust's *mémoire involontaire*—like the mimesis that Benjamin says formerly pervaded macrocosm and microcosm, or the mimesis that for him now pervades language.

The world in a state of resemblance has a special relationship to the consciousness that perceives it. It is not a matter of the ordinary self's perceiving or observing objects or even a world. Rather, there is an emptying disfiguring of the self such as we saw in the *Berlin Childhood* miniature "The Mummerehlen." If the stocking game is the dreamworld, the self is "the Pouch." But this disfiguring is equivalent to, constitutes, a kind of continuity and discontinuity between self and objects in the world. This relationship is one of mutual gazing. In his essay on Baudelaire, Benjamin quotes Paul Valéry on the dreamworld: "To say, 'Here I see such and such an object' does not establish an equation between me and the object. . . . In dreams, however, there is an equation. The things I see, see me just as much as I see them."[11] On the one hand, the subject has become part of the dreamworld of resemblances; this is the equation. On the other hand, the mutual gazing implies some distance between subject and object and therefore a degree of otherness.

This notion of the object that returns our gaze links the Proustian "world in a state of resemblance" with the domain of the aura as Benjamin elaborates it in his essay on Baudelaire. There Benjamin defines the aura as "the associations, which, at home in the *mémoire involontaire,* tend to cluster around the object of a perception" ("Baudelaire," 186). "To perceive the aura of an object we look at," Benjamin says, "means to invest it with the ability to look at us in return. This experience corresponds to the data of the *mémoire involontaire.*" (The camera, in contrast, he points out here, is an instrument of the *mémoire volontaire;* it does not return our gaze.) This investment pulls the subject into the

world of the *mémoire involontaire* in such a way that a sense of
autonomy on the part of the things of that world is created, and
with it the sense of distance that characterizes the aura as well:
"Whenever a human being, an animal, or an inanimate object
thus endowed by the poet lifts up its eyes, it draws him into the
distance. The gaze of nature thus awakened dreams and pulls
the poet after its dreams" ("Baudelaire," 200, n. 17). The aura,
then, gives a measure of the depths of time and memory that
only the *mémoire involontaire* can traverse. And the cluster of
associations that Benjamin says constitutes the aura would seem
to be the same as the web of opaque similarities that form the
basis of the "world distorted in a state of resemblance" for Proust
and that also constitute the particular kind of image that is the
enigmatic image or picture puzzle. The aura of any particular
object thus indicates its continuity with the whole tissue of opaque
similarities that is the world of the *mémoire involontaire*.

With the aura, we have entered the domain of the aesthetic,
and Benjamin makes it clear that beauty, too, is none other than
this same cluster of opaque resemblances that gaze at us from
across the depths of memory. "One would define beauty," he says,
commenting on Goethe's notion of correspondences, "as the
object of experience in the state of resemblance. This definition
would probably coincide with Valéry's formulation: 'beauty may
require the servile imitation of what is indefinable in things'"
("Baudelaire," 199, n. 13). (We will see shortly how Adorno uses
this same quotation from Valéry to similar effect.) Beauty, then,
is the opaque similarity between the work and the object of
experience as perceived in the state of resemblance. Beauty is the
signal that the work as an object participates in the state of
resemblance; the aura that is the hallmark of beauty is precisely
a reflection of the web of similarities that characterizes that state.
Beauty is mimesis of the indefinable in objects, because the in-

definable is precisely their participation in the enigmatic coherence of opaque similarities.

Language and words, too, can become part of this state of resemblance; they too can be defined in terms of a cluster of associations in the gaze that looks back at us from across a distance. "Words too can have an aura of their own," says Benjamin, and he quotes Karl Kraus: "The closer one looks at a word, the greater the distance from which it looks back" ("Baudelaire, 200, n. 17). And not only "The Mummerehlen" but other miniatures in the *Berlin Childhood* as well provide examples of the auratic yet distorting mimetic capacities of words.[12] Whereas in "On the Mimetic Faculty" Benjamin indicated that mimesis had migrated into language, here it seems that language participates in the "world in a state of resemblance" governed by mimesis, the world of aesthetic experience. Language is thus capable both of being absorbed into that world and of absorbing that world into itself. The enigmatic relationship of language and mimesis will bear further exploration. First, however, I will return to *Aesthetic Theory* to examine Adorno's conceptions of enigma and mimesis in the light of what we have just seen.

The Mute Languages of Nature and Art

As indeterminate, and hostile to definition, natural beauty is undefinable. . . . [T]he beautiful in nature flashes out, only to disappear immediately when one tries to pin it down. Art does not imitate nature . . . but rather natural beauty as such. . . . "The beautiful may require the servile imitation of what is indefinable in things" [Valéry].

—Aesthetic Theory

In Benjamin's essays on Proust and Baudelaire, we saw how mimesis as resemblance is intertwined with the notion of an indeterminate cluster of associations from the depths, and how that clustering is experienced as aura, as the return of our gaze by its objects. For Benjamin, language is one more phenomenon that both leads into those depths and participates in the phenomenon of the auratic gaze. It is as though there is a state of resemblance as such, a mimetic state in which nature—or the cosmos, or the world of matter—and consciousness are on the same footing. A quality of depth, distance, and otherness is built into that state even at the same time as it loosens the separateness of consciousness. This is its enigmatic quality.

Benjamin's reflections on the "world in a state of resemblance" might be thought of as an extended meditation on similarity and on the relationships that characterize the state of resemblance. What we find in *Aesthetic Theory*, in contrast, is not a meditation on resemblance so much as a focus on the question of what is imitated and what form the imitation takes. One of Adorno's answers to that question—the one I want to pursue here—is a discourse on nature and language.

"Art does not imitate nature, nor even individual natural beauty, but rather natural beauty as such" (113/107), says Adorno in an important assertion about mimesis in art. What does it mean to imitate natural beauty as such? Natural beauty, he says, is indeterminable, indefinable; it cannot be conceptualized. This is so because of its particularity, its individuality: "Natural beauty cannot be defined by means of general concepts, because the very substance of the category lies in something that eludes a generalizing conceptualization. Its essential indeterminacy is manifested in the fact that every piece of nature . . . is capable of becoming beautiful" (110/104). At the same time, the individuality or autonomy of each instance of natural beauty is shown by the fact that "every single object of nature that is experienced as beautiful presents itself as though it were the only beautiful thing in the whole world" (110/104).

What Adorno says about how natural beauty is perceived sheds light on another aspect of this autonomy. The individual instance of natural beauty has a strange quality of strength and power vis-à-vis the capacities of subjective perception. He speaks of "the weakness of thought—of the subject—in the face of natural beauty and its objective strength" (114/107–8). Natural beauty seems to stand apart from the subjective perceiver and to be independent from it: "Such objective expression could not exist without [subjective] receptivity, but it is not reducible to the subject; natural beauty testifies to the primacy of the object in subjective experience" (111/104). One indicator of this relative weakness of subjective perception is that natural beauty appears in perception as fleeting: "[T]he beautiful in nature flashes out, only to disappear immediately when one tries to pin it down" (113/107). This strength and its converse, fleetingness, mean that natural beauty is best perceived nonrationally, blindly: "Unconscious perception knows more about the beauty of nature than does the intense concentration with which we regard works of art. Natural beauty opens up, at times suddenly, in the continuity of unconscious perception. . . . The objectification brought about by attentive observation damages the eloquence in nature" (108/102). It is as though, Adorno says with a nod to Proust and Bergson, natural beauty can be perceived only in the *temps durée*. As a result of these qualities, natural beauty is perceived both as "compellingly valid and as something unintelligible that poses a question and awaits its solution" (111/104–5)—in other words, as enigmatic.

Art's mimetic relationship to natural beauty can be understood both as a response to these qualities and in the context of increasing rationality in the course of history. On the one hand, consciousness perceives this fleetingness of natural beauty as a problem, which inspires the desire to capture it in art, which is not fleeting but has duration. At the same time, natural beauty is increasingly seen as defective and archaic in its blindness (hence, Adorno says, its disappearance from aesthetic theory since Kant).[13] As consciousness and rationality mature, blind perception is no longer felt to be acceptable or adequate, just as the unfreedom that is also inherent in nature and instinct is no longer acceptable or adequate. Hence, increasingly "beauty lends itself to analysis," and hence the demand that "the enigmaticness of natural beauty be reflected in art and thereby define itself in relation to concepts although, again, not as something inherently conceptual" (114/108). Art, in other words, will both fix and reflect natural beauty, though nondiscursively.

As he himself points out, much of what Adorno says about natural beauty is similar to what he says about works of art. Like fragments of nature, human artifacts—which become second nature—can become beautiful, and works of art, too, present themselves as though they were the only beautiful things in the world. Works of art may also need to be perceived in the *temps durée* and through a kind of blind apperception—the kind of mimetic behavior that the performer engages in. Works of art, too, are enigmatic. We are dealing here, in other words, with a continuity, in which art is a modification of natural beauty but is still continuous with it. Aesthetic philosophy too, as we will see, is similarly both a modification of art and continuous with it. How consciousness, rationality, and conceptuality enter into this continuity and discontinuity is a central theme of *Aesthetic Theory*. One of the ways in which Adorno presents the theme is as a matter of language.

Let me approach the question of language by returning to what it means to imitate natural beauty as such. First, it does not mean, as Adorno emphatically tells us, to copy nature, because natural beauty is something that appears, and appears as image, and to copy an image is to destroy its autonomous quality: "Nature as something beautiful cannot be depicted. For natural beauty, as something that manifests itself, is itself an image. There is something tautological about copying it" (105/99). The Old Testament taboo on graven images, Adorno tells us, has an aesthetic implication. It implies "that no such image is possible. In being duplicated in art, that in nature which manifests itself or appears is robbed of its inherent being, which is what the appreciation of nature feeds on" (106/100). But the appearing quality in nature, its being-in-itself, is also defined as a special kind of language, the language of nature, which, Adorno says, may be the closest thing we have to the language of creation, the language of things. This linguistic capacity of nature, its speaking quality, Adorno calls expression: "What qualitatively distinguishes the beautiful in nature is to be sought, if anywhere, in the degree to which something not made by human beings speaks, in its expression" (110–11/104). This language of nature as expression is what art imitates, trying to give voice in another, further sense to the language of nature: "Under the prevailing rationality, the subjective elaboration of art as a nonconceptual language is the only form in which something like the language of Creation appears. . . . If the language of nature is mute, art seeks to help this muteness speak" (121/115). Art, in other words, imitates the nonconceptual language of nature, "the model of a non-conceptual language, a language not pinned down in significations," as Adorno calls it elsewhere (105/99). When art copies not nature but natural beauty, it achieves something that converges with the language of nature. Adorno comments, for instance, that in Schubert's "Wanderers Nachtlied," "the subject falls silent within what it creates, as in every authentic work of art; but through its language the poem imitates the unsayable element of the language of nature" (114/108). Similarly, the pure sound in the most authentic works of Anton Webern, he says, turns into "the sound of nature; of an eloquent nature—nature's language—and not a copy of a piece of nature" (121/115).

Conversely, we could say that art takes over the enigmatic but authoritative quality of natural beauty, that this is what it imitates, and it can do so only insofar as it can create nonconceptual and enigmatic forms of language: "Art is imitation not of nature but of natural beauty. This aspect is entwined with the allegorical intention that it displays without decoding; with meanings that never become objectified as they do in discursive language" (111/105). Not attempting to decode nature's enigmas, this language of art retains an enigmatic quality. It is a language "without meaning, or, more precisely, a language whose meaning is severed or covered over" (122/116). Clearly this "language" of art is to be distinguished from discursive or communicative language. And of course it need not involve words or sentences at all. On the other hand, the artistic use of verbal language may transform it into the nonconceptual language of art, as when James Joyce and other modern writers, Adorno says, attempt "to transform communicative language into a mimetic language" (171/164).

What is this nonconceptual language that art uses to imitate natural beauty and that converges with the language of creation? It is none other than artistic form as such, which gives articulation to its material, its subject matter: "In form, all that is quasi-linguistic in works of art becomes concentrated" (217/208). The notion of articulation draws attention to the dual function of this languagelike quality of form. On the one hand, it allows the thing imitated to "speak," to become articulate. On the other hand, as articulation in the sense of organization—differentiation and integration—it is languagelike in providing structure and coherence, something analogous to a syntax, and thus a degree of rationality and universality, without becoming a formal discursive, conceptual language: "Works of art approximate the idea of a language of things only through their own language, through the organization of their disparate moments; the more they are immanently syntactically articulated, the more eloquent they become, together with their various moments" (211/203).[14] In other words, the cognitive but nonconceptual nature of art—its logicity, to use another term of Adorno's—is its languagelike quality; the language of form is akin to reason in its organization and articulation. But at the same time, the language of art, or, more accurately, the languagelike quality of art, retains its continuity with mimesis, with the specific and the particular and thus also the opaque and enigmatic: "The quasi-linguistic moment in art is the mimetic moment. . . . The basis of the paradox that art both says something and does not say it is that the mimetic moment through which it makes its statement is opaque and particular and as such at the same time resists speech" (305/293).

The fact that the "language" of art retains its opaqueness, its mimetic character, is what gives it its affinity with silence and muteness and therefore with the enigmatic quality of natural beauty, or the language of nature. This is one of the crucial paradoxes of the aesthetic as Adorno conceives it. To give expression to natural beauty, to let the thing itself speak, is at the same time to become mute and speechless, to fall silent. Expression is the achievement of the work of art and is languagelike in that it becomes the naturelike voice of things, but at the same time it is speechless and mute because it is not a discursive language: "The epitome of expression is the linguistic character of art, which is totally different from language as a medium of art. . . . In fact, the true language of art is speechless" (171/164). Adorno emphasizes this in referring to Samuel Beckett, in whose work the moment of muteness is so striking:

Aesthetic transcendence and disenchantment achieve unison in falling silent: in Beckett's oeuvre. It is the fact that a language removed from meaning is not a speaking language that creates its affinity with muteness. Perhaps all expression, which is the closest thing to transcendence, is this close to muteness, just as in great modern music nothing is so expressive as the sound that dies away, the tone that emerges naked from the density of form, the note in which art opens out into its natural aspect by virtue of its own movement. (123/117)

Here, with the element of speechlessness and muteness, we find ourselves again in the domain of the aura, for the muteness of natural beauty, or of the work of art, is at the same time a gaze, a mute enigmatic gaze. Indeed, expression, Adorno says, is "the gaze of works of art" (172/165). It is this speechless expressiveness, this mute enigmatic gaze that they turn on us in their imitation of natural beauty, that gives works of art their paradoxical autonomy. "The mimesis of works of art is their resemblance to themselves," Adorno says in one of the most enigmatic formulations in *Aesthetic Theory* (159/153). What this means is that what works of art express is their own beingness, their *haecceitas*. Commenting on the Etruscan vases in the Villa Giulia, Adorno says that "their similarity to language accords most closely with something like 'this is me' or 'here I come,' asserting a selfhood which is not carved out of the interdependent totality . . . by identifying thought but stands on its own. In the same way a speechless animal, say a rhinoceros, seems to be saying 'I am a rhino,'" (171–72/164). (Here Adorno cites Rilke's line about there being "no place which does not see you.") With this evocation of an interdependent totality, a sphere of mute, gazing presences that resemble themselves by virtue of their resemblance to something enigmatic and indefinable, we have reached Adorno's equivalent of Benjamin's "world in a state of resemblance," just as with art's imitating not nature but natural beauty and in fact the language of nature we have reached Adorno's elaboration of the aesthetic domain as one of "nonsensuous similarity." In both cases, this domain is one in which the subject-object paradigm as we know it does not hold—one in which subject and object, consciousness and matter, the human and nonhuman are on equal footing; one in which a language is "spoken" without subsuming the object to concepts through definition and conceptual identification.

There remains, however, the question of philosophical language, the language of aesthetic theory, which is not the language of things and not, certainly, identical with the language of art. Earlier, I showed how enigma was the point of continuity and discontinuity between art and aesthetic reflection. With this investigation of natural beauty as what is imitated in art, we see something that looks more like a linear progression in which the enigmatic quality is transferred, in a series of shifts both continuous and discontinuous, from nature to art to philosophy or aesthetic theory. The language of nature is mute, and art tries to help it speak. But art speaks and does not speak; it too is speechless. The speechlessness of art in turn calls forth the speech of philosophy: "[A]rt needs philosophy, which interprets it in order to say what art cannot say, whereas in fact it is only art that can say it—by not saying it" (113/107). But just as it is the enigmatic quality of natural beauty that gives rise to art and is continued in the enigmatic quality of art, so too something of the enigmatic quality of art—or at least its paradoxical quality—is continued in aesthetic philosophy. To return to the context from which I just quoted, "Art [imitates] natural beauty as such. This [states] the aporia of aesthetics as a whole. Its subject matter is defined negatively, as indefinable. This is why art needs philosophy. . . . The paradoxes of aesthetics are imposed on it by its subject matter" (113/107).

Thus we have the semblance of a progression that is characterized both by a continuity of enigma or paradox and by an increase in rationality. At the same time, we seem to have an attempt to return to some of the qualities of natural beauty and its perception. Thus Adorno says of the "second reflection" of aesthetic analysis, "Second reflection takes up the work of art's mode of proceeding, its language in the broadest sense, but it aims at blindness" (47–48/40)—the blindness of that continuity of unconscious apperception in the *temps durée* that I referred to earlier. Equally, however, we may say that these appearances of linear progression and return are complementary, and that the structure we are really dealing with in aesthetic mimesis is one of convergence. Like his comments on Webern's music, cited earlier, Adorno's comments on the analysis of beauty, which resemble his comments on the mimetic nature of aesthetic experience, can be read to suggest this structure of convergence: "Analysis returns beauty to spontaneity and would be fruitless if there were not a moment of spontaneity hidden within analysis. When faced with beauty, analytic reflection restores the *temps durée* through its antithesis. Analysis terminates in something beautiful. . . . In doing so it retraces, subjectively, the trajectory described objectively by the work of art" (109/103).

This notion of a structure of convergence, or, in Benjamin's term, "convolution," is, I believe, linked with the experience of fleeting perception or flashes of perception that we saw in Adorno's description of natural beauty and that figures so strikingly in Benjamin's comments on language as a repository of nonsensuous similarity. I will return to Benjamin's work to pursue this connection more fully and link it with the question of philosophical form, the domain in which, if Jameson's suggestion is accurate, Adorno's mimesis of Benjamin ultimately takes place.

The Flashing of Constellational Form

To observe the interaction of aging and remembering means to penetrate to . . . the universe of convolution. It is the world in a state of resemblances, the domain of the correspondences. . . . When the past is reflected in the dewy fresh "instant," a painful shock of rejuvenation pulls it together once more.

—*Benjamin, "The Image of Proust"*

In "On the Mimetic Faculty," Benjamin presents the idea of language as a refuge for the mimetic faculty, and hence an archive of nonsensuous similarity, in several versions, including the image of words in different languages arrayed in a configuration around a common center and the image of similarity flashing up like a flame. Configuration and flashing flame would seem to have little in common, but they come together in the image of a constellation of sparkling stars. In what follows, I explore what this conjunction suggests for a philosophical language and form consonant with the aesthetic dimension and its basis in mimesis, a philosophical language and form in which we would expect the mimetic dimension of language to play a role. I begin by drawing attention to some of the ideas linked with these two images in Benjamin's texts.

"If words meaning the same thing in different languages are arrayed about that thing as their center, we have to inquire how they all—while often possessing not the slightest similarity to one another—are similar to what they signify at their center" ("Mimetic Faculty," 335). What is interesting about Benjamin's description of this mimetic linguistic configuration is that the "thing" at the center, which is not language, binds the dissimilar and in fact alien words together. The nonverbal thing at the center plays the role of a crucial but enigmatic blank space, somewhat as the child-narrator of the *Berlin Childhood* can resemble things but not his own image. At the same time, it is only in the configuration as a whole that the similarities become evident. Described in this way, the configuration of words resembles the Proustian world of mute, gazing autonomous presences bound together by opaque similarities. Benjamin's description of the way nonsensuous similarity flashes up also links it to the image of the configuration and the world of opaque similarities: "The coherence of words or sentences is the bearer through which, like a flash, similarity appears. For its production by man—like its perception by him—is in many cases, and particularly the most important, limited to flashes" ("Mimetic Faculty," 335). The moment of entry into the world of opaque similarities takes the form of a flash in which there is a conjunction of the present moment with a moment in the past. Benjamin speaks of the "concentration . . . in which things consume themselves in a flash" and the "painful shock" that pulls time together ("Proust," 211).

Clearly, consciousness plays a role in this moment of "convoluted time" that opens into and constitutes the "universe of convolution" ("Proust," 211). In his texts on mimesis, Benjamin describes the mind as "participating" in the moment, in the production of nonsensuous similarity, through the speed of reading and writing, which allows the semiotic and mimetic aspects of language to fuse and the constellation to be illuminated, as it were, in a flash: "So speed, that swiftness in reading or writing which can scarcely be separated from this process then becomes, as it were, the effort or gift of letting the mind participate in that measure of time in which similarities flash up fleetingly out of the stream of things" ("Doctrine of the Similar," 68). Similarly, with regard to the astrologer's "reading" of the stars, "The perception of similarities . . . seems to be bound to a time-moment. It is like the addition of a third element, namely the astrologer, to the conjunction of two stars which must be grasped in an instant" ("Doctrine of the Similar," 66).

Let me now turn to the implications of these ideas for textual form. I begin by returning to the miniatures of the *Berlin Childhood*, which Benjamin describes as "excursions into the depths of memory" and which we might thus expect to demonstrate some of what he elaborated with respect to Proust. The miniature entitled "Winter Evening" does in fact provide a very eloquent demonstration of how perceiving and remembering, image and language can be wrapped together in the convolutions of textual form:

Winter Evening

On winter evenings my mother often took me with her when she went shopping. It was a dark and unfamiliar Berlin that lay before me in the gaslight. We did not leave the old West End, whose streets were more pleasant and less pretentious than those that later became fashionable. The overhanging balconies and the columns were no longer visible, and the lights had come on in the housefronts. Whether it shone on gauze curtains or blinds or on a gas jet under a hanging lamp, this light revealed little about the rooms it illuminated. It was concerned only with itself. It attracted me and made me pensive. It does that even now when I recall it. Its favorite thing is to lead me to one of my postcards. The card depicted a square in Berlin. The buildings surrounding it were a pale blue, and the night sky with the moon was a darker blue. The moon and all the windows had been cut out of the layer of blue pasteboard. One was supposed to hold the card up against the light, and then a yellow glow shone from the clouds and the rows of windows. I was not familiar with the district portrayed. "The Halle Gate" was the caption. "Gate" and "Halle" merged in it to form the illuminated grotto in which I come upon the memory of Berlin in winter. (*Berlin Childhood*, 414)

We might initially try to understand this miniature as a picture puzzle in the sense of a rebus, presenting a series of pictures of objects that bear some relationship to one another and, taken together, make up some other thing that is the answer to their puzzle. In these terms, the miniature is made up of a sequence something like this: houses in the darkened streets of the old West End, gaslight, picture postcard, illuminated grotto. But this is not a satisfying construction. It seems to leave out too much, and the elements in this series are too disparate to fit the kind of series that would make up a conventional rebus. Looking again at the miniature, we might see that the similarity among these elements seems to consist in the fact that they are transformations of one another, with the precise transformational function, so to speak, remaining opaque. The picture postcard described has no one-to-one correspondence with the lighted houses; nor does the illuminated grotto in the mind have direct correspondences to the postcard or the original scene. Yet there is some kind of resemblance between them—a nonsensuous similarity. Further, there is light, an illumination, that pervades the whole text in different forms that again seem to be transformations of one another. In the initial scene, the light is described as "preoccupied with itself"; then it "leads" the narrator to the postcard and returns as the light to which the postcard is held up, and it persists as the illumination in the interior grotto formed by the words of the caption. This light and its transformations, however, are of a different order again from the houses, the postcard, the grotto, and their transformational relationships. Still, there does indeed seem to be some kind of sequence of transformations here, beginning with an actual cityscape, moving to an image of a cityscape (the postcard), and then to the words that title that image, and finally to the metaphor of the interior grotto.

But these attempts to identify linear sequences, even of different kinds of elements that are transformations of one another, are upset by the presence here of convoluted time. Past and present are joined enigmatically and indefinably as the light leads from the exterior scene to the postcard both then and now: "It made me pensive. It does that even now when I recall it. Its favorite thing is to lead me to one of my postcards. The card depicted. . . ." Further, the last element in the text, the interior grotto, is the space in which the memory of Berlin in winter is encountered in the present—the same memory that has been recounted in its transformations leading up to the grotto in which it is contained. Finally, it is language in the form of the words of the postcard caption, "the Halle Gate," that forms the container for the memory. But this container of words is then redescribed as an illuminated grotto, only then to be reincorporated into the text as a whole as a linguistic structure—the text—which in turn incorporates external scene, artifactual image (the postcard), the words of the caption and the image of the illuminated grotto.

We might say, then, that this is a text that both demonstrates its own genesis in childhood experience and recontextualizes the notion of such a genesis through its structure of convoluted time in which the genesis touches the present moment of its unfolding. The presence of the light in its different forms here might then be a muted equivalent of the flash that pulls time together, itself subjected to the distortions that govern the world in a state of resemblance. Further, we might say that the structure of convoluted time that governs this miniature is the structure that allows its language to form a constellation out of the disparate kinds of elements within it, a constellation in which they can be read as transformations of one another. And finally, we might say that language has this capacity to represent convoluted time and to name these disparate elements, suggesting at the same time that they are transformations of one another, because it is indeed an archive of nonsensuous similarities. These comments, which only crudely articulate the complex textual form of this miniature, nevertheless begin to convey the sense in which Benjamin's notion of language as the repository of the mimetic faculty can be actualized in textual form.

The miniatures of the *Berlin Childhood* are not, of course, works of philosophy or aesthetic theory. In such works, we are still more directly concerned with the cognitive moment, the moment of truth or knowledge, which is nevertheless present to some degree in works of art and indeed in works of memory. Benjamin links enigmatic and convoluted time with truth and knowledge, just as he links them with the aesthetic dimension and the "world in a state of resemblance." There is a cognitive moment in the perception of nonsensuous similarity, as we saw in the miniature "The Stocking," with its message about truth in its discontinuous continuity with narrative. And the enterprise of understanding and awakening from historical experience that underlies not only the *Berlin Childhood* but also such works of original philosophical form as the *Passagen-Werk* or the "Theses on the Philosophy of History" also turns on convoluted time and the flash of constellational perception that is a flash of understanding or knowledge.[15]

There is much to suggest, then, that Benjamin's conception of language as the repository of the mimetic faculty provides the basis of his original conception of philosophical form, the conception through which, as Jameson puts it, Adorno achieved liberation by mimesis. Accordingly, our final task is to see whether the very philosophical form of Adorno's *Aesthetic Theory* can be illuminated by Benjamin's notions of language, and thereby of philosophical form as well, as the repository of the mimetic faculty. For one last time, however, I want to proceed by way of Benjamin, and to ask specifically what the philosophical form of the *Passagen-Werk*—surely his most daring example of a form based on this enterprise of historical awakening through the achievement of a convoluted time—might suggest for *Aesthetic Theory*, which as a culminating, enigmatic, and uncompleted work is certainly its analogue in Adorno's oeuvre.

Of course it is with a degree of irony that I speak of the philosophical form of the *Passagen-Werk,* since it consists of an unwritten book in the form of a collection of materials.[16] Here I will simply speculate briefly on Benjamin's idea, which at least Adorno considered with interest,[17] that the *Passagen-Werk* might be a book consisting solely of quotations. Were that the case, the quotations would function something like the words in various languages arrayed around a "thing" at their center that they all mean, as in the image from "On the Mimetic Faculty." They would be linguistic, discursive in form in their original contexts, but not discursive in function in the context of the *Passagen-Werk*. There, on the contrary, their mimetic function would come to the fore—language as artifact. Indeed, on another level, many of the quotations have to do with cultural artifacts or with the materials of material culture, such as iron and glass. Reading these groupings of quotations would presumably allow them to be constellated in a flash of perception that would illuminate them in their relation to one another and to that unspoken center that they all mean but cannot say directly; this constellation would be the convolution of the present with the historical moment, the convolution that permits awakening.[18]

But how does this idea of a work consisting wholly of quotations illuminate the form of *Aesthetic Theory,* a work of some five hundred pages that is, in contrast, almost strikingly devoid of quotations? There are a few quotations from Valéry, and from

Benjamin himself, to be sure, but essentially the book is one long series of sentences by Adorno himself, in which even paragraph or section breaks are infrequent and inconspicuous. The materials from which Adorno forms his constellations are simply different; broadly speaking, his materials consist of contexts rather than quotations. Once we see this, Benjamin's notions about constellational form in its relation to nonsensuous similarity, as exemplified for instance in the *Berlin Childhood* or in the *Passagen-Werk* conceived as a book of quotations, suggest a number of perspectives on the form of *Aesthetic Theory*.

We see the idea of a constellation composed of contexts in one of Adorno's favorite analogies for constellational form as he expounds it in "The Essay as Form": the analogy referred to earlier of learning a foreign language without a dictionary, an analogy that bears a striking resemblance to Benjamin's notion of arraying words in various languages around the thing they all mean as their center:

The way the essay appropriates concepts can best be compared to the behavior of someone in a foreign country who is forced to speak its language instead of piecing it together out of its elements according to rules learned in school. Such a person will read without a dictionary. If he sees the same word thirty times in continually changing contexts, he will have ascertained its meaning better than if he had looked up all the meanings listed, which are usually too narrow in relation to the changes that occur with changing contexts and too vague in relation to the unmistakable nuances that the context gives rise to in every individual case. (13)[19]

Aesthetic Theory itself, as I suggested earlier, may be seen as composed of the disparate concepts from previous aesthetic theories, now taken out of their original contexts and set in relation to one another. In particular, we may think of mimesis as the undefined foundational concept, the blank center itself, surrounded by innumerable contexts of exposition, a number of which I listed earlier in my short display of contexts in which mimesis appears in *Aesthetic Theory*. In this sense, *Aesthetic Theory* might be described as a tracing around the various points in this constellation of contexts with mimesis at its center. Hence the feeling that there is no natural starting or ending point to it. This feeling Adorno shared, as he indicated in the letter about the "presentational difficulties" of the book cited earlier: "The sequence of first and afterwards which is almost indispensable to a book proves to be incompatible with the matter itself" (541/496). Mimesis is also like that blank, "disfigured" center in that it remains alien, despite its implication in these numerous contexts. Its presence is felt everywhere in *Aesthetic Theory*, but it is linked to the other that is not subject in such a way that the subject can never fully participate in it and still retain the sense of self; mimesis means assimilation to the other. In this sense, the enigmatic and indefinable quality of mimesis can be thought of as generating the seemingly infinite irresolvable set of contexts around it.

The contexts in *Aesthetic Theory*, however, are formed from individual sentences and the links between them. As I said earlier, *Aesthetic Theory*, perhaps more strikingly than other works, consists of one long series of Adorno's sentences. Let us see if we can specify the role these sentences play in the form of *Aesthetic Theory*. Two critics have made suggestive, if not wholly satisfying, comments on Adorno's sentences and their role in the form of his works. In "Subversive Mimesis," his essay on mimesis in *Aesthetic Theory*, Michael Cahn notes that, although Adorno considers the languagelike quality of artistic form to consist in its resemblance to syntax, sentences do not seem to be the basic syntactic units of Adorno's constellations, any more than individual words are: "The syntactic order of a mimetic configuration, while following in some respects the Wittgensteinian turn from a word to sentence, nevertheless upsets this basic syntactic unit. Against the sentence it adopts the fragmentary as paradigm."[20] In fact, however, though technically unfinished, *Aesthetic Theory* does not have a fragmentary character. In contrast to Adorno's essays, which are often constructed of relatively self-contained segments, *Aesthetic Theory* seems to go on and on, each sentence linked with the next one.

Fredric Jameson, in contrast, who devotes some insightful comments to the mimetic or gestural quality of Adorno's sentences, points to the way the sentences create a kind of spatiality that expands outward: "Adorno's sentences try to recover the intricately bound spatial freedom of Latinate declension, objects that grandly precede subjects, and a play of gendered nouns that the mind scans by means of the appropriately modified relative. Chiasmus here becomes the structural echo by one part of the sentence of another, distant in time and space; and the result of these internal operations is the closure of the aphorism itself; definitive, yet a forthright act that passes on, not into silence, but into other acts and gestures."[21] Jameson is not talking specifically about *Aesthetic Theory* here, and indeed *Aesthetic Theory* is not constructed of aphorisms and has perhaps less of an aphoristic feel than many of Adorno's other works. Nevertheless, it is composed of aphorism-like sentences that pass quickly on to related or opposing ideas and from there to still others. Despite the limitations of their comments, Cahn is helpful, I believe, in pointing us beyond the sentence in looking at constellational form in *Aesthetic Theory,* and Jameson is helpful in pointing us to the way the interconnections between sentences in Adorno expand the space of the text outward into act and gestures that cross the boundaries of sentences.

Can these suggestions be linked back with what we have derived from Benjamin's work? Let me attempt to do so by proposing that we think of the sentences in *Aesthetic Theory* as the bearers of the flame in which we perceive the resemblance of one context to another, the flash in which the constellation around mimesis is created. The gestures and acts, to use Jameson's phrase, that make up *Aesthetic Theory*—the deconstruction and recontextualizing of one historical aesthetic theory and its concepts after another—are this flame. In them we perceive the connections and resemblances in which mimesis continues to operate in its enigmatic and indefinable way. For the sentences are linked in this activity of recontextualizing, but without discursive adjudication. One assertion of position is transformed into another on the basis of resemblance, but the resemblance that permits the transformation is never definitively specified. "Logicity," that analogue in expository prose of the languagelike quality in art, is this state of resemblance at the conceptual, linguistic level. It retains the enigmatic quality that both constitutes and plagues beauty and the aesthetic, from natural beauty through art to aesthetic theory. And as if to put the seal on its enigmatic quality, *Aesthetic Theory* remains an unfinished torso, asserting, as if were, its incapacity ever to take on definitive form.

Let me say a little more about this notion of the flame of resemblance in contextualization that passes through the sentences of *Aesthetic Theory*. In *One-Way Street,* Benjamin has a suggestive passage on the tractatus form, a form characterized by its unobtrusive, undifferentiated exterior. Benjamin describes it in ways that invite comparison with *Aesthetic Theory:* "The surface of its deliberations is not pictorially enlivened but covered with broken, proliferating arabesques. In the ornamental density of this presentation the distinction between thematic and excursive

expositions is abolished."[22] And while Benjamin does not make
the connection explicit, the arabesque form, which consists of
intertwining lines, also appears in the Proust essay as a spatial
analogue of convoluted time: "When the past is reflected in the
dewy fresh 'instant,' a painful shock of recognition pulls it together once more as irresistibly as the Guermantes way and
Swann's way became intertwined for Proust" ("Proust," 211).
Although *Aesthetic Theory* is not labeled as a tractatus, the notion
of "unbroken, proliferating arabesques" seems peculiarly appli-
cable to it. The series of sentences across which the flame of
contextual resemblance passes has an internal structure that is
reminiscent of such nonpictorial arabesques (*Aesthetic Theory* is
curiously devoid not only of quotations but also of examples or
"pictures.") Each sequence of sentences points in several directions, and the various themes contained in any sequence of sentences are interlaced, so that a certain theme can be traced
through a sequence of sentences by omitting certain phrases or
sentences, while a completely different theme can be followed in
the same sequences of sentences by omitting other phrases or
sentences. The full series is rarely usable in support of any one
idea or position.

This arabesque quality of interlacing themes has in fact been
reflected in the way I have quoted from *Aesthetic Theory* in this
essay. Take the passage, for instance, which I used in discussing
Adorno's notion that art imitates natural beauty:

Natural beauty is defined by its indeterminateness, which is the un-
definedness of the object as much as that of the concept. As indeterminate, and hostile to definition, natural beauty is indefinable, and in that
it is akin to music. . . . As in music, the beautiful in nature flashes out,
only to disappear immediately when one tries to pin it down. Art does
not imitate nature, nor even individual natural beauty, but rather natural beauty as such. This goes beyond the aporia of natural beauty to

state the aporia of aesthetics as a whole. Its subject matter is defined negatively, as indefinable. This is why art needs philosophy, which interprets it in order to say what art cannot say, whereas in fact it is only art that can say it—by not saying it. The paradoxes of aesthetics are imposed on it by its subject matter: "The beautiful may require the servile imitation of what is indefinable in things" (113/107).

This passage appears in parts throughout my discussion, the parts appearing in conjunction with parts of other passages, both preceding and following it. Embedded here, for instance, is the statement that art imitates natural beauty, a statement that seems to present a key idea. But this statement appears here in the context of the idea of natural beauty's indefinability, an idea that is better understood in relation to an earlier context in which it appears (110/104). The notion of natural beauty's flashing out is not explicitly connected here with either of those ideas, but it can be understood on the basis of comments in the earlier passage about the subject's relative lack of priority or strength in the face of natural beauty, a notion that then reappears in the paragraph following this one. The notion of language too (what art can and cannot *say*), flashes out here but can be understood only in connection with comments that appear in a number of other contexts. Art's need for philosophy is stated here, first in a context that suggests that philosophy can speak when art cannot, because of the indefinability of art's subject matter, and then in a context that suggests that aesthetics retains the paradoxes of what it talks about, namely, both art and natural beauty.

Thus, on the one hand, the ideas here do not follow directly from one another from sentence to sentence but must be amplified through their connections with other passages, as though this text were foregrounding its nature as a complex weaving. On the other hand, there is some sense of coherence from one sentence to the next, a sort of opaque resemblance. (The same thing is true of Benjamin's writing, whose sentences also seem to be linked by opaque connections.) The coherence from one sentence to the next is provided by the concept or image in a sentence showing first one face, which links it to the sentence preceding, and then another face, which links it to the sentence following. In this way, we may imagine each concept or image to be faceted like a jewel, with several faces that point in different directions.[23]

This comparison of the individual concepts and sentences in *Aesthetic Theory* to faceted jewels expands the idea of the constellational form of *Aesthetic Theory*. We may now imagine it as an interlacing of multitudinous constellations—a whole night sky, perhaps—whose nodes are those faceted jewels. This allows us in turn to imagine the difficulty of grasping this text; the various interlaced constellations and their nodes of connection flash up at one moment and are gone the next, for what reader has the speed to perceive and retain all of these interlaced constellations in the same act of concentration?[24]

5
Adorno and Benjamin, Photography and the Aura

Two Kafka Photographs

There is a childhood photograph of Kafka, a rarely touching portrait of the "poor, brief childhood." It was probably made in one of those nineteenth-century studios whose draperies and palm trees, tapestries and easels placed them somewhere between a torture chamber and a throne room. At the age of approximately six the boy is presented in a sort of greenhouse setting, wearing a tight, heavily lace-trimmed, almost embarrassing child's suit. Palm branches loom in the background. And as if to make these upholstered tropics still more sultry, the model holds in his left hand an oversized, wide-brimmed hat of the type worn by Spaniards. Immensely sad eyes dominate the landscape prearranged for them, and the auricle of a big ear seems to be listening for its sounds.

—*Walter Benjamin, "Franz Kafka"*

Students of Benjamin's work will be familiar with this photograph of Kafka, which Benjamin possessed, and with a similar one of Benjamin himself, taken in a similar studio. Students of Benjamin and Adorno will also be aware that Adorno was highly critical of Benjamin's essay "The Work of Art in the Age of Mechanical Reproduction," written shortly after Benjamin's essay on Kafka. In the Artwork essay, as I will refer to it, Benjamin credits the invention of photography with having decisively transformed the nature of art and in particular with having, by immensely facilitating the possibility of mechanical reproduction of images, destroyed the aura of uniqueness and authenticity surrounding the original of a work of art. In one of a series of well-known letters that make up Adorno's contribution to what has come to be called the "Adorno-Benjamin dispute," Adorno criticized Benjamin's espousal of mass culture, and film in particular, in the Artwork essay at the expense of what Adorno calls "autonomous art."[1] In his *Aesthetic Theory*, some thirty years later, Adorno, who speaks there of photography's "thing-likeness," which he associates disparagingly with "copy-realism," claims that the "simplifications" of the Artwork essay have "contributed in no small way to its obtrusive popularity." Benjamin's negative assessment of the aura, he says, is "easily extended to real modern art, which puts distance between itself and the logic of practical action" (*Aesthetic Theory* 89–90/82–83).

Readers who have followed the history of photography (and film) criticism since Benjamin's essay, however, know that in fact the Artwork essay has set the terms for much of contemporary thought on the nature of photography, providing not only a lens through which one can see photography's "re-auratization" in the museum galleries but also a lens through which one can see the still more final demise of the original in digital imaging.[2] The farsightedness of Benjamin's ideas suggests that something more than "obtrusive popularity" is at stake. This in turn casts doubt on Adorno's criticisms of the Artwork essay and thus on the contemporary relevance of his notions of an authentic modernism, in the name of which his criticisms were made.

What most students of Adorno and Benjamin are not so keenly aware of, however, is that Adorno not only praises Benjamin's "Short History of Photography," written a few years earlier than

183

Adorno and Benjamin, Photography and the Aura

the Artwork essay, but also, in a 1934 letter to Benjamin about
Benjamin's Kafka essay, criticizes him for not explicating that
childhood photograph of Kafka, and offers his own association
between Kafka and photography as evidence of the common
ground between himself and Benjamin. He has never before—
before reading Benjamin's Kafka essay, that is—been so aware of
their agreement on central philosophical issues, Adorno says; as
evidence of this agreement, he cites his own earlier attempt to
interpret Kafka's work as "a photograph of earthly life from the
perspective of the redeemed life, nothing of the latter appearing
in the photograph but a corner of the photographer's black cloth,
while the horribly distorted optic of the picture is none other
than that of the obliquely placed camera itself" (Dec. 17, 1934,
p. 103).

This letter of Adorno's, which invokes photography in a positive light as an image for Kafka's work and which stresses his and
Benjamin's common association of photography and Kafka as
evidence for their common philosophical ground, precedes by
less than a year the famous Hornberger letter of March 18, 1936,
that initiated the so-called Adorno-Benjamin dispute in which
Adorno's criticisms of the Artwork essay figure so prominently.
Although we are all well aware that Adorno and Benjamin share
much common ground (and several of the essays in the present
volume have been concerned with exploring it), the place we
might least expect to find Adorno affirming it is with regard to
photography, and in the complex of letters that represent his side
in the dispute. This letter indicates, certainly, that their positions
are not so antithetical as it might seem. Rather, as Adorno himself
says in the letter devoted to the Artwork essay, it is a matter of a
fine differentiation against a background of much common
ground. The two men agree that technology and modernity have
moved art beyond a magical aura, and that the same processes

have threatened the autonomous individual. But Adorno claims that modernist art itself is antiauratic and yet aesthetic, that it has a dialectical relationship to the moment of magical aura it retains. In these terms, from Adorno's point of view, the problem with the Artwork essay is that Benjamin is being insufficiently dialectical and is in this sense oversimplifying. Benjamin is identifying art as such with the magical aura that he claims has been destroyed by the technological processes of which photography and film are the exemplars and has thrown himself behind the demolition of art and of the individual subject in favor of the unmediated realities of mass culture and all it implies, rather than seeing modernist art as both a reflection of, and a protest against, those processes. In these terms, far from confirming that Adorno is an outmoded modernist, the contemporary relevance of Benjamin's Artwork essay might simply indicate that Adorno's analysis could provide a still more dialectical interpretation of that situation.

As we know, much of Adorno's work is devoted to attempting to articulate this dialectical character of modernist art and its relation to these late stages of technical rationality and mass culture. But it may be fruitful to examine the differences between Adorno and Benjamin on a portion of the ground that Benjamin has defined for them with his Artwork essay, namely photography. Benjamin's interpretation of the nature and impact of photography construes it as "late" technology in the sense in which I have been using the term. Namely, the new media of photography and film raise the possibility of a complete disjunction between image and aura (and of subjectivity along with aura), between the sociopolitical and the aesthetic, and between image and gesture on the one hand and language on the other. If the aim of Adorno's work on aesthetics is precisely to articulate the nature of a mediated but still genuine and truth-bearing relationship between these terms in a late situation in which such a complete disjunction threatens, then the dispute between Adorno and Benjamin can be said to be about whether the image character of photography is consonant with the possibility of an aesthetic experience that remains genuine even at the cost of incorporating disjunction and scarring. What I propose to do here is to examine the fine differences between Adorno and Benjamin on the question of the aura—that is, on the question of art and subjective experience in late modernity—by way of their differing conceptions of photography. As my touchstone in this exploration I will use the conjunction of Kafka, a figure of the utmost importance for both men, and photography, the conjunction we saw in Adorno's letter to Benjamin about the essay on Kafka.[3]

That letter provides us with an initial glimpse of how Adorno's imagination uses photography, and the reader who approaches Adorno's work with that image of Kafka as photographer in mind will discover that photography figures as an element in an inconspicuous but rich constellation in Adorno's work. Photography and photographs, real or figurative, appear frequently in Adorno's writings, as do the various elements in his image of Kafka as photographer. The image of the earth seen from a point of view outside it, for instance, recurs in an important passage in Adorno's discussion of the *Abschied* [farewell] section of Mahler's *Das Lied von der Erde:* "For *Das Lied von der Erde* the earth is not the universe, the totality, but rather something that the experience of those flying at high altitudes fifty years later could recoup—a star. To the gaze of the music that is in the process of leaving it, the earth becomes rounded to a sphere which one can see the whole of, just as it has now been photographed from space, not the center of creation but something tiny and ephemeral."[4] Photographs of the earth from space also take the form in

Adorno's writing of aerial photographs of bombed-out cities, to which he compares both Kafka's work and the miniatures of Benjamin's *Berlin Childhood,* also comparing the latter to snapshots by fairy "aeronauts."[5]

This "view of earth from somewhere else," as we might provisionally call it, is central to the constellation in which photography figures in Adorno's imagination. Benjamin, Kafka, and Mahler, all of whom are intimately linked for Adorno, all figure in this constellation. Adorno's published characterizations of Benjamin—which, in striking contrast to the detailed criticisms in the letters of the "dispute," are almost completely adulatory and express Adorno's admiration and awe of the older man—enrich our view of this constellation by furnishing associated ideas and images. To select some of the most telling phrases, Benjamin's gaze, Adorno says, "revealed the ordinary world in the eclipse which is its permanent light." The world that lies before Benjamin in eclipse is the world "seen from the perspective of the dead man," but also the world "as it appears to the redeemed man"—as it really is. Benjamin's ideas "glow with a color that rarely occurs within the spectrum of concepts," and his gaze "turns its objects to stone." Everything that falls "under the scrutiny of his words is transformed, as though it has become radioactive," and his "intellectual energy might well be described as a mental atomic fission."[6]

What is at stake for Adorno in all these characterizations of Benjamin is first of all a kind of vision. It is a vision that is in many senses an outside one, radically discontinuous with what it sees and revealing a different—more internal, more inorganic or deathlike—aspect of what it sees. Allied to the penetrating and dangerous processes made possible by twentieth-century science, it is a vision that both negates and transforms, a vision both nonmundane and extramundane. In these terms, the "view of earth from somewhere else" implies an outside location for the photographer that is not so much a place as a perspective that negates and transforms. The unearthly light employed in this process can be conceived as a transformation of the radiance associated with the aura. Thus, although Adorno nowhere speaks explicitly about photography and the aura in this vein, we may speculate that for him photography has the capacity—as do Benjamin and Kafka—to present a version of the world in negative. This negative image may then entail a different kind of aura, a negative aura—or, to follow the language of the miniature in Benjamin's *Berlin Childhood* entitled "The Moon," a piece that fascinated Adorno (Aug. 2, 1933, p. 121)—a "para"- or "counter"-aura.[7]

Ironically, despite their common ground and despite the fact that, for Adorno, Benjamin exemplifies as much as Kafka does what we might call "the photographic perspective" or "photographic vision" in the positive meaning Adorno gives it (i.e., as negation, as the capacity to see things in an unearthly light), the aspects of photography that Benjamin's and Adorno's imaginations seize on are different in subtle ways. These differences lead, one might say, to the differences that give rise to the dispute around the Artwork essay. A comment in Roland Barthes' book on photography, *Camera Lucida,* is helpful in defining this difference of interests. Barthes notes that one can consider photographs from the point of view of the operator (the photographer), the spectator (the one looking at the photograph), or the target (the person or thing being photographed).[8] In these terms, Adorno, as his image of Kafka the photographer indicates, is interested primarily in the photographer's gaze, which in turn reveals what we might call the "photographic negative"—indeed Adorno uses this term in his essay on Surrealism, as we will see—that is, the difference between the thing

seen in its ordinary light and seen under the gaze of the photographer. Benjamin, as his description of the Kafka photograph
indicates, is far more concerned with the experience of the "target" of photography. He is particularly concerned with the fate
of the face, that prime object of photography, which is also the
prime seat of the target's sense of self. In contrast, the face hardly
enters into the constellation Adorno associates with photography.
This difference, which neither man remarks on, is decisive for
their different conceptions of photography and its relation to
subjectivity. To understand its implications, we need to follow
Benjamin's construal of the history of photography in terms of
the relationship between the face and the aura.

The Face, the Interior, and the City

The face is the locus par excellence of the aura. We find this
acknowledged in religious and mystical traditions, in which the
saintly face may be surrounded by an aura or halo, and in which
the divine may manifest itself in the form of the *caro spiritualis*
that is perceived as radiantly beautiful.[9] And we find it acknowledged in depth psychology, where the baby's rapturous gazing
at the mother's mirroring face while nursing has been interpreted as the root of the significance of the face.[10] Hence, it is
not surprising that Benjamin should see photography, which
began by usurping the function of the portrait painter, as the
medium in which the fate of the aura is decided, and that his
"Short History of Photography" should deal so extensively with
the fate of the face in photography.

The "Short History of Photography" (1931) begins by presenting the destruction of portrait painting by the peculiarly auratic
early photographs of the mid 1850s and the special role of the

face and the gaze in them. It traces the disappearance of this aura as the face became engulfed in the bourgeois interior of the late nineteenth century, the substitution of the empty cityscape for the face in the "cleansing" initiated by Atget, and the return of a nonauratic portrait face in the physiognomic photography of the 1920s under August Sanders.[11] It thus provides the background for what Benjamin will present in the Artwork essay as an anti-auratic and anticontemplative role for the face in photography on the part of the politicized masses of the twentieth century.

It is precisely because Benjamin wrote, in the "Short History of Photography," about the aura around the first photographs that Adorno preferred that text to the Artwork essay, and it is important to see how Benjamin construes that aura. He defines it there as a "strange web of time and space: the unique appearance of a distance, however close at hand" (49). In these first photographs, the inextricable connection between past and future, that is, between the present moment of the subject in the photograph and the present moment of the viewer looking at the photograph, and thus between life and death, is experienced as something new and unique. Thus, Benjamin comments on Hill's photograph: "One encounters something strange and new: in that fishwife from Newhaven who looks at the ground with such relaxed and seductive modesty something remains that does not testify merely to the art of the photographer Hill, something that is not to be silenced, something demanding the name of the person who had lived then, who even now is still real and will never entirely perish into art" (47). This new element is connected precisely with the photograph's fidelity to nature, which Rosalind Krauss calls its indexical (as opposed to iconic) quality: the photograph has been touched directly (through the physical action of light) by the empirical reality it shows.[12] This indexical quality gives the early photographs a kind of empirical aura, so to speak, which is very different from anything found in a painted portrait. As Benjamin puts it,

This most exact technique can give the presentation a magical value that a painted picture can never again possess for us. All the artistic preparation of the photographer and all the design in the positioning of his model to the contrary, the viewer feels an irresistible compulsion to seek the tiny spark of accident, the here and now. In such a picture, that spark has, as it were, burned through the person in the image with reality, finding the indiscernible place in the condition of that long past moment where the future is nesting, even today, so eloquently that we looking back can discover it. (47)

For Benjamin, as for the mother and her nursing baby, the aura is also a phenomenon of the reciprocal gaze[13] and is thus dependent on the presence of the face, as exemplified in the experience with which Barthes begins his book on photography: "I am looking at eyes that looked at the Emperor," he exclaims on viewing an 1852 photograph of Napoleon's brother.[14] This does not necessarily mean that the subjects in the early photographs look directly into the camera. Rather, in these photographs the mere presence of the human being has the quality of a gazing face. The face with its capacity to gaze stands, as it were, for the living presence of the human being. It is in the reciprocal gaze of subject and viewer in this sense that past and future encounter one another so pointedly. Hence it is the early photographs of faces in which the new, strange photographic aura is so striking. Hence, too, the almost embarrassing intensity of the photographic encounter and the consequent modesty and reserve of both model and photographer:

It has been said that Hill's camera maintained a discreet reserve. But his models, for their part, are no less reserved; they maintain a certain shyness in the face of the apparatus. The motto of a later photographer, from the period of photography's boom—"Never look at the camera"—could have been derived from their stance . . . [in] the sense in which old Dauthendey spoke of the daguerreotype: "At first one does not trust himself," he reported, "to look for very long at the first pictures he has made. One shies away from the sharpness of these people, feels that the puny little faces of the people in the picture can see him, so staggering is the effect on everyone of the unaccustomed clarity and the fidelity to nature of the first daguerreotypes." (47–48)

This moment of the new, intense photographic aura was historically specific and dependent on the precise state of technology at that time. (As Adorno points out in his critique of the Artwork essay, where he notes that it is autonomous art rather than mass art that has integrated and used technological developments, technology and the aura were quite compatible at that point). On the one hand, the face was just on the brink of self-consciousness. Newspapers, as Benjamin points out, were still a luxury, and people were not yet accustomed to seeing faces reproduced in them. Accordingly, "the human face had a silence about it in which its glance rested" (48). The technical requirement of long exposures also produced this sense of resting in time: "the procedure itself caused the models to live, not *out of* the instant, but *into* it; during the long exposures they grew, as it were, into the image" (48). This quality of silent resting in time also contributed to the sense of fusion of life and death in these early photographs, which were appropriately, Benjamin notes, often set in the cemetery.

In facilitating this silent resting gaze, the camera also brought it to self-consciousness. And photography, which made the ubiquity of images possible, helped to destroy the unique photographic aura of the face and the world in which it flourished. Benjamin presents the bourgeois interior, the correlate of self-conscious inwardness, as the next step in this process.

The childhood photograph of Kafka appears in this context in the "Short History of Photography" as a "pendant to the early photographs in which people did not yet look out into a world as isolated and godforsaken as the boy here." In Benjamin's description of this photograph here, which differs slightly from that in his Kafka essay, we see the struggle of the face as it is about to vanish into a different configuration of time and space and a different version of the aura: "He would surely vanish into this arrangement [the artificial decor of the photographer's studio] were not the boundlessly sad eyes trying so hard to master this predetermined landscape" (48). The isolated and godforsaken world into which the face of the early photographs vanished was the bourgeois interior. For the photographer's studio, midway between torture chamber and throne room, as Benjamin says, outfitted with exotic palms and Alpine landscape, with draperies and Gobelins, exemplifies the mixture of exoticism and historicism that characterized the bourgeois interior of the late nineteenth century, in which the face with its aura of depth and certainty was mortified and the face as ego image and decor was enthroned.

The photographer's studio as torture chamber—as it appears both in Benjamin's description of the childhood photograph of Kafka and in the passage from the *Berlin Childhood* miniature "The Mummerehlen," in which Benjamin describes the screens, cushions, and pedestals of the photographer's decor as "thirsting for [his] image the way the shades in Hades thirst for the blood of the sacrificial animal" (*Berlin Childhood, Schriften* version, 607)[15]—bears witness to the self's struggle against its total assimilation to the interior. For the most part, however, Benjamin notes, the generation after the first photographs "withdrew . . . into its living space . . . like Schopenhauer, in the Frankfurt picture of around 1850, receding into the depths of his armchair" (50). If the aura represents the authenticity of the original work of art, it also signaled the uniqueness of the individual person in the early photographs. Precisely at the point when bourgeois subjectivity as inwardness was flourishing, the uniqueness of the individual person was disappearing, replaced by the commodification of the living space—in the interior—and the face as image. Kierkegaard, whom Adorno used as the spokesperson for the shift into the bourgeois interior, recognized early on the potential link between photography and the disappearance of the individual face: "With the daguerreotype everyone will be able to have their portrait taken—formerly it was only the prominent, and at the same time everything is being done to make us all look exactly the same—so that we shall need only one portrait."[16] This destruction of the aura of the individual face accompanies a technological shift: it is contemporaneous with instituting the practice of retouching photographs, that is, with the creation of an artificial aura.

We can see, then, that photography has the potential for a true if new form of the aura, linked to its indexical quality, but also for a false, artificial form of aura, linked to the commodification and standardization that became the keynote of late–nineteenth-century culture. Although Adorno is quite aware of this dual potential of the aura,[17] he does not explicate it specifically with regard to photography or to the bourgeois interior of the late nineteenth century. And although Benjamin documents the shift we have just shown, he does not make the ambivalent nature of the aura explicit. In their discussions of the bourgeois interior, however, which are found in Adorno's 1933 book on Kierkegaard and especially in the file marked "Interior" in Benjamin's notes and materials for his *Passagen-Werk*, it is clear not only that the two men agree substantially on their analysis of the interior but also that the nature of the bourgeois interior itself represents a transformation of the characteristics of the aura.[18] The aura as Benjamin defines it in the "Short History of Photography" is a kind of container or casing, an exterior with an interior, an exterior or husk that creates the sense of distance in time and space, despite all closeness of presence. It signals, one might say, this illusion of distance in closeness. All these elements, in their own way, are constitutive of the bourgeois interior; it is a perverted version, as it were, of the kind of aura we saw in the early photographs. That aura combined depth with presence, whereas the perverted aura of the bourgeois interior combines surface with an emptiness that is absence.

The exoticism of time and space in the furnishings of the bourgeois interior—what we would now call historicism and Orientalism—represents this perversion of distance in time and space. Separated from their use value, these furnishings provide only the illusion of distance in time and space, according to Adorno's critique of Kierkegaard's notion of inwardness, in a passage that Benjamin transcribed in his notes for the *Passagen-Werk:*

It is not by accident that [Kierkegaard] readily compares inwardness with a fortress. Under the sign of the fortress as that of the primordial past, and under the sign of the *intérieur* as that of the incalculably distant, which are stamped upon the present and the nearest, semblance gains its power. The contents of the *intérieur* are mere decoration, alienated from the purposes they represent, deprived of their own use-value, engendered solely by the isolated apartment that is created in the first place by their juxtaposition.[19]

This supposed era of bourgeois subjectivity or "inwardness" is in fact the era of semblance as mere exterior. "The self is overwhelmed in its own domain by commodities and their historical essence. Their illusory quality is historically-economically produced by the alienation of things from use-value," Adorno continues (*Kierkegaard*, 44). The self becomes an empty, standardized self in the midst of the empty—because stripped of their meaning—objects that make up the interior. "Living in the interior rooms of that era," as Benjamin puts it, "was having woven, spun oneself tightly into a spider web in which world events hung all around like the bodies of insects whose insides had been sucked out" (*Passagen-Werk*, 286).

The soft, encasing quality of this artificial aura is signaled by the importance of velvet and plush in that era.[20] Describing his grandmother's flat in the *Berlin Childhood* miniature "Blumeshof 12," Benjamin notes that "it was called not Blumes-Hof but Blumezoof, and it was a giant plush flower that shot out at my face from its ruffled coverings" (411). Benjamin's description of this flat and its furnishings shows that the security the child felt in his grandmother's flat was based on its denial of history and thus of death: "What ruled here was a type of furniture that was imbued with itself and its permanence through the stubborn will with which its ornamentation combined that of many centuries. Poverty could have no place in these rooms, where even death had none. . . . That is why they seemed so comfortable by day and became the scene of bad dreams at night" (412). Photography participated in the creation of this artificial aura, for the exotic furnishings derive from a world in which colonialism has turned the distant into a commodity, and the picture postcards spawned by tourism bear witness to that: "Madonna di Campiglio and Brindisi, Westerland and Athens and wherever else she sent picture postcards from on her journeys—all of them were filled with the air of Blumeshof. And the large, comfortable handwriting that played around the bottom of the pictures or formed clouds in their skies showed them to be so completely inhabited by my grandmother that they became colonies of Blumeshof" (411).

This phase of the interior, with its perverted aura (and its correlate, the colonial city in the atmospheric haze of tourist postcards), is followed, both in art and in photography, by a period of what Benjamin characterizes as "cleansing." From a penetrating radiance, the aura had become a haze, and Atget, photographer of empty streets and small, neglected details, "disinfected the sticky atmosphere spread by conventional portrait photography in that age of decline." His pictures "turn reality against the exotic, romantic, show-offish resonance of the city name: they suck the aura from reality like water from a sinking ship" ("Short History," 49). The empty city thus becomes a more truthful image than the only apparently full bourgeois interior with its standardized face. The city supplants the face as the exemplary object of photography, and it would seem that with the face the aura has disappeared from photography altogether.

Benjamin's "Short History of Photography" skips quickly over Surrealism, which continued what Atget had begun, moving to the return of the face in twentieth-century photography and film—thus, as I have indicated, preparing the ground for the Artwork essay—and showing that when the face reappears in the most advanced photography it is in scientific or political form, as with the masses in Russian film or in August Sanders's comparative anatomy of social classes. (By that time, as Benjamin says in the Artwork essay, "The cult of remembrance of loved ones, absent or dead, offers a last refuge for the cult value of the picture.")[21] Nor does Benjamin discuss the Surrealists' use of photography in his provocatively subtitled essay on Surrealism, "the last snapshot of the European intelligentsia," with its comments on "the most dreamed-of of [the Surrealists'] objects, the city of Paris itself."[22] Surrealism, however, is the movement many of Adorno's own mentions of photography refer to, and the links he makes among Surrealism, photography, and the city are decisive for understanding his position on photography and the aura and the related issues at stake in the Adorno-Benjamin dispute. Here again, differences in emphasis between Adorno and Benjamin form the basis for differences in interpretation.

Although the essay Adorno devoted to Surrealism is not primarily concerned with the Surrealists' use of photography, any more than Benjamin's was,[23] it defines the terms in which Adorno construes photography, terms that enable us to understand his criticisms of Benjamin more fully. The essay highlights the importance of Surrealist shocks. Although it does not play a major role in the "Short History of Photography," the link between photography and shock, with its moments both of violence and of instantaneousness (as we hear in the English "snapshot" and the German "Momentaufnahme"), is central not only to Adorno but also to Benjamin in the Artwork essay. Further, Adorno interprets Surrealist shocks as having both prospective and retrospective import, as both awakening from the nineteenth century and anticipating the twentieth century. It is for the absence of such dialectical Janus-faced interpretation that Adorno criticizes not only Benjamin's Artwork essay but also the other writings discussed in the letters of the mid 1930s.[24] The same terms and the same criticisms, as we will see, apply to Adorno's and Benjamin's interpretations of Kafka.

Adorno's essay on Surrealism is intent on giving Surrealist shocks ("explosions") a sociohistorical, as opposed to a psychologistic, interpretation. Surrealist images are emphatically not symbols of the unconscious or dream images, he says; such an interpretation would eliminate their historical dimension. Instead, they look both forward and backward in time. The Surrealist concern with the city looks forward to the explosive destruction of cities to come: "After the European catastrophe the Surrealist shocks lost their force. It is as though they had saved Paris by preparing it for fear: the destruction of the city was their center."[25] At the same time, the Surrealist images, created through a montage technique, looked backward to reveal the libido encapsulated in the fetishized commodity objects of the late–nineteenth-century interior. They are not, Adorno says, "images of something inward; rather, they are fetishes—commodity fetishes—on which something subjective, libido, was once fixated" ("Surrealism," 89). Surrealism, in short, shares Adorno's and Benjamin's critique of nineteenth-century bourgeois interiority in both its senses.

Photography plays a key role in Adorno's interpretation of Surrealism as sociohistorical critique; he uses it as a metaphor for the critical historical consciousness he takes Surrealist images to embody. When he compares the modernist artworks of this era to the later photographs of bombed-out cities, he is affirming photography as a means of capturing the essence of historical reality. Still more emphatically, he ends his essay by comparing Surrealism to photography. It is photography as snapshot and as negative that best captures his interpretation of Surrealism as awakening rather than dreaming and as awareness of denial rather than symbolism of the unconscious:

As a freezing of the moment of awakening, Surrealism is akin to photography. Surrealism's booty is images, to be sure, but not the invariant, ahistorical images of the unconscious subject to which the conventional view would like to neutralize them; rather, they are historical images in which the subject's innermost core becomes aware that it is something external, an imitation of something social and historical. . . . If Surrealism now seems obsolete, it is because human beings are now denying themselves the consciousness of denial that was captured in the photographic negative that was Surrealism. (89–90)

Adorno's notion of Surrealist shock as awakening converges with Benjamin's conception of his *Passagen-Werk* as an attempt to awaken from the nineteenth century. And whereas the link between shock and photography/film is central to Benjamin's Artwork essay, it is, as I have indicated, strangely absent from the "Short History of Photography." It is almost as though there is an elision in Benjamin's conception of the development of photography that is filled by Adorno's interpretation of Surrealism. Since Adorno makes the kind of prospective-retrospective interpretation here that he accuses Benjamin of failing to make, we can infer that the link between photography and shock will be important in understanding his dissatisfaction with Benjamin's work. In fact, the differences in the way the two men interpret the photography–shock link are related to the difference between understanding photography as negative vision, as Adorno does, and focusing on the fate of the targeted face in photography, as Benjamin does. We can observe these differences being played out in Adorno's criticisms of Benjamin's Kafka essay. For Adorno, the essence of Kafka's work is shock, whereas for Benjamin Kafka represents rather a depiction of engulfment in the archaic world of the nineteenth-century bourgeois interior.

Shock, Violence, and the Mute Epic Gesture

Let me return to Adorno's letter on Benjamin's Kafka essay. Adorno has a comment regarding the childhood photograph of Kafka that Benjamin describes there. He criticizes Benjamin for not having "raised the relationship between *Urgeschichte* [prehistory] and modernity to the level of a concept"—something crucial to the success of any Kafka interpretation, as far as Adorno is concerned, who, as we have seen, insists that objects must be interpreted prospectively as well as retrospectively—and having given the "forgetting" of *Urgeschichte* an archaicizing rather than a fully dialectical interpretation. "It is no accident," he continues, "that of the anecdotes you explicate, one, namely the childhood photograph of Kafka, remains without explication. Its interpretation would be equivalent to a neutralization of the cosmic epoch *[Weltalter]* in a flash of lightning" (Dec. 17, 1934, pp. 105–6). (Adorno refers here to the distinction between the contemporary period, or *Zeitalter,* and the cosmic epoch, or *Weltalter,* that Benjamin makes in his essay on Kafka. The notion of a cosmic epoch, Adorno says, needs to become dialectical so that the primeval past can be seen to reflect our petrified present.) Adorno does not explicate the Kafka photograph any more than Benjamin did, but we can trace its meaning for him by exploring the constellation associated with it, beginning with the element of shock contained in the image of the flash of lightning.

The shock capacity of images is closely allied with violence—as we see, variously, in the notion of the photographer's studio as torture chamber, or Surrealist images as akin to photos of bombed-out cities, or Dadaist art as "an instrument of ballistics" that "hit the spectator like a bullet," as Benjamin says in the Artwork essay ("Work of Art," 238). Adorno makes it clear that the shocks in Kafka's work are a form of violence.[26] The demand for interpretation that Kafka's Surrealist images exert, he says, is a kind of "aggressive physical proximity" that destroys the contemplative relationship between text and reader by collapsing the distance between them, agitating the reader's feelings "to a point where he fears that the narrative will shoot towards him like a locomotive in a three-dimensional film" ("Notes on Kafka," 246).

For Adorno, the shocks and violence in Kafka's work are inevitably linked with photography. They were for Kafka as well, if we are to believe this story from Gustav Janouch's *Conversations with Kafka,* cited by Barthes: "'The necessary condition for an image is sight,' Janouch told Kafka; and Kafka smiled and replied: 'We photograph things in order to drive them out of our minds. My stories are a way of shutting my eyes.'"[27] Adorno picks out a moment like this in Kafka's *Castle* to illustrate the way Kafka's work freezes the moment with a violent motion equivalent to the shock of a snapshot:

Josef K. opens the lumber-room, in which his warders had been beaten a day earlier, to find the scene faithfully repeated, including the appeal to himself. "At once K. slammed the door shut and then beat on it with his fists, as if that would shut it still more securely." This is the gesture of Kafka's own work, which . . . turns away from the most extreme scenes as though no eye could survive the sight. ("Notes on Kafka," 253)

Another way of shutting the eyes on something as if by snapping it in a photograph is to approach it obliquely. Apropos of the title of the Kafka story in which Odradek appears, Adorno comments, "'The Cares of a Family Man' corresponds precisely to the oblique perspective from which the story is written. Only that perspective allowed the writer to deal with a monstrousness that would have struck his prose dumb or driven it mad if he had looked it straight in the eye" ("Titles," 7). If Adorno says, in the description of Kafka's work as photography with which he begins his letter to Benjamin, that the "horribly distorted optic of the picture is none other than that of the obliquely placed camera itself," it is because all of Kafka's work takes this indirect approach to the monstrousness it photographs.

An oblique and distorted perspective, an aerial view of bombed-out cities, and the inverted perspective of one hanging upside down—another image Adorno uses for Kafka's work[28]— all these images indicate that the violent shocks associated with Kafka and photography are incompatible with the "web of space and time" that characterized the early aura. For one thing, the shock effects associated with photography and film make orientation in space impossible. Benjamin and Adorno agree on this point. Benjamin locates the shock effect of film in its rapid shifting of place such that the viewer cannot project himself into what he sees:

The distracting element of film is . . . primarily tactile, being based on changes of place and focus which periodically assault the spectator. Let us compare the screen on which a film unfolds with the canvas of a painting. The painting invites the spectator to contemplation; before it the spectator can abandon himself to his associations. Before the movie frame he cannot do so. No sooner has his eye grasped a scene than it is already changed. It cannot be arrested. ("Work of Art," 238)

Similarly, in his essay "Titles," from which his comments on the Odradek story above were taken, Adorno introduces a photograph from his edition of the *Stoker,* the early fragment of what later became Kafka's novel *America:* "The work has as much to do with America as the prehistoric photograph 'In New York Harbor' that is included in my edition of the *Stoker* fragment of 1913. The novel takes place in an America that moved while the picture was being taken, the same and yet not the same America on which the emigrant seeks to rest his eye after a long, barren crossing" ("Titles," 7).[29] While we might trace the movement of the ground here to the motion of the boat, we might also link the emigrant's inability to rest his eye to the destruction of the capacity for stable contemplation that characterizes film. It is equally associated with the destruction of memory, a stable relation to time, as the continuation of this little piece of Kafka's title shows: "Nothing could fit that better than *The One Who Was Never Heard of Again [Der Verschollene],* a blank space for a name that cannot be found. The perfect passive participle *verschollen,* never heard of again, has lost its verb the way the family's memory loses the emigrant who goes to ruin and dies" (7).

In his "Notes on Kafka," the only essay he devoted explicitly to Kafka, Adorno claims Kafka for Surrealism, and his interpretation of Kafka's work as a critique of the bourgeois interior and bourgeois inwardness runs along lines similar to his interpretation of Surrealism. This is critique as awakening, the "lightning flash" contained in the childhood photograph of Kafka that will neutralize Benjamin's undialectical identification of Kafka with the archaic "cosmic epoch." As in Surrealism, "the crucial moment . . . toward which everything . . . is directed," Adorno says of Kafka's work, "is that in which men become aware that they are not themselves—that they themselves are things" (255). Kafka's work is explicitly described as a critique of Kierkegaardian inwardness. It is as though Kafka takes that inwardness and critically depicts its hellish distortion of space and time. All Kafka's stories "take place in the same spaceless space" (256). Kafka is Kierkegaard's pupil not as an existentialist but "solely with regard to 'objectless inwardness'": "What is enclosed in Kafka's glass ball is even more monotonous, more coherent and hence more horrible than the system outside, because in absolute subjective space and in absolute subjective time there is no room for anything that might disturb their intrinsic principle, that of inexorable estrangement" (261). Again, this effort to depict a hellish, spaceless space is incompatible with the web of space and time that made up the early aura. Yet the flash of unearthly vision that illuminates spaceless space may, as I have indicated, be seen as a negative aura that illuminates what would otherwise be too mundane to be visible.

In these remarks about shock, we can see how close Adorno and Benjamin are. It is the emphasis on shock as awakening—the prospective moment that links it with modernity—that most separates them. Most of Adorno's criticisms of Benjamin's Kafka essay, however, revolve around the role of gesture in Kafka's work, something that might at first seem unrelated to the link between photography and shock. The theme of gesture, however, serves to elaborate and enrich the constellation introduced by shock. Benjamin assimilates the gestic element in Kafka to the archaic world he saw Kafka portraying and conceives gesture in terms of theater; he links Kafka's Nature Theater of Oklahoma to Chinese gestic theater and proposes that many of Kafka's stories are best understood as acts in the Nature Theater of Oklahoma.[30] For Adorno, however, by placing gesture in this constellation, Benjamin has once again failed to capture the dialectic of the modern and the archaic that is so crucial in interpreting Kafka: "If one were to look for the basis of gesture," Adorno says, "it might be less to be found in Chinese theater than, it seems to me, in 'modernity,' that is, in the withering away of language. In Kafka's gestures the creature whose words have been taken away finds release" (Dec. 17, 1934, p. 108). Kafka is less like theater, in fact, than like film—silent film. Kafka's novels, Adorno says, "are the last, fading captions for silent film (which, not by chance, disappeared at almost precisely the same time as Kafka's death)" (Dec. 17, 1934, p. 109).

It is not only the "modernity" of silent film that makes Adorno find this comparison fitting but also the jerkiness of the gestures in it, which reflect the shocks contained in it, as we saw earlier. Indeed, Adorno links gesture and shock. He compares Kafka's gestures to the shocklike freezing accomplished by snapshot: "Eternalized gestures in Kafka are the momentaneous brought to a standstill. The shock is like a surrealistic arrangement of that which old photographs convey to the viewer" ("Notes on Kafka," 252). Violence and shock, that is, are implicit in gesture, as they are in photography; and of course photography, being mute, captures not language but gesture.

The theme of gesture evokes the theme of language. Adorno reminds Benjamin that he had identified writing (*Schrift*) in Kafka as both relic and prolegomenon, in short as a locus of the dialectic of the archaic and the modern and the retrospective and prospective. Gesture, a phenomenon associated with the decay of language, is important as an intermediate zone in that dialectic. "The ambiguity of gesture," Adorno continues his comment on Kafka's work as captions for silent film, "is that between sinking into muteness (with the destruction of language) and rising out of it into music" (Dec. 17, 1934, p. 109). The mute gesture expresses at the same time the impossibility of clear and definitive interpretation and its urgency. This is the role of gesture in that "aggressive proximity" of Kafka's, the appeal that goes out from the work to the reader like an onrushing locomotive.

On gesture and language, gesture and music, Adorno continues, "The most important item for the constellation gesture-animals-music is the depiction of the group of dogs silently making music in 'The Investigations of a Dog'" (Dec. 17, 1934, p. 109). Indeed, it is precisely in that depiction that we can see how gesture as the intermediate zone is at one and the same time the locus of the aesthetic, the locus of shock and violence, and a version of that web of time and space that constitutes the aura. Here is the core of Kafka's depiction:

Seven dogs stepped into the light. . . . They did not speak, they did not sing, they remained, all of them, silent, almost determinedly silent; but from the empty air they conjured music. . . . The music gradually got the upper hand, literally knocked the breath out of me and swept me far away from those actual little dogs, and quite against my will, while I howled as if some pain were being inflicted upon me, my mind could attend to nothing but this blast of music which seemed to come from all sides . . . , seizing the listener by the middle, overwhelming him, crushing him, and over his swooning body still blowing fanfares so near that they seemed far away and almost inaudible.[31]

"Fanfares so near they seemed far away and almost inaudible": this is a distance in closeness, but one whose closeness is violent and whose distance borders on vanishing. Like the strange light that illuminates the earth from space, these violent but inaudible fanfares are figures of the negative or para-aura that characterizes the modern aesthetic of shock. It is the particular combination of that intermediate zone, which signals the dialectic of archaic and modern, with the shock that is characteristically modern, that seems to be the condition for this kind of aura.

The notion of gesture as a kind of borderline or intermediate phenomenon is not confined to the realm of sound. Immediately after criticizing Benjamin for not explicating the Kafka photograph, Adorno introduces Odradek (whereas Benjamin, at least in the surviving text, follows the photograph with the Nature Theater of Oklahoma). For Adorno, Odradek is the most important case of Benjamin's failure to follow out the dialectic of myth; he should have read him both as part of the prehistoric world and as prolegomenon: "Certainly Odradek as the reverse side of the world of things is a sign of distortion—but as such precisely a motif of transcendence, namely of the removal of the boundary and reconciliation of the organic and the inorganic or of the *Aufhebung* of death: Odradek 'survives.' To put it another way, only to life that is inverted in an object-like way is escape from the context of nature promised" (Dec. 17, 1934, p. 106). Odradek, in other words, exists in an intermediate zone between the organic and the inorganic that is as shocking to our sensibilities as Kafka has shown the intermediate zone between music and muteness to be. Odradek's laughter, too, occurs in the intermediate zone between noise and voice; it is "the kind that has no lungs behind it. It sounds rather like the rustling of fallen leaves."[32] This is the monstrousness for which, as we have seen, Kafka adopted an oblique optic. It reflects the dialectic of modern art as late art, which becomes increasingly inorganic while retaining a refracted mimetic relation to nature and thus a dialectical negative relation to the early aura. Photography itself, a fossilized form of shock, exists in this intermediate zone, in some sense a mere inorganic empirical trace of reality and in some sense a negative auratic preservation of past life in the present moment.

Not only does Adorno reinterpret the role of gesture in Kafka to locate it within this intermediate zone of modernity—as opposed to the context of Chinese gestic theater where Benjamin had located it—he disputes more broadly Benjamin's association of Kafka's work with theater and links it instead with the novel and thus the epic as opposed to the dramatic. Even the Nature Theater of Oklahoma, Adorno says, is not theater, and Kafka's work as a whole is novelistic and the antithesis of theater. This reinterpretation stems from something more fundamental than Adorno's discomfort with Brecht's influence on Benjamin. It forms part of the context for Adorno's development of the dialectic of violence and nonviolence in art. The epic and the gestural in Kafka testify not only to the role of shock and violence in modern experience but to the nonviolent strategies through which the modern aesthetic transcends and survives domination.

For Adorno, all art is engaged in a dialectic of domination. Though it is not logic, art is logiclike, and, through artistic form with its implicit striving for totality, it imposes structure on its materials. The phrase "tour de force" points to this element of domination (and implicitly of violence as well) in art, for which Viennese classicism and Beethoven's music in particular, as we have seen, are an exemplary focus.[33] Great art struggles with this dialectic. Here, too, Beethoven's music, in which the heroic gesture of symphonic language in the middle period gives way to a kind of renunciation of the striving for totality in the late period, is exemplary. This dialectic of violence and nonviolence, this allowing, as it were, of nonintegration, can be seen in the high points of modernist art: "The utmost in integration is the utmost in illusion, and that sets the reversal in motion: since the late Beethoven, the artists who have managed this have mobilized disintegration. The truth content of art, whose organ was integration, turns against art, and at these turning points art has some of its greatest moments" (*Aesthetic Theory* 73–74/67). The turn from integration to nonintegration means that nothingness—in the form of the trifling, the insignificant, the amorphous—enters the work and becomes the agent, or better said, the medium, of coherence: "In great music the so-called primal elements unearthed by analysis are often trifling. It is only insofar as these elements approach nothingness asymptotically that they fuse into a whole as pure becoming" (154/148). This emphasis on the importance of the nonidentical and nonsubsumable detail is, by another name, Adorno's aesthetic nominalism, and it is part of the dialectic of aesthetic illusion or semblance *(Schein)*; in modernist art certain constitutive illusions like totality are called into question—as is, we might add, the prephotographic aura.

For Adorno, the opposition of theater and the novel—or more broadly, of the dramatic to the epic element in art—stands for the distinction between an art that more fully approximates to the laws of logic and one in which the nominalist tendency predominates (although of course Adorno would recognize nominalist tendencies in modern theater, as in the work of Beckett).[34] This is why it is so important for him to interpret Kafka's work as fiction rather than theater. We can best understand what he means by the epic in art by looking at his characterization of it in music. Just as he uses Beethoven to exemplify the shift from integration to nonintegration, he uses Mahler, whom he repeatedly compares to Kafka, to exemplify the epic element. It represents renunciation of pregiven pattern or design and abandonment to a logic of form that proceeds from individual figures:

In Viennese classicism the concept of totality was the undisputed master. Its musical ideal could therefore be called dramatic. If that is so, then Mahler's may be described as epic; it is a cousin to the large-scale novel. Reminiscent of the novel are the rise and fall of passion; the unexpected, seemingly coincidental, but in reality necessary event; the detours, which are actually the main road. . . . Since the music has been composed from the bottom up, it must be heard from the bottom up. The listener must abandon himself to the flow of the work, from one chapter to the next, as with a story when you do not know how it is going to end. You then become aware of a second and superior logic. It follows from the definition of the individual figures, rather than an abstract, preordained design. ("Mahler," 87)

The ultimate exemplar of this epic element in Mahler's music is to be found in certain notes in which the music comes to a halt or is suspended. They "do not represent any build-up of power," says Adorno. "Nor are they simply a pause in which the movement temporarily comes to rest, but something different again: they are the seal of permanence, of the music's inability to fight free of itself." They represent the overcoming of dramatic violence by epic nonviolence: in them, "the epic sense of form of Mahler's symphonies has penetrated right down into the motivic cell and there resists non-violently the essentially dramatic thrust of the symphony" ("Mahler," 104–5).

Such notes are the musical equivalent of Kafka's uninterpretable gestures. One might say that it is the presence of an unassimilated and in that sense alien material element in any medium—the unintegrated note in a work of music, the gesture in a written work—that constitutes for Adorno the movement of nonviolence. Narrative as such does not guarantee the epic element in Mahler's music, in the sense in which Adorno describes it; language, like musical form, participates in the logic of domination through concepts. Hence, in the case of Kafka, Adorno must pose the question how it is possible to be an expressionist novelist: that would seem to be a contradiction in terms, given expressionism's focus on immediacy. But Kafka mastered "the task of . . . finding words for the space of objectless inwardness, in spite of the fact that the scope of every word transcends the absolute immediacy of that which it is supposed to evoke . . . through the visual element. As the medium of gestures, it asserts its priority" ("Notes on Kafka," 264). In other words, gesture is the place in which the element of visual immediacy can enter a linguistic work. That is why it is so important, as both Adorno and Benjamin point out, to take Kafka's gestures not symbolically but literally—as uninterpretable allegories, literal rebuses.[35] As part of the dialectic of language, gesture lies not only between muteness and music but also between language and the muteness of matter.

At the same time, the fall away from language and logic into gesture reflects the imperiled state of the subject. Kafka's work is not theater, and the Nature Theater of Oklahoma is not theater, also because Kafka's characters are not free enough as subjects to engage in dramatic action and because there can be no outside, no totalizing point of view—no spectator's point of view—from which the Nature Theater of Oklahoma can be viewed (Dec. 17, 1934, p. 108). When full subjecthood is not possible, nonviolence is nonviolent resistance to myth, a strategy of cunning designed to preserve a little of the subject in an inconspicuous and uninterpretable survival on the model of that Ulysses whom Kafka found as fascinating as Adorno and Horkheimer did.[36]

Understanding gesture in Kafka as part of this complex of epic nonviolence that eludes both the ambiguity and the dominating logic of language reveals once again what Kafka and photography share for Adorno. Photography as index, bearing the trace of the original object in the actual light that struck it at the specific instant, is literal to a fault and nonlinguistic as well. At the same time, it is capable of retaining, in negative perhaps, the possibility of subjectivity. The individual photographic print, exemplar of reproducibility, is as subject to fading and oblivion as the refuse of which Kafka, as Adorno says, makes his art. One such photograph, as Adorno points out, makes its appearance in *The Castle:* "only with difficulty can K. recognize anything on it" ("Notes on Kafka," 253). Yet like Odradek, it may contain within it, in the dialectic of its negativity, a whisper, a glint, of utopia.

This movement of nonviolence that is linked with the preeminence of the *nichtig,* the trifling (literally, nothing-ish), of the inscrutable but literal detail, is akin to aura as a negative reflection, an intangible and uncoercive radiance. It is, we might say, aura that is one step further in its evolution, aura in the era of the crisis of illusion, now become a para- or counteraura. Given the implicit commitment of Adorno's work on the aesthetics of modernism to tracing the continued existence of aura in this new form, one can see how he would feel that Benjamin's Artwork essay, which seems to applaud and embrace the shocks and violence that destroy aura without embracing the tiny movements of nonviolent resistance in modernist works of art, constituted an act of identification with the aggressor.[37]

The Chinese Painter and the Sacrifice of the Self

For Benjamin, however, the theme of shock and violence plays itself out differently, and Adorno fails to see this.[38] Whereas for Adorno the crucial factor in the dynamics of that theme is the epic element, for Benjamin it is something I will refer to as the "Chinese element." Like the epic element in Adorno, the Chinese element in Benjamin is two-sided and intimately linked to the dimension of gesture. On the one hand, the Chinese element is part of the mythic, archaic world that Kafka evokes; Benjamin refers to the Jews and the Chinese as "among Kafka's ancestors in the ancient world" ("Franz Kafka," 117) and quotes Franz Rosenzweig's depiction of the Chinese ancestor cult (132). At the same time, the Chinese element takes the form of the impersonal, characterless "elemental purity of feeling" in the Confucian "average man" (120; Benjamin is again quoting Rosenzweig). Both the purity of feeling and the incomprehensibility of the ancestor world are conveyed through gesture.

Although Adorno may have been familiar with Scholem's remark about Benjamin's "Chinese politeness,"[39] he seems to have made too little of Benjamin's extensive references to things Chinese in his essay on Kafka. Further, Adorno does not seem to have understood that this impersonal Chinese element is itself a reaction to shock in Benjamin, but one quite different from identification with the aggressor. It is a reaction that is intelligible from the point of view of the subject or "target" of shock—a point of view that, as noted earlier with respect to photography, is very much Benjamin's. Benjamin describes a progressive stripping away of the subjective dimension from Kafka's gestures, and his own autobiographical writings can help to elucidate this connection between shock and the Chinese element. In fact, it is through another text that alludes to the experience of being the target of photography that we can best begin to explicate the connection. The text is an early version of what became the *Berlin Childhood* miniature "Announcement of a Death." This version, which appears in Benjamin's uncompleted *Berlin Chronicle,* begins as follows:

Anyone can affirm that the length of time in which we receive impressions has no correlation to the fate of those impressions in our memories. Nothing precludes the fact that we retain, more or less, memories of rooms in which we spent twenty-four hours, while others, where we lived for months, are totally forgotten. . . . Perhaps more frequent are the cases in which the twilight of habitude for years denies the place the necessary light, until one day it flares up from an outside source like ignited magnesium, and now the image is captured as a snapshot on the plate. But we ourselves always stand at the center of these curious pictures. And that is not so puzzling, because such moments of sudden illumination are at the same time moments of being-outside-ourselves, and while our wakeful, habitual, daytime self mixes, active or sorrowful, into events, our deeper self rests elsewhere, and is stricken by shock like the magnesium by the flame of a match. This sacrifice of our deepest self to shock is what creates the most indestructible images for our memory.

This is the preamble to the narration of the announcement referred to in the title. The text continues: "So the room in which I slept at the age of six would have been forgotten had not my father come in one night—I was already in bed—with the news of a death."[40] The text breaks off in midsentence shortly afterward. In the final version, from the *Fassung letzter Hand* of the *Berlin Childhood*, the preamble has disappeared. This version reads,

I may have been five years old. One evening when I was already in bed my father appeared. He came to say goodnight to me. Perhaps half against his will, he told me the news of the death of a cousin. The cousin had been an older man who was of little importance to me. My father embellished the announcement with details. I did not take in all of his narrative. But that evening I impressed my room upon my memory as though I had known that I would have business there again one day. I was already long grown when I heard that my cousin had died of syphilis. My father had come in order not to be alone. But it was my room he had sought out and not me. The two of them needed no confidant. (410)

With the announcement of a death and the sacrifice of our deepest self to a shock like that of a photographic flash in the process of creating the memory image in which the room remains, not only has the self been sacrificed, but, as Linda Rugg has noted, the depiction of the experience as one of shock has been erased as well.[41]

In another early version of this text, also in the *Berlin Chronicle*, which becomes the sole version in Adorno's 1955 edition of the *Berlin Childhood*, the photographic shock in the preamble is replaced by a discussion of the "déjà écouté." The shock with which a moment comes to our consciousness as having already been experienced, Benjamin says, tends to assault us in the form of a sound, perhaps a rustling or a knocking (*Berlin Chronicle*, 59–60). With this echoing of past and future in the image container of memory, we have once again a form of the aura as a "strange web of time and space," this time a web created through the sacrifice of the self to shock. But in the final version of "Announcement of a Death," the role of sound is erased. We are left only with the "indestructible image" of a room awaiting the future—a room containing a death, an exclusion, and a deception. Something analogous occurs in the "Short History of Photography"; the role of shock in Surrealism and Surrealist photography is omitted from the history. When it returns in the Artwork essay, it will be in disguised form.

In a letter about Kafka to his friend Gershom Scholem, written in 1938, thus four years after the Kafka essay we have been discussing, Benjamin reconstrues Kafka in terms that echo these. Kafka's relation to the modern world in which technology is capable of annihilating us all verges on the edge of what an individual can experience, and it is characterized by the act of listening to indistinct sounds. "This reality [of the modern world]," Benjamin says, "can virtually no longer be experienced by an individual." At the same time, he notes shortly afterward, "if one says that [Kafka] perceived what was to come without perceiving what exists in the present, one should add that he perceived it essentially as an individual affected by it. . . . But his

experience was based solely on the tradition to which [he] sur-
rendered; there was no far-sightedness or 'prophetic vision'.
Kafka listened to tradition, and he who listens hard does not
see."[42] Vision is replaced by listening; listening to the indistinct
sounds of the past produces a complementary vision of the future. Looking back, Benjamin notes the "apologetic character"
of his earlier essay and emphasizes instead the importance of
failure in Kafka: "To do justice to the figure of Kafka in its purity
and its peculiar beauty one must never lose sight of one thing: it
is the purity and beauty of a failure" ("Reflections on Kafka,"
144–45).

If we consider the progression over the years in Benjamin's
revisions of "Announcement of a Death" and his reflections on
Kafka, we see, as I have said, a process in which the experience
of shock itself tends to disappear and what is left is a containing
structure in which past and future reverberate and in which
listening, rather than the visual element, plays a major role. At
the same time, this structure might also be described as a stance—
on the part of both Kafka and Benjamin—in which purity and
failure are the prominent elements and in which what is listened
to is faint and unintelligible. In Benjamin's work, then, we find
a complex that relates shock to disappearance, containment, failure, and purity. Although one could certainly find thematic links,
Adorno's complex relating of shock to freezing, obliqueness, survival, and awakening is clearly different. The constellation that
Adorno develops, derived from Kafka and Surrealism, is the one
that is elided in Benjamin's work.

In the form of an anecdote about a Chinese painter who
disappears into his painting, however, the Chinese element in
Benjamin's work appears in a number of contexts in which its
connection to shock and photography is more explicit. One of
them, in the Artwork essay, is perhaps Benjamin's most blatant

defense of shock as the antithesis of aura. Here he uses the story to illustrate the contrast between "absorption," the old aesthetic stance of contemplation, and "distraction," the new aesthetic stance that film compels: "Distraction and concentration form polar opposites which may be stated as follows: A man who concentrates before a work of art is absorbed by it. He enters into this work of art the way legend tells of the Chinese painter when he viewed his finished painting. In contrast, the distracted mass absorbs the work of art" ("Work of Art," 239). On the surface—the deceptive surface that the text of the Artwork essay is—the contrast is very clear, and this passage exemplifies the sort of assertions that make Adorno accuse Benjamin of identifying with the aggressor. But in fact this anecdote and the exoticism that it reflects were a part of the cultural context Adorno and Benjamin shared; Adorno, too, recounts the anecdote, citing a text by Ernst Bloch as its source. His use of it helps to illuminate its meaning for Benjamin. Adorno cites the anecdote in his comments on Mahler's *Lied von der Erde,* in which the Chinese element is pervasive. Adorno is speaking about one of the songs that make up this work: "The pavilion song, which ends like a transparent fata morgana, is reminiscent of the Chinese story about the painter who disappears into his painting, a futile and indelible pledge *[Unterpfand].* A miniaturization, this vanishing is the appearance of death, in which music preserves at the same time what perishes" (*Mahler,* 152). Adorno's gloss on the Chinese story gives an added dimension to what Benjamin calls absorption (and in any case the use of that term is suspicious, given Benjamin's well-known statement about theology in his work being like something absorbed by blotting paper). Here the absorption is a disappearance into the depths that is a miniaturization and a death, but also a preservation. The disappearance is a sacrifice, a pledge, which allows the image to be retained and which is retained in the image.

Adorno's interpretation of the exoticism reflected in *Das Lied von der Erde* confirms and extends his comments on the story of the Chinese painter. Mahler's exoticism, Adorno says, was "a prelude to emigration." Mahler went to New York and broke down—much like the emigrant in Adorno's improvisation on Kafka's title, who went to America and was never heard of again. This migration into something other, which in Mahler's case as well as the painter's is the work itself, is both a sacrifice of one's identity and a preservation of it in hiding. For Adorno, it is Mahler's Jewishness that is given this sacrificial concealment: "This Orient," he continues, "is pseudomorphous as a cover for Mahler's Jewish element. One can no more put one's finger on this element than in any other work of art; it shrinks from identification yet remains indispensable to the whole" (149).[43]

Adorno's interpretation of the anecdote about the Chinese painter is confirmed in turn by the other context in Benjamin's work in which it appears, one that links it again with photography. This context is the early version of the *Berlin Childhood* miniature "The Mummerehlen," cited earlier, a piece that Benjamin originally intended as his self-portrait.[44] The theme of "The Mummerehlen" is distortion, disguise, and disappearance. It begins with the child's disappearing into, or disguising himself in, the cloud of words, as well as coming to resemble the interiors he lives in, and then moves into a description of Benjamin's childhood experience in a photography studio like the one in Kafka's boyhood photograph. Just as we saw the face and its aura disappear in Benjamin's "Short History of Photography," here the child Benjamin finds himself incapable of resemblance to himself. At the end of "The Mummerehlen," talking about his experience painting on porcelain, Benjamin introduces the story of the Chinese painter as "the story that led [him] back to the work of the mummerehlen many years later":

It comes from China and tells of an old painter who showed his friends his most recent painting. In it a park was represented, a narrow path along the water and through a stand of trees, coming out in front of a little door that gave access to a little house at the back. But when the friends looked for the painter, he was gone and in the picture. There he wandered up the narrow path to the door, stopped in front of it, turned around, smiled, and disappeared into its opening. So I too, there by my plates and brushes, was suddenly transposed into the picture. I came to resemble the porcelain, into which I made my entrance with a cloud of color. (*Berlin Childhood, Schriften* version, 609)

This disappearance, in short, is at the same time a way of permeating what one disappears into, becoming part of the cloudiness. The context tells us that it is inseparable from the kind of sacrifice of the self the child experiences in the photographer's studio. Disguise and sacrifice are two sides of the same coin, which is both death and preservation, oppression and artistic activity.

As Adorno's notion of *Unterpfand,* which suggests something that has been given over in the form of a substratum, and his description of the Jewish element in Mahler's work as something one cannot put one's finger on but that is nevertheless indispensable to the whole, should tell us, the mention of clouds in "The Mummerehlen" is neither accidental nor trivial. It very accurately combines the suggestion of obscurity and concealment and the suggestion of dispersal—in fact absorption, to recall the term Benjamin uses in the Artwork essay. As we will see, for Benjamin it also stands for the shock and violence that are at the heart of this process of disguise and disappearance. But just as Adorno overlooks the significance of the Chinese element for Benjamin, he also overlooks the significance of cloudiness for him. Referring to Odradek in his letter on Benjamin's Kafka essay, he says, "Here is something more than 'cloud,' namely dialectic, and not so much to 'clear up' the cloud form but to thoroughly render it thoroughly dialectical—to cause the parable to rain, as it were—remains the most essential task for an interpretation of Kafka" (Dec. 17, 1934, pp. 106–7).

The passage in Benjamin's Kafka essay to which Adorno was probably referring deals with gesture and, implicitly, with violence and sacrifice. "This Abraham," Benjamin writes—the Abraham Kafka envisioned, who would be fully prepared to sacrifice Isaac but who simply could not get away to do so, thus effecting an indeterminate postponement—"appears 'with the promptness of a waiter.' Kafka could understand things only in the form of a gestus, and this gestus which he did not understand constitutes the cloudy part of the parables. Kafka's writings emanate from it" ("Franz Kafka," 129). For Benjamin as well as Kafka, cloudiness is at the center—the interior—of things. The link between cloudiness and the violence and shock contained and preserved in the interiors of things is quite apparent in the *Berlin Childhood* miniature "Boys Books," in which words and reading are compared with snow falling and in which their interior seems clouded and colored by a strange violent light of slaughter: "To open one [of the books] would have led me right into the middle of the womb in which a changing and obscure text clouded up, a text pregnant with colors. They were effervescent and fugitive colors; they always ended in a violet that seemed to come from the inside of a slaughtered animal" (397).[45] The mummerehlen herself, who originates in the distortion of a children's verse, and who stands for the distorted, fictitious, yet fascinating disappearance that the miniature bearing her name is devoted to—miniaturization, preservation and sacrifice all together—comes in the final version to live in the indeterminacy of snow and to resemble Odradek in the faintness and indeterminacy of her voice: "The mummerehlen herself confided nothing to me. She may have had almost no voice. Her gaze fell from the indecisive flakes of the first snow. If it had fallen on me even once I would have been consoled for a lifetime" (418).[46] The search for the mummerehlen requires the same kind of listening to the indeterminate that Benjamin describes Kafka as practicing, the kind that the ear/auricles of those boys in the childhood photographs were practicing and that Benjamin, in lines from "The Mummerehlen" cited earlier, depicts as his method for understanding the nineteenth century: "As a mollusk lives in its shell, I lived in the nineteenth century, which now lies hollow before me like an empty shell. I hold it to my ear" (417).

The gesture of the Chinese painter, which as Adorno and "The Mummerehlen" have shown us is inseparable from this cloudiness with all its implications, is the essential gesture of Benjamin's own work. Voluntarily and involuntarily, as a strategy of survival derived from childhood experience and responding to the disappearance of the face into the bourgeois interior and the experience of Jewishness, however we may interpret the reasons for the gesture, Benjamin has not so much become absorbed in the contemplation of a work of art as disappeared into his own work, miniaturized himself within it, bid farewell to his friends and disappeared, hidden in the interior of his own work. Adorno's evocation of the futile but indelible *Unterpfand* is a far more accurate figure for the meaning of the story than Benjamin's disingenuous invocation of traditional aesthetic contemplation.

The Artwork essay itself can be seen as a disguised version of the story of the Chinese painter. In that essay, Benjamin describes the actor whose image has been chopped up into bits and reassembled in film, and who must operate with no aura at all, no grounding in time and space; he describes the spectators who have become critical observers but are also actors, and he notes the universal quest for similarity that has destroyed distance and aura. As Robert Hullot-Kentor has indicated, these descriptions are best understood as images of Benjamin's own stance; the Artwork essay describes the processes to which Benjamin has both been submitted and has subjected himself.[47] In fact, the disingenuous Artwork essay shows the final stage, the result, of the process of disappearance. In the boyhood pictures of Benjamin and Kafka, with their tortured smiles and their ear/auricles attending to the faint whisperings—are they really whisperings?—of Odradek and the mummerehlen, we see the process when it is underway but not yet complete. The successive deletions of the references to photography and shock in the *Berlin Childhood* and the increasing condensation—miniaturization—of its texts are, as noted earlier, the traces of this disappearance of the self into the text.

This process of disappearance, I would argue, is Benjamin's response to shock. We see this in the connection between the magnesium flash and the sacrifice of the self in "Announcement of a Death" and in the violet light of slaughter in the interior of the cloud in "Boys Books." The death or vanishing that occurs is actually the destruction of the self through shock that Benjamin chronicles not only in the "Short History of Photography" but also in the Artwork essay. But the works that result from and contain this gesture of disappearance demonstrate that these shocks to the self do not necessarily entail the destruction of the aura. The Chinese painter smiles, certainly enigmatically, at his friends before disappearing, and his friends continue to gaze—in puzzled fascination, no doubt—at his work. Benjamin's works, to say nothing of Benjamin himself, retain the ability to fascinate. They have, that is, an aura of their own.

This aura is a version of the modernist or para-aura that we have met in connection with photography. Benjamin's works, produced through the sacrifice of the self, contain that admixture of death and disintegration that Adorno invokes when he speaks of Benjamin's radioactivity-inducing gaze or compares the *Berlin Childhood* miniatures to ruins and fairytale snapshots. "When it snows what is far away leads not into the far distance but into the interior," says Benjamin in "Boys Books" (*Berlin Childhood,* 396–97). In his texts the relationships of interior and exterior, foreground and background, near and far, and past and future are constantly shifting. The shocks and violence that reverberate through them have caused the firm ground of time and space to shake, creating a truly "strange web of time and space."

Paradoxically, Adorno's criticisms of Benjamin's Kafka essay have guided us in elaborating the full constellation of shock, photography, and aura in Benjamin's work. Yet Adorno, whose descriptions of Benjamin's intellectual powers invest him with precisely this negative modernist aura, and who characterized Benjamin as an exemplar of the kind of self-divesting he admired in Hegel as well, did not grasp the constellation of shock and self-sacrifice that links Benjamin's essay on Kafka to his autobiographical writings and to the Artwork essay. He did not penetrate the ruse that is the Artwork essay, Benjamin's own cunning mode of survival. In the final analysis, his criticisms of Benjamin's interpretations as oversimplified and undialectical seem oversimplified themselves. Yet the light they shed illuminates the theme of the negative aura in Adorno's own work.

Mahler's Death Mask

I will close my attempt to define the "distance, however close" between Adorno and Benjamin by counterposing the image of

Mahler's death mask to the gesture of the Chinese painter. As we have seen, Adorno is keenly aware of the similarities between Mahler and Kafka (and by extension, Benjamin) with regard to the themes of emigration, exoticism, and a strategy of nonviolent resistance. Adorno's comments on Mahler's death mask extend these connections to the question of hope and hopelessness, which, as we—and Adorno himself—have seen, preoccupied Kafka and Benjamin as well. There seems to be a smile on Mahler's face in death as it is preserved in his death mask, Adorno says, and that smile is more than a mere illusion caused by some muscular reflex:

In Mahler's face, which seems both imperious and full of a tender suffering, there is a hint of cunning triumph, as if it wished to say: I have fooled you after all. Fooled us how? If we were to speculate we might conclude that the unfathomable sorrow of his last works had undercut all hope in order to avoid succumbing to illusion, rather as if hope were not unlike the superstitious idea of tempting fate, so that by hoping for something you prevent it from coming true. Could we not think of the path of disillusionment described by the development of Mahler's music as by no other as an example of the cunning not of reason but of hope? ("Mahler," 110)

The smile on Mahler's death mask seems to me the precise analogue of the smile on the face of the Chinese painter as he vanishes into the interior of his painting. Like Mahler, whose smile in death reflects the cunning of hope, Benjamin, who liked to quote Kafka's remark that there is all the hope in the world, only not for us, played a cunning game with hope. What appeared to be a sacrifice and a death was a strategy for achieving permanent and indestructible images permeated by a self no one could put his finger on. Film and photography in Benjamin's work both enact and explicate this process. Adorno knew this. For him, too, the various images of photographs of the earth from space, whether he uses them in connection with Mahler, Kafka, or Benjamin, are emblems of hope in hopelessness. "Kafka, the land-surveyor," Adorno says in a passage referred to earlier, "photographs the earth's surface just as it must have appeared to those Jewish victims hung head down during the endless hours of their dying." "It is for nothing less than such unmitigated torture," he continues, "that the perspective of redemption presents itself to him" ("Notes on Kafka," 269).

But the images of the death mask and the photograph of the earth also demonstrate the slight but significant distance between Adorno and Benjamin in this regard. What is important for Adorno is a surface—a mask, the surface of the earth—which is looked at from a point of view outside it. What is seen is full of feeling, full of suffering, and Adorno reads this easily; then, in a kind of extrapolation by negation, as in a photographic negative, the possibility of hope, of happiness, of redemption is read as well. This is the essence of what photography means for Adorno. For Benjamin, in contrast, it is the tactile and especially the aural, rather than the visual, that are important, because the subject of the experience is enclosed in the interior, and the surface turned to the viewer is a disguise. Perhaps more accurately, it is because in Benjamin's complex spatiality the surface is permeated with a reverberating interior, which is also the subject, and which does not hold still long enough to be grasped visually.

Adorno's sensibility befits one concerned with the aesthetic dimension in its late, modern form, in which the dialectic of semblance is crucial. This dialectic is a matter of the coexistence in disjunction of the organic and the inorganic, of surface appearances and their negations, and at the same time of the transience and the leavetaking that have always been associated with the aesthetic. As Adorno says of the photograph of the earth from space to which he compares Mahler's music: "To the gaze of the music that is in the process of leaving it, the earth becomes rounded to a sphere which one can see the whole of, just as it has now been photographed from space, not the center of creation but something tiny and ephemeral" (*Mahler,* 154). Benjamin's work, concerned with the dialectic of destruction and the indestructible and entailing a sacrifice beyond emotion, is less unambiguously located in the aesthetic dimension and the aura that is inseparable from it, whatever form it may take. It is almost as though there is a will in his work to elide the aesthetic between the opposites of theology and politics; hence Adorno's criticism that Benjamin does not respect the distance between art and the logic of practical action. Yet Adorno's fascination with Benjamin, his repeated assertions of their common ground, and his ability to see and read the depths and distances in the aesthetic surfaces Benjamin presents have made him the best guide to penetrating to the elided defense of the aura in Benjamin's work.

Notes

Published translations from the German have sometimes been amended or re-translated.

Introduction

1. See Rainer Nägele, ed., *Benjamin's Ground: New Readings of Walter Benjamin* (Detroit: Wayne State University Press, 1988); and Susan Buck-Morss, *The Dialectics of Seeing: Walter Benjamin and the Arcades Project* (Cambridge, Mass.: MIT Press, 1989). This spectrum reflects Benjamin's popularity with deconstructionists and postmodernists as well as those more closely allied with the Frankfurt School. See also *Diacritics* 22:3–4 (fall–winter 1992), which was devoted to Benjamin.

2. I am thinking of Adorno's importance for such prominent musicologists and cultural critics concerned with music as Charles Rosen, Richard Taruskin, Leon Botstein, and Edward Said. For an appraisal of Adorno's influence on twentieth-century musicology, see Harold Blumenfeld, "Ad vocem Adorno," *Musical Quarterly* 75:4 (winter 1991): 263–95.

3. My comments are in no way intended to minimize the importance of this work of situating and appraising Adorno. To provide just a few examples from the extensive literature on Adorno: The foundational work on Adorno and the Frankfurt School by Martin Jay, Gillian Rose, and Susan Buck-Morss requires no comment. For readings oriented around evaluations of Adorno's relation to Marxism, or his utopianism, see Russell Berman, "Adorno, Marxism, and Art," *Telos* 34 (winter 1977–78): 157–66; and Richard Wolin, "Mimesis, Utopia, and Reconciliation: A Redemptive Critique of Adorno's *Aesthetic Theory*," in his *Terms of Cultural Criticism: The Frankfurt School, Existentialism, Poststructuralism* (New York: Columbia University Press, 1992), 68–79. For a comparison of Adorno with recent

French thought, see Peter Dews, "Adorno, Post-Structuralism, and the Critique of Identity," in Andrew Benjamin, ed., *The Problems of Modernity: Adorno and Benjamin* (London and New York: Routledge, 1989), 1–22. Attempting to reverse the common notion of Adorno as a deconstructionist avant la lettre, Dews argues, quite convincingly, that while sharing with that thought a critique of constitutive subjectivity, Adorno avoids the mistake of simply prioritizing the particular and the nonidentical. For a more narrowly focused comparison that similarly differentiates Adorno from poststructuralism, see Martin Jay, "Mimesis and Mimetology: Adorno and Lacoue-Labarthe," in Tom Huhn and Lambert Zuidervaart, eds., *The Semblance of Subjectivity: Essays in Adorno's Aesthetic Theory* (Cambridge, Mass.: MIT Press, 1997). The feminist appraisal of Adorno has been slower to come, but see Sabine Wilke and Heidi Schlipphacke, "Construction of a Gendered Subject: A Feminist Reading of Adorno's *Aesthetic Theory*," in Huhn and Zuidervaart's collection, as well as Maggie O'Neill's anthology *Adorno, Culture, and Feminism*, to be published by Sage. For an interesting and useful discussion of the various strands in Adorno's reception, see Peter Uwe Hohendahl, "Approaches to Adorno: A Tentative Typology," in his *Prismatic Thought: Theodor W. Adorno* (Lincoln and London: University of Nebraska Press, 1995).

4. Fredric Jameson, *Late Marxism: Adorno, or the Persistence of the Dialectic* (London: Verso, 1990). Jameson's book has inspired my work more than any other, not so much because I agree with him on any particular detail but because his remarks are so suggestive and reflect an appreciation of the formal dimension of Adorno's work, and because I appreciate the scope of the claims he makes for Adorno's importance. On *Late Marxism*, see Hohendahl's comments in *Prismatic Thought*, including his discussion of Robert Hullot-Kentor's and Eva Geulen's reviews, which appeared in *Telos* 90 (fall 1991), and my review article, "Adorno in Postmodern Perspective," in *Thesis Eleven* 34 (1993): 178–85.

5. See Lambert Zuidervaart, *Adorno's Aesthetic Theory: The Redemption of Illusion* (Cambridge, Mass.: MIT Press, 1991); David Roberts, *Art and Enlightenment: Aesthetic Theory after Adorno* (Lincoln: University of Nebraska Press, 1991); and J. M. Bernstein, *The Fate of Art: Aesthetic Alienation from Kant to Derrida and Adorno* (State College: Pennsylvania State University Press, 1992). Zuidervaart's book is particularly useful in providing a thorough grounding in the historical-intellectual context for, as well as the chief arguments of, *Aesthetic Theory*. Max Paddison's detailed and careful *Adorno's Aesthetics of Music* (New York: Cambridge University Press, 1993) accomplishes something similar for Adorno's work on music. Most recently, Hohendahl's *Prismatic Thought* addresses issues central to Adorno's aesthetics, including Adorno's philosophy of language, and Huhn and Zuidervaart's anthology on *Aesthetic Theory* marks a further level of detailed investigation of Adorno's aesthetic work in the Anglo-American context. At the same time, I concur with Zuidervaart's comment, in the introduction to that collection, that the reception of Adorno's aesthetics by Anglo-American philosophy has barely begun.

6. The second development is related to the first, for Jameson provided the earliest and still one of the best formulations of the formal dimension of Adorno's work in his "T. W. Adorno: Or, Historical Tropes," in *Marxism and Form* (Princeton, N.J.: Princeton University Press, 1971). The new translation of *Aesthetic Theory* by Robert Hullot-Kentor is being published by the University of Minnesota Press.

7. Adorno, *Negative Dialectics*, trans E. B. Ashton (New York: Continuum, 1987), xx.

8. As Paddison points out, "authentic" has a very different meaning when Adorno uses it with regard to artworks (or, I would add, aesthetic experience) than it does in his polemic against Heideggerian/existentialist jargon (where the German word in question is *Eigentlichkeit*) in the *Jargon of Authenticity*. See Paddison's review of *Aesthetic Theory* in *Music Analysis* 6 (1987), cited in Roberts, *Art and Enlightenment*, 233, n. 1.

9. I have translated Adorno's term "exakte Phantasie" as "exact imagination" rather than, for instance, "precise fantasy." One could make valid arguments for either rendering of *Phantasie*. My choice is based on my sense that Adorno means to evoke Kant and the aesthetic rather than Freud. (Adorno does not use the term *Einbildungskraft* as a contrast to *Phantasie* in the text in question.)

10. Adorno, "Die Aktualität der Philosophie," *Gesammelte Schriften* 1 (Frankfurt am Main: Suhrkamp, 1973), 325–45, here 342. *Gesammelte Schriften* will hereafter be cited as GS. Translated as "The Actuality of Philosophy," *Telos* 31 (spring 1977). Hereafter cited in the text as "Actuality of Philosophy."

11. Adorno, "Schöne Stellen," GS 18 (Frankfurt am Main: Suhrkamp, 1984), 685–718, here p. 699. Hereafter cited in the text as "Beautiful Passages."

12. For an elaboration of Adorno's notion of the "speculative ear" in the context of English Romantic poetry, and in particular Keats's notion of negative capability, see Robert Kaufman, "Negatively Capable Dialectics: Keats, Vendler, Adorno, and the Theory of the Avant-Garde," unpublished essay.

13. Jürgen Habermas, *The Philosophical Discourse of Modernity*, trans. Frederick Lawrence (Cambridge, Mass.: MIT Press, 1987), chap. 5. (Adorno himself, of course, rejects the possibility of a regression behind the Weberian differentiation of reason.) In his "Concerning the Central Idea of Adorno's Philosophy," in Huhn and Zuidervaart, Rüdiger Bubner also makes a case against Adorno's advocacy of the essay form for philosophical discourse. Bubner argues that Adorno's effort to place truth in the aesthetic dimension via the mimetic does not succeed; philosophy must remain external to art. (The original title of Bubner's essay was "Kann Theorie aesthetisch werden?")

14. Albrecht Wellmer, "Truth, Semblance, Reconciliation," in *The Persistence of Modernity,* trans. David Midgeley (Cambridge, Mass.: MIT Press, 1991), 1–35.

15. Habermas's and Wellmer's criticisms have been enormously influential. Both Zuidervaart and Bernstein provide discussions of them. Zuidervaart argues, persuasively in my view, that Adorno does not so much fall into an outmoded subject-object paradigm as explode it. Cf. *Adorno's Aesthetic Theory,* chap. 11. In his *Perversion and Utopia: A Study in Psychoanalysis and Critical Theory* (Cambridge, Mass.: MIT Press, 1995), Joel Whitebook defends Castoriadis against Habermas's criticisms, arguing along lines similar to the ones I take here. "The philosophy of language does not . . . sublate the philosophy of consciousness without residue," says Whitebook (164).

16. Jameson, *Late Marxism,* 239.

17. See Adorno, "Spätstil Beethovens," in *Moments Musicaux* (Frankfurt am Main: Suhrkamp, 1964), 13–17; now also GS 17, 1982). Hereafter cited in the text as "Beethoven's Late Style." For additional texts and notes on Beethoven's late work and late style, see Adorno, *Beethoven: Philosophie der Musik,* ed. Rolf Tiedemann (Frankfurt am Main: Suhrkamp, 1993).

18. Cf. Adorno, "Spätkapitalismus oder Industriegesellschaft?" GS 8 (1972), 354–70; translated as "Late Capitalism or Industrial Sociology?" in Volker Meja, Dieter Misgeld, and Nico Stehr, eds., *Modern German Sociology* (New York: Columbia University Press, 1987).

19. See "Beethoven's Late Style," 66. For a sample of the catastrophic reception of *Aesthetic Theory,* see the review by Henry L. Shapiro in the *Philosophical Review* 95 (April 1986), 288–89, in which Shapiro calls the book "shockingly difficult" and refers to its "enormous obscurity" and "long-winded manner."

20. Cf. Wellmer, "Truth, Semblance, Reconciliation," 35.

21. Cf. Adorno, "The Essay as Form," in *Notes to Literature,* vol. 1, trans. Shierry Weber Nicholsen (New York: Columbia University Press, 1991), 21–22.

22. This despite the existence of books with titles like "Adorno and Benjamin." Cf. Pierre Missac, *Walter Benjamin's Passages,* trans. Shierry Weber Nicholsen (Cambridge, Mass.: MIT Press, 1995). Missac comments that Benjamin's "reciprocal interaction" with Adorno "ought to be studied in both directions, beginnning with the seminar the young Privatdozent Adorno devoted to Benjamin's book on the German Trauerspiel in 1929 and extending to works Adorno published after the war, in which the authority of Benjamin is often invoked" (26). Richard Wolin has made a start on this in his discussion of the "Adorno–Benjamin dispute," which he characterizes as "one of the most significant aesthetic controversies of our century." See his *Walter Benjamin: An Aesthetic of Redemption,* rev. ed.

(Berkeley and Los Angeles: University of California Press, 1994). For Wolin's nuanced account of Benjamin's stance on Surrealism and Adorno's stance on Benjamin's, see his "Benjamin, Adorno, Surrealism," in Huhn and Zuidervaart. The final essay in the present volume, "Adorno and Benjamin, Photography and the Aura," covers some of the same ground, adducing a different layer of the textual material, so to speak.

1 Subjective Aesthetic Experience and Its Historical Trajectory

1. On Adorno and reception aesthetics, see Hans Robert Jauss, "Negativität und aesthetische Erfahrung. Adornos aesthetische Theorie in der Retrospektive," in *Materialien zur aesthetischen Theorie: Th. W. Adornos Konstruktion der Moderne*, ed. Burkhardt Lindner and W. Martin Lüdke (Frankfurt am Main: Suhrkamp, 1979); and Pauline Johnson, "An Aesthetics of Negativity/An Aesthetics of Reception: Jauss's Dispute with Adorno," *New German Critique* 42 (fall 1987): 51–70. For a productivist view of Adorno, see Russell Berman, "Adorno, Marxism, and Art" and, in a slightly different sense, Jameson's *Late Marxism*. See also Robert Kaufman, "Red Kant, or, The Persistence of the Third Critique in Adorno and Jameson," presented to the annual meeting of the Modern Language Association, December 1995. Kaufman explicitly opposes Adorno's constructivism, which is his focus, to a productionism.

2. Adorno, *Aesthetische Theorie*, GS 7 (Frankfurt am Main: Suhrkamp, 1970). English translation *Aesthetic Theory*, trans. Christian Lenhardt (London: Routledge & Kegan Paul, 1984). All translations from *Aesthetic Theory* are my own. Hereafter cited in the text as *Aesthetic Theory*, followed by the page number first in the German original and then in Lenhardt's English translation.

3. Adorno, "Presuppositions," in *Notes to Literature* vol. 2, trans. Shierry Weber Nicholsen (New York: Columbia University Press, 1992), here 97.

4. The conception is clearly Kantian, as are Adorno's formulations of the nature of aesthetic experience generally. Adorno's *Aesthetic Theory* is as much a reframing of Kantian aesthetics as it is a reframing of Hegelian aesthetics—with, crudely, Kant providing the experiential structure and Hegel providing the perspective on the end of art—and a number of scholars are pursuing the theme of the relationship between Kant and Adorno. See, for instance, Robert Kaufman, "Red Kant"; Tom Huhn, "Kant, Adorno, and the Social Opacity of the Aesthetic," in Huhn and Zuidervaart; J. M. Bernstein, *The Fate of Art;* and Peter Osborne, "Adorno and the Metaphysics of Modernism: The Problem of a 'Postmodern' Art," in Andrew Benjamin, *The Problems of Modernity*. Osborne correctly points out that, whereas for Kant aesthetic experience is a generic category of experience, for Adorno it is primarily an artistic category (p. 30). Conversely, the ability

of Adorno's aesthetics to surpass, in my opinion, both Kant's and Hegel's is based
on the fact that Adorno adds aesthetic experience of all kinds—including that of
the composer and the performer—to his philosophical expertise. Jameson's discussion of Kant and Adorno, in contrast, is concerned primarily to distinguish
Adorno from traditional philosophical aesthetics, despite the appearances
aroused by Adorno's "stubborn commitment to some notion of 'genuine aesthetic
experience.'" See *Late Marxism*, 127–28.

5. Adorno, "Schwierigkeiten," in *Impromptus*, GS 17 (Frankfurt am Main:
Suhrkamp, 1982), 253–91, here 298. Hereafter cited in the text as "Difficulties."

6. Adorno, "Skoteinos, or How to Read Hegel," in *Hegel: Three Studies*, trans.
Shierry Weber Nicholsen (Cambridge, Mass.: MIT Press, 1993), 89–148, here
139. Adorno's discussion of association and the descriptions of aesthetic experience in "Beautiful Passages" that I will cite later both bring to mind Robert Bly's
notion of "leaping poetry": "My idea . . . is that a great work of art often has at
its center a long floating leap, around which the work of art in ancient times used
to gather itself like steel shavings around the magnet. . . . Thought of in terms
of language, . . . leaping is the ability to associate fast. In a great ancient or
modern poem, the considerable distance between the associations, the distance
the spark has to leap, gives the lines their bottomless feeling, their space, and the
speed of the association increases the excitement of the poetry." Robert Bly,
Leaping Poetry: An Idea with Poems and Translations (Boston: Beacon Press, 1975)
3–4.

7. For a more complex, though differently focused, treatment of this subject-object reversal in Adorno, which comes to the fore when one looks at his aesthetics
in relation to Kant, see Tom Huhn, "Kant, Adorno, and the Social Opacity of the
Aesthetic."

8. Adorno, "Im Jeu de Paume gekritzelt," in *Ohne Leitbild* (Frankfurt am Main:
Suhrkamp, 1967), 42–47, here 46–47.

9. Adorno, "Motifs," in *Quasi una fantasia: Essays on Modern Music*, trans. Rodney
Livingstone (London and New York: Verso, 1992), 9–36, here 34–35 (translation
altered).

10. Adorno, *Moments Musicaux* (Frankfurt am Main: Suhrkamp, 1964; now also
GS 17), 7.

11. For a delightful exposition of the historicity of the work of art in this sense,
see Robert Hullot-Kentor's "Is Aesthetics Still for the Birds?"

12. Adorno, "Reaktion und Fortschritt," in *Moments Musicaux*, 153–60. Hereafter
cited in the text as "Reaction and Progress." For musical materialism, see "Nachtmusik," in *Moments Musicaux*, 66.

13. For an extended discussion of Adorno's concept of musical material, see Paddison, *Adorno's Aesthetics of Music*.

14. Adorno, "Nachtmusik," in *Moments Musicaux*, 58–66, here 58. Hereafter cited in the text as "Night Music."

15. Adorno, "Neue Tempi," in *Moments Musicaux*, 74–83, here 81. Hereafter cited in the text as "New Tempos."

16. Adorno, "Schubert," in *Moments Musicaux*, 18–36, here 18.

17. On Adorno on Beethoven and on late style, see Paddison, *Adorno's Aesthetics of Music*, 233–42; Carl Dahlhaus, "Zu Adornos Beethoven-Kritik," in Lindner and Lüdke, eds., *Materialien zur aesthetischen Theorie*, 494–505; Rose Rosengard Subotnik, "Adorno's Diagnosis of Beethoven's Late Style: Early Symptom of a Fatal Condition," in her *Developing Variations: Style and Ideology in Western Music* (Minneapolis: University of Minnesota Press, 1991), 15–41; and, in a broader context, Edward Said, *Musical Elaborations* (New York: Columbia University Press, 1991), especially 12ff.

18. Adorno, "Verfremdetes Hauptwerk. Zur Missa Solemnis," in *Moments Musicaux*, 167–85. English translation, "Alienated Masterpiece: The *Missa Solemnis*," *Telos* 28 (summer 1976), 113–24. Hereafter cited in the text as "Alienated Masterwork."

19. Adorno's "Schwierigkeiten" has two sections: first, "Difficulties in Composing," dated 1964; second, "Difficulties in Grasping Contemporary Music," dated 1966.

20. Adorno never completed this project, but the notes and texts that formed the material for it are now published as *Beethoven: Philosophie der Musik*.

21. Adorno, "On the Final Scene of *Faust*," in *Notes to Literature*, vol. 1, 111–20, here 112. Hereafter cited in the text as "*Faust*."

22. Adorno, "Toward a Portrait of Thomas Mann," in *Notes to Literature*, vol. 2, 12–19, here 19.

23. Adorno, "Aspects of Hegel's Philosophy," in *Hegel*, 1–51, here 49–50.

24. Adorno, "Benjamin the Letter Writer," in *Notes to Literature*, vol. 2, 233–39, here 236.

25. Adorno, "Introduction to Benjamin's *Schriften*," in *Notes to Literature*, vol. 2, 220–32, here 223.

26. Adorno. "Titles," in *Notes to Literature*, vol. 2, 3–11, here 5. Hereafter cited in the text as "Titles."

27. On Adorno as émigré, see Martin Jay, "Adorno in America," in his *Permanent Exiles* (New York: Columbia University Press, 1985), 120–37. For the image of the émigré learning a language, see "The Essay as Form," 13; and "Skoteinos," 107.

28. Adorno, "Words from Abroad," in *Notes to Literature*, vol. 1, 185–99, here 187.

29. Adorno, "Parataxis: On Hölderlin's Late Poetry," in *Notes to Literature*, vol. 2, 109–49, here 118.

30. Walter Benjamin, *Berliner Kindheit um 1900*, in *Gesammelte Schriften* 7.1, ed. Rolf Tiedemann and Hermann Schweppenhäuser (Frankfurt am Main: Suhrkamp, 1989), 385–432, here 385. Hereafter cited in the text as "Berlin Childhood." The translations are from my unpublished translation of this work.

2 Language: Its Murmuring, Its Darkness, and Its Silver Rib

1. Adorno talks about Odradek in his 1934 letter to Walter Benjamin on the latter's essay on Kafka: "Certainly Odradek, as the reverse side of the world of things, is the sign of distortion—but precisely as such a motif of transcendence, namely of the removal of the boundary and the reconciliation of the organic and the inorganic, or the *Aufhebung* of death: Odradek 'survives.'" Theodor W. Adorno, *Über Walter Benjamin* (Frankfurt am Main: Suhrkamp, 1970) 106. See "Adorno and Benjamin, Photography and the Aura," in this volume, for a further discussion of Adorno's criticisms of Benjamin's Kafka essay.

2. For explicit discussions of Adorno's notions about language, although from a more philosophical than literary and a more theoretical than practical perspective, see Susan Buck-Morss, *The Origin of Negative Dialectics* (New York: Free Press, 1977); and Peter Uwe Hohendahl, *Prismatic Thought*.

3. Adorno, "Thesen über die Sprache des Philosophen," GS 1, 366–71, hereafter cited in the text as "Theses." I am indebted to Hohendahl's essay on Adorno and the problem of language in his *Prismatic Thought* for drawing my attention to this essay as well as the other early essay "The Actuality of Philosophy."

4. Adorno, "Skoteinos," 107. As noted earlier, a similar passage occurs in "The Essay as Form," 13. The fact that many of the essays in *Notes to Literature* that are most relevant to the theme of language deal with German poets whose work is little known in English—and that these essays play a prominent role in my own essay on Adorno and language—should make this image still more compelling for the English-language reader.

5. Adorno, "Charmed Language: On the Poetry of Rudolf Borchardt," in *Notes to Literature*, vol. 2, 193–210, here 193. Hereafter cited in the text as "Borchardt."

6. Adorno, "In Memory of Eichendorff," in *Notes to Literature*, vol. 1, 55–79; here 68–69. Hereafter cited in the text as "Eichendorff." *Verhallen*, the word I have translated as "dying away," is used of sounds.

7. For an extensive discussion of Adorno's conception of mimesis, see my "*Aesthetic Theory*'s Mimesis of Walter Benjamin," in this volume.

8. Adorno's critique of reason is a far more familiar dimension of his work than his discussions of language. See especially *Dialectic of Enlightenment* (jointly with Max Horkheimer), trans. John Cumming (New York: Seabury, 1972); and *Negative Dialectics*. Adorno's critique of the communicative dimension of language further helps us understand why he would not be drawn to a Habermasian paradigm of communicative rationality.

9. Although Adorno does not refer explicitly to the pragmatic (as opposed to the semantic or syntactic) dimension of language, it is clear that at least a portion of his criticism of the communicative dimension is aimed at what Habermas would call the "strategic" uses of communicative action.

10. Adorno, "On Epic Naiveté," in *Notes to Literature*, vol. 1, 3–23, here 27. Hereafter cited in the text as "Epic Naiveté."

11. Buck-Morss points out (in *The Origin of Negative Dialectics*, p. 89) that Adorno has a second, Marxian conception of the name, in which naming something dissolves its mythical power.

12. Cf. "The determinable flaw in every concept makes it necessary to cite others; this is the font of the only constellations which inherited some of the hope of the name." *Negative Dialectics*, 53, cited in Buck-Morss, *Origin of Negative Dialectics*, 90.

13. Adorno, "Music and Language: A Fragment," in *Quasi una fantasia*, 1–6, here 5. In this connection, it is interesting to note that Adorno figures prominently in the fall 1993 issue of *Musical Quarterly*, which is devoted to the topic of music and language. On Adorno's conception of the relationship between music and language, see also Paddison, *Adorno's Aesthetics of Music*, 143–44; and Andrew Bowie, "Music, Language, and Modernity," in A. Benjamin, *Problems of Modernity*. Bowie emphasizes the similarities between music and a language divorced from representation, and stresses Adorno's interest in music and the unsayable. As we see here, however, when Adorno addresses the topic of music and language directly, he reverts to a conventional notion of language.

14. Adorno, "Stefan George," in *Notes to Literature*, vol. 2, 178–92; here 184.

15. Michael Eigen elaborates this hard/soft polarity in his "Soft and Hard Qualities," in *The Electrified Tightrope* (Northvale, N.J.: Jason Aronson, 1993), 105–8.

16. Adorno, "Mahler," in *Quasi una fantasia,* 81–110, here 104–5.

17. For further discussion of Adorno's conception of the epic element in connection with Mahler and the dialectic of violence and nonviolence, see "Adorno and Benjamin, Photography and the Aura," in this volume. Jameson also notes the central place that epic holds for Adorno. For him it exemplifies the combination of a residual interest in truth with violent discontinuities of logic, thus marking Adorno as a modernist rather than a postmodernist writer. See Jameson, *Late Marxism,* pp. 18–19. I have chosen to emphasize the way epic, with its paratactic qualities, breaks the violence inherent in logic. These are simply alternate descriptions of the same constellation.

18. Adorno, "On Lyric Poetry and Society," in *Notes to Literature,* vol. 1, 37–54, here 53.

19. For a further discussion of "Parataxis" and of the polemic against Heidegger contained in it, which I have not dealt with here, see Sabine Wilke, "Kritische und ideologische Momente der Parataxis: Eine Lektüre von Adorno, Heidegger und Hölderlin," *Modern Language Notes* 102 (April 1987): 627–47.

20. Adorno, "On the Use of Foreign Words," in *Notes to Literature,* vol. 2, 286–91. The editors of Adorno's collected works indicate only that this was a manuscript found among his papers. No date is given. Judging by its bold assertions and vivid images, I would date it to the late 1920s or early 1930s. I note that there is a passage in "Motifs," in *Quasi una fantasia,* on foreign words in operetta texts, dated 1927 (p. 10).

21. See note 4. But note conversely the following comment: "If one writes in a truly foreign language one is—admittedly or not—compelled to communicate, to say it in a way that others can also understand. In one's own language, however, were one only to say something as exactly and uncompromisingly as possible, one might also hope through such relentless effort to become understandable as well. In the domain of one's own language, it is this very language which stands in for one's fellow human beings." Adorno, "On the Question: 'What Is German?,'" trans. Thomas Y. Levin, *Theory Culture & Society* 2:3 (1985): 121–31. Here pp. 129–30.

22. Cf. Walter Benjamin, *One-Way Street,* in *Reflections,* trans. Edmund Jephcott (New York: Harcourt Brace Jovanovich, 1978), 85: "With the cautious lineaments of handwriting the operator makes incisions, displaces internal accents, cauterizes proliferations of words, inserts a foreign term as a silver rib."

23. Cf. Adorno, "On the Classicism of Goethe's *Iphigenie,*" in *Notes to Literature,* vol. 2, 153–70, for a discussion of the notion of *Humanität* and *das Humane* in relation to the opposition of civilization and barbarism.

24. Cf. Adorno, "Skoteinos," 118: "[Hegel's] linguistic praxis follows a slightly archaic conception of the primacy of the spoken over the written word, the kind of notion held by those who cling stubbornly to their dialect."

25. The musicologist Rose Subotnik has commented that Adorno's writings on nineteenth-century music "often seem to work less as explanations of particular musical effects than as verbal equivalents, homologues, or even models of those effects." Rose Rosengard Subotnik, *Developing Variations: Style and Ideology in Western Music* (Minneapolis: University of Minnesota Press, 1991), 213.

26. Jameson, always alert to matters of textual form, devotes some interesting notes to Adorno's style. See his *Late Marxism,* 256, n.38. See also Rainer Hoffman, *Figuren des Scheins: Studien zum Sprachbild und zur Denkform Theodor W. Adornos* (Bonn: Bouvier Verlag, 1984), for a discussion of several aspects of Adorno's style, including his use of foreign words. On constellational form, see also my explication of a section from "Titles" in "Configurational Form in the Aesthetic Essay and the Enigma of *Aesthetic Theory,*" in this volume, which provides a more detailed examination of the "slackening of the logical function" in the transitions between sentences.

27. On the notion of a personal idiom or lexicon, see Christopher Bollas's writings on individuals' elaboration of their own idioms through life activities, the choice of objects, and so on. See his *Being a Character: Psychoanalysis and Self Experience* (New York: Hill and Wang, 1992).

28. These are the final sentences of the essays "On Epic Naiveté," "Looking Back on Surrealism," and "The Artist as Deputy," respectively, all from *Notes to Literature,* vol. 1.

29. Constellation is not system, as Adorno says in "Skoteinos." The comparison between Adorno's writing and Hegel's discussion of method in his *Logic* would bear further elaboration. I am indebted to Jeremy J. Shapiro for suggesting it to me, although I have not taken it in the direction he suggested.

3 Configurational Form in the Aesthetic Essay and the Enigma of *Aesthetic Theory*

1. See the introduction to this book, especially n. 5, regarding recent work on Adorno's aesthetics.

2. Wellmer, "Truth, Semblance, Reconciliation," 2, 35.

3. Many readers of Adorno, I am sure, prefer the aesthetic essays to *Aesthetic Theory*. For an attempt to ground this preference in a discussion of problems of form and content in *Aesthetic Theory*, see Hendrik Birus, "Adorno's 'Negative Aesthetics'?" in *Languages of the Unsayable: The Play of Negativity in Literature and Literary Theory*, ed. Sanford Budick and Wolfgang Iser (New York: Columbia University Press, 1989), 140–64.

4. Adorno's conception of the essay form and the constellation are indebted both to the earlier development of the essay form in German letters and to Benjamin's conceptions of constellational and paratactic form. "The Essay as Form" makes early reference to Lukács's "On the Nature and Form of the Essay," in his *Soul and Form*, and *Philosophy of Modern Music* begins by quoting Benjamin's *Origin of German Tragic Drama* on configuration. See R. Lane Kauffman, "The Skewed Path: Essaying as Un-Methodical Method," *Diogenes* 143 (fall 1988): 66–92.

5. For a detailed exposition of Adorno's conception of the structure of subjective aesthetic experience, which is presupposed here, see "Subjective Aesthetic Experience and Its Historical Trajectory," in this volume. While it may be scarcely possible to speak of the aesthetic unaesthetically, it is hardly usual. See Robert Hullot-Kentor's discussion of the externality of conventional aesthetics in his "Is Aesthetics Still for the Birds?" Hullot-Kentor's essay moves between Barnett Newman's quip, "Aesthetics is for me like ornithology must be like for the birds," and Adorno's early aphorism, "We don't understand music; it understands us."

6. One might say, however, that there is an invisible center to "Titles," a center not named and present only negatively in several senses: Walter Benjamin's concept of the true name. Adorno alludes to it in the conclusion of one of the segments: "The work no more knows its true title than the zaddik knows his mystical name" (p. 5).

7. The issues raised by the use of the term "concrete elements" are usefully explored in the philosophical analysis of referentiality. See Israel Scheffler, *Beyond the Letter: A Philosophical Inquiry into Ambiguity, Vagueness, and Metaphor in Language* (London: Routledge & Kegan Paul, 1979).

8. The German original reads as follows: "Für den Amerika-Roman wäre der Titel Der Verschollene, den Kafka im Tagebuch benutzte, besser gewesen als der, unter dem das Buch in die Geschichte einging. Schön ist auch dieser: weil das Werk soviel mit Amerika zu tun hat wie die prähistorische Photographie Im Hafen von New York, die als loses Blatt in meiner Ausgabe des Heizer-Fragments von 1913 liegt. Der Roman spielt in einem verwackelten Amerika, demselben und doch nicht demselben wie das, an dem nach langer, öder Überfahrt das Auge des Emigranten Halt sucht.—Dazu aber passte nichts besser als Der Verschollene, Leerstelle eines unauffindbaren Namens. Diesem participium perfecti passivi kam sein Verb abhanden wie dem Andenken der Familie der Ausgewanderte,

der gestorben und verdorben ist. Der Ausdruck des Wortes verschollen, weit über seine Bedeutung hinaus, ist der des Romans selber." Theodor W. Adorno, *Noten zur Literatur* (Frankfurt am Main: Suhrkamp, 1981), 330.

9. For an elaboration of the role of photography in Adorno's imagination, see "Adorno and Benjamin, Photography and the Aura," in this volume. Russell Berman's insightful comment on this passage (in a letter to me) illustrates the generative effect of Adorno's compact and allusive references: "I take [the reference in the third sentence] to refer to the illusion that the shore is moving while it is in fact the position of the emigrant's ship that is constantly shifting. But it is also the objective dynamism of a society that will certainly not offer the emigrant anything like rest, except in the sense of a final resting-place. And that intimated death-threat—ergo, der Verschollene—flows into a second material: the emigrant, trying to take a snapshot of the momentous arrival in the New World, wants to make the landscape hold still, but America, it turns out, is a moving picture. So it's also about a conflict between photography and film, between a late version of the iconography of bourgeois identity and the terror of the culture industry, the bad non-identity of the same and not the same America."

10. See Theodor W. Adorno, *Philosophy of Modern Music*, trans. Anne G. Mitchell and Wesley V. Blomster (New York: Seabury, 1973), 105.

11. For an extended discussion of the role of such interweaving in the form of *Aesthetic Theory*, see "*Aesthetic Theory*'s Mimesis of Walter Benjamin," in this volume.

12. This effect on the reader, namely, inciting the creation of a mobile and decentered point of view, corresponds to the way Habermas and Wellmer conceptualize the effect of aesthetic experience. Wellmer and his students talk about art's potential to expand and transform subjective capacities. Habermas, following Piaget, talks about a "decentered" subjectivity and a developmental logic in which a postconventional dissolution of conventional norms may be followed by reconstruction on a different basis. See especially Karl-Heinz Bohrer, *Plötzlichkeit. Zum Augenblick des aesthetischen Scheins* (Frankfurt am Main: Suhrkamp, 1981); and Jürgen Habermas, "Moral Consciousness and Communicative Action," in his *Moral Consciousness and Communicative Action*, trans. Christian Lenhardt and Shierry Weber Nicholsen (Cambridge, Mass.: MIT Press, 1990). For a discussion of Habermas's views on the aesthetic dimension, see David Ingram, *Habermas and the Dialectic of Reason* (New Haven: Yale University Press, 1987), esp. pp. 177–88.

13. For an illuminating discussion of virtuosity in historical perspective that is both indebted to, and critical of, Adorno, see Edward Said, *Musical Elaborations*, especially chap. 1, "Performance as an Extreme Occasion."

14. Cf. Charles Rosen's discussion of the late piano sonatas, in *The Classical Style: Haydn, Mozart, Beethoven* (New York: Norton, 1972), esp. pp. 436–48.

15. These formulations are drawn from Adorno's "Night Music." See "Subjective Aesthetic Experience and Its Historical Trajectory," in this volume.

4 *Aesthetic Theory*'s Mimesis of Walter Benjamin

1. See especially "Subjective Aesthetic Experience and Its Historical Trajectory" and "Adorno and Benjamin, Photography and the Aura," both in this volume.

2. Jameson, *Late Marxism*, 52, 64.

3. See Josef Früchtl, *Mimesis: Konstellation eines Zentralbegriffs bei Adorno* (Würzburg: Konigshausen & Neumann, 1986); and Karla Schultz, *Mimesis on the Move: Theodor W. Adorno's Concept of Imitation* (Berne: Peter Lang, 1990), neither of which has figured prominently in English-language discussions of Adorno's aesthetics. Schultz's work is designed to lay the groundwork for an examination of mimesis in *Aesthetic Theory* but does not deal with *Aesthetic Theory* itself. For accounts that foreground the centrality of mimesis in Adorno's aesthetics, see Bubner, "Concerning the Central Idea of Adorno's Philosophy," and Wolin, "Mimesis, Utopia, and Reconciliation." For a detailed discussion of Adorno's conception of mimesis in relation to its vicissitudes in contemporary French thought, see Martin Jay, "Mimesis and Mimetology."

4. Walter Benjamin, "On the Mimetic Faculty," in Walter Benjamin, *Reflections* (New York: Harcourt Brace Jovanovich, 1978). Hereafter cited in the text as "Mimetic Faculty." "Doctrine of the Similar" is to be found in *New German Critique* 17 (1979): 65–69.

5. Cf., for instance, Michael Taussig, *Mimesis and Alterity* (New York: Routledge, 1992), with its repeated references to Benjamin and Adorno; or, specifically on Jakobson, Ann Jefferson, "Literariness, Dominance and Violence in Formalist Aesthetics," in Peter Collier and Helga Geyer-Ryan, eds., *Literary Theory Today* (Ithaca, N.Y.: Cornell University Press, 1990), 125–41.

6. By the "semiotic element" here, we must assume that Benjamin means language as characterized by signs with no inherent resemblance to what they signify. In "Doctrine of the Similar," however, he amplifies this by referring to the "semiotic or communicative element of language," making it clear that he means not only this technical linguistic idea but the ordinary discursive use of language: "The nexus of meaning implicit in the sounds of the sentence is the basis from which something similar can become apparent instantaneously, in a flash." "Doctrine of the Similar," 68.

7. Jameson, *Late Marxism*, 256.

8. For a fuller elaboration of Adorno's conception of subjective aesthetic experience and the role of mimesis in it, see "Subjective Aesthetic Experience and Its Historical Trajectory," in this volume.

9. The question of language can be approached from different directions. In "Truth, Semblance, Reconciliation," Albrecht Wellmer argues that although mimesis in art, on the one hand, and philosophical reflection with its rationality, on the other, may both be required for full aesthetic understanding, they nevertheless remain unreconcilable. In Wellmer's reformulation of the aesthetic in terms of a paradigm of intersubjective communicative rationality, language becomes the medium of reconciliation. In contrast, I have explored the implications for language of the notion of mimesis that is implicit in Adorno's and Benjamin's work, with particular reference to the suggestion of a continuity or affinity between subject and object in the mimetic or aesthetic dimension.

10. Walter Benjamin, "The Image of Proust," in his *Illuminations,* trans. Harry Zohn (New York: Schocken, 1969), 201–15, here 204. Hereafter cited in the text as "Proust." In "Proust," Benjamin offers none other than the stocking game described in the *Berlin Childhood* as the symbol of the dreamworld with its deep, pervasive, and opaque similarities: "Children know a symbol of this world: the stocking which has the structure of this dream world when, rolled up in the laundry hamper, it is a 'bag' and a 'present' at the same time. And just as children do not tire of quickly changing the bag and its contents into a third thing—namely a stocking—Proust could not get his fill of emptying the dummy, his self, at one stroke in order to keep garnering that third thing, the image which satisfied his curiosity—indeed, assuaged his homesickness" (204–5).

11. Walter Benjamin, "On Some Motifs in Baudelaire," in *Illuminations,* 155–200, here 188–89. Hereafter cited in the text as "Baudelaire."

12. Cf. this passage from the earlier version of "The Mummerehlen," in Walter Benjamin, *Schriften,* ed. Theodor and Gretel Adorno, vol. 1 (Frankfurt am Main: Suhrkamp, 1955); hereafter cited in the text as *Berlin Childhood, Schriften* version: "Thus it happened once that people talked in my presence of copper engraving, *Kupferstichen.* The day afterwards, I stuck my head out from under a chair; that was a 'head-poking,' a 'Kopfverstich.'" Such distortion of language leads, via the child's mimetic behavior, to "the whole distorted world of childhood": "The Muhme Rehlen, Old Aunt Rehlen, appears in an old church verse. Because the word 'Muhme' meant nothing to me, in my mind this creature became a spirit: the mummerehlen. The misunderstanding shifted the world around for me. But in a good way; it pointed out the paths that led to its interior" (607).

13. Recent interest in the relationship between Adorno's and Kant's aesthetics has often taken the form of an interest in the concepts of natural beauty and the sublime. See, for instance, Heinz Paetzold, "Adorno's Notion of Natural Beauty:

A Reconsideration," in Huhn and Zuidervaart; and Thomas Huhn, "The Kantian Sublime and the Nostalgia for Violence," *Journal of Aesthetics and Art Criticism* 53:3 (summer 1995): 269–75. It may well be that Adorno's aesthetics will prove influential in the developing field of environmental aesthetics.

14. The importance of articulation as an aesthetic concept has not been sufficiently recognized. But see Konrad Wolff, *The Teaching of Artur Schnabel* (London: Faber & Faber, 1972).

15. Benjamin's "Theses on the Philosophy of History" are full of formulations of this kind. To cite just a few (all from *Illuminations*, 253–64): "The true image of the past flits by." "The past can be seized only as an image which flashes up at the instant when it can be recognized and is never seen again." "History is the subject of a structure whose site is not homogeneous empty time, but time filled by the presence of the now [*Jetztzeit*]." "Where thinking suddenly stops in a configuration pregnant with tensions, it gives that configuration a shock, by which it crytallizes into a monad." "The present, . . . as a model of Messianic time, comprises the entire history of mankind in enormous abridgement." "[The historian] grasps the constellation which his own era has formed with a definite earlier one."

16. For an imaginative improvisation on the status of these quotations, see Pierre Missac's *Walter Benjamin's Passages*, 169–72.

17. Theodor W. Adorno, "A Portrait of Walter Benjamin," in his *Prisms*, trans. Samuel and Shierry Weber (Cambridge, Mass.: MIT Press, 1981), 329.

18. Here we are reminded of Benjamin's statement in *One-Way Street* to the effect that quotations in his works are like highway robbers who fall upon the reader and rob him of his convictions (*Schriften*, vol. 1, 591). This is the reverse or "shock" face of the speed of reading that allows the reader to snatch a glimpse of nonsensuous similarity, as a passage from "Doctrine of the Similar" makes clear: "Even profane reading, if it is not to forsake understanding altogether, shares this with magical reading: that it is subject to a necessary speed, or rather a critical moment, which the reader must not forget at any cost unless he wishes to go away empty-handed" (68).

19. Adorno himself, of course, talks extensively about his own use of constellational form. See "Configurational Form in the Aesthetic Essay and the Enigma of *Aesthetic Theory*," in this volume.

20. Michael Cahn, "Subversive Mimesis: Theodor W. Adorno and the Modern Impasse of Critique," in *Mimesis in Contemporary Theory*, ed. Mihai Spariosu (Philadelphia: John Benjamins, 1984), vol. 1, p. 41.

21. Jameson, *Late Marxism*, ix. See also Jameson's comments on chiasmus in Adorno, 256, n. 38, and my discussion of Adorno's use of language in "Language: Its Murmuring, Its Darkness, and Its Silver Rib," in this volume.

22. Benjamin, *Reflections*, 82.

23. Compare the phrase from Mallarmé's *Le Mystère dans les lettres* that Pierre Missac uses to conceive the relationship between Benjamin and Mallarmé: a "distant sparkling reciprocity, or one presented obliquely, as a contingent event" leading back to its source (*Walter Benjamin's Passages*, 23).

24. I am reminded here of Christopher Alexander's book on the aesthetics of early Turkish carpets, *A Foreshadowing of 21st Century Art* (New York: Oxford University Press, 1993). Alexander argues that these carpets attain the wholeness and density of "beings" by virtue of being composed of a multitude of highly differentiated centers integrated across a number of levels. He talks at one point about asking his students to try to draw the design of a specific carpet and the difficulty they have doing so given their inability to "see" the various centers and their relations to one another. Similarly, he points out that the weavers who wove these carpets would have had to attend to each knot with a concentration that encompassed the relationship of that particular knot to perhaps eight centers at once (see pp. 177–79). Some similar concentration must be required to properly read *Aesthetic Theory*. Cf. Adorno's evocation of the carpet in "The Essay as Form": "Thought does not progress in a single direction; instead, the moments are interwoven as in a carpet. The fruitfulness of the thoughts depends on the density of the texture" (13).

5   Adorno and Benjamin, Photography and the Aura

1. For a synopsis and discussion of the Adorno–Benjamin dispute, see Richard Wolin, *Walter Benjamin: An Aesthetic of Redemption*, chap 6. The letters that make up Adorno's contribution to the dispute are collected in Theodor W. Adorno, *Über Walter Benjamin*. Individual letters hereafter cited in the text by the date of the letter. On the Adorno–Benjamin debate, see also Robert Kaufman, "Negatively Capable Dialectics." Kaufman makes the interesting point that "the most acute literature on the Frankfurt School (and related) aesthetics has implicitly or explicitly ceased to 'take sides' in the earlier controversy, or has essentially re-routed a Benjaminian utopianism away from the paths of surrealism and mechanical reproducibility, subtly referring that utopianism to an Adornian focus on critical (albeit imaginative) analysis." On this way of framing the essential difference between Benjamin and Adorno, see also Wolin's essay on Adorno's utopianism, "Mimesis, Utopia, and Reconciliation"; and his "Benjamin, Adorno, Surrealism," in Huhn and Zuidervaart, eds., *The Semblance of Subjectivity*.

2. For contemporary discussions that situate Benjamin's stance on photography in relation to later developments, see especially Martin Jay, "Photography and the Mirror of Art," *Salmagundi* 84 (fall 1989): 14–23; and William J. Mitchell, *The Reconfigured Eye: Visual Truth in the Post-Photographic Era* (Cambridge, Mass.: MIT Press, 1992). Testimony to the importance of Benjamin's theses is widespread. See, for instance, Douglas Crimp, "On the Museum's Ruins," in *The Anti-Aesthetic,* ed. Hal Foster (Seattle: Bay Press, 1983). Susan Sontag's *On Photography,* perhaps the single most influential reading of photography in recent times, acknowledges its debt to Walter Benjamin. For more detailed discussions of Benjamin's work on film and photography, see Susan Buck-Morss, *The Dialectics of Seeing;* Miriam Hansen, "Benjamin, Cinema and Experience: 'The Blue Flower' in the Land of Technology," *New German Critique* 40 (winter 1987): 179–224; and Heinz Puppe, "Walter Benjamin on Photography," *Colloquia Germanica* 12:3 (1979), 273–91. For a critical view of the historical background on reproducibility, see Paul Mattick, Jr., "Mechanical Reproduction in the Age of Art," *Theory Culture & Society* 10:2 (May 1993): 127–47.

3. Robert Alter's *Necessary Angels: Tradition and Modernity in Kafka, Benjamin and Scholem* (Cambridge, Mass.: Harvard University Press, 1991), which might profitably be read in connection with the present essay, uses a similar strategy of triangulation via Kafka.

4. Theodor W. Adorno, *Mahler: A Musical Physiognomy,* trans. Edmund Jephcott (Chicago: University of Chicago Press, 1992). p. 154.

5. See Adorno's "Nachwort" to Walter Benjamin, *Berliner Kindheit um neunzehnhundert* (Frankfurt am Main: Suhrkamp, 1987).

6. See, respectively, Adorno, "Introduction to Benjamin's *Schriften,*" 228; "Zu Benjamins Gedächtnis," in *Über Walter Benjamin,* 10; "Introduction to Benjamin's *Schriften,*" 228; "A Portrait of Walter Benjamin," 220, 230; and "Introduction to Benjamin's *Schriften,*" 221.

7. Benjamin's miniature "The Moon" opens with these lines: "The light that streams down from the moon is not intended for the scene of our everyday existence. The sphere it illuminates in such a confusing manner seems to belong to a counter-world, a para-earth" (*Berlin Childhood,* 426).

8. Roland Barthes, *Camera Lucida* (New York: Hill and Wang, 1981), 9.

9. Cf. Henry Corbin, *The Man of Light in Iranian Sufism* (Boulder: Shambhala, 1978).

10. Cf. Michael Eigen, "The Significance of the Face," in his *Electrified Tightrope* (Northvale, N.J.: Jacob Aronson, 1993), 49–60.

11. Walter Benjamin, "A Short History of Photography," trans. Phil Patton, *Artforum* 15:6 (February 1977): 46–51. Hereafter cited in the text as "Short History."

12. See Rosalind Krauss, "Notes on the Index," in her *Originality of the Avant-Garde and Other Modernist Myths* (Cambridge, Mass.: MIT Press, 1986).

13. For a discussion of the aura in relation to mimesis that complements this material, see "*Aesthetic Theory*'s Mimesis of Walter Benjamin," in this volume.

14. Barthes, *Camera Lucida*, 3.

15. Benjamin's *Berlin Childhood* was not published as a whole during his lifetime. The version Adorno assembled for the 1955 edition of Benjamin's *Schriften* differs in many respects from the *Fassung letzter Hand* or final draft, discovered later and published in vol. 7 of the *Gesammelte Schriften*. Some of the differences are discussed later in this chapter.

16. Cited in Susan Sontag, *On Photography* (New York: Farrar, Straus & Giroux, 1977), 208.

17. Cf., for example, *Aesthetic Theory*, 73/66–67.

18. Cf. Walter Benjamin, *Das Passagen-Werk*, ed. Rolf Tiedemann (Frankfurt am Main: Suhrkamp, 1982), vol. 1, pp. 290–91. For further comments on Adorno's notion of the interior, see Tom Huhn, "Kant, Adorno, and the Social Opacity of the Aesthetic," in Huhn and Zuidervaart, eds., *The Semblance of Subjectivity*.

19. The passage is found in Theodor W. Adorno, *Kierkegaard: Construction of the Aesthetic*, trans. Robert Hullot-Kentor (Minneapolis: University of Minnesota Press, 1989), 43–44.

20. Cf. Benjamin, *Passagen-Werk*, 292: "The nineteenth century understood the residence as a casing for human beings and embedded them with all their belongings so deeply into it that one might think of the interior of a round case in which an instrument with all its spare parts lies embedded in deep, usually violet, velvet hollows." Or p. 294: "Plush—the fabric in which the imprint of traces is especially easily made."

21. Walter Benjamin, "The Work of Art in the Age of Mechanical Reproduction," in his *Illuminations*, 226. Hereafter cited in the text as "Work of Art."

22. Walter Benjamin, "Surrealism," in his *Reflections*, 182.

23. On the Surrealists' use of photography, see Rosalind Krauss, *L'Amour Fou: Photography and Surrealism* (New York: Abbeville Press, 1985).

24. Cf. especially the so-called Hornberger letter of August 2, 1935, on Benjamin's 1935 exposé of the *Passagen-Werk*, in *Über Walter Benjamin*, 111–25.

25. Theodor W. Adorno, "Looking Back on Surrealism," in *Notes to Literature*, vol. 1. Hereafter cited in the text as "Surrealism."

26. Cf. Theodor W. Adorno, "Notes on Kafka," in *Prisms*, 254: "The Penal Colony and the Metamorphosis [were] reports that had to await those of Bettelheim, Kogon and Rousset for their equals, much as the bird's eye photos of bombed-out cities redeemed, as it were, Cubism, by realizing that through which the latter broke with reality." Adorno also describes Kafka's texts as anticipatory images of bombed-out cities.

27. Barthes, *Camera Lucida*, 53.

28. Cf. "Notes on Kafka," 269: "In the middle ages, Jews were tortured and executed 'perversely'—i.e., inversely: . . . offenders were hung head-down. Kafka, the land-surveyor, photographs the earth's surface just as it must have appeared to those victims during the endless hours of their dying."

29. Cf. also Adorno, *Mahler*, 250: "[Mahler's] utopia is worn out like the Nature Theater of Oklahoma. The ground trembles under the feet of the assimilated Jew—as of the Zionist; by the euphemism of foreignness the outsider seeks to appease the shadow of terror."

30. See especially Benjamin, "Franz Kafka," in *Illuminations*, 120–21.

31. Franz Kafka, "Investigations of a Dog," in *Selected Stories of Franz Kafka*, trans. Willa and Edwin Muir (New York: Modern Library, 1952), 206–8.

32. Franz Kafka, "The Cares of a Family Man," in *The Penal Colony*, trans. Willa and Edwin Muir (New York: Schocken, 1948), 161. For further discussion of this description, see "Language: Its Rustling, Its Darkness, and Its Silver Rib," in this volume.

33. On the intrinsic connection between art and domination, see Adorno, "Music and Language," 4: "Musical form, the totality in which a musical context acquires authenticity, cannot really be separated from the attempt to graft the gesture of decision ['This is how it is'] onto the nondecisive medium. On occasion this succeeds so well that the art stands on the brink of yielding to assault from the dominating impulse of logic." On the relationship between domination, tour de force, and the dialectic of violence and nonviolence in art, see also *Aesthetic Theory* 163/156 and 276/265. For a related discussion, see "Language: Its Rustling, Its Darkness, and Its Silver Rib," in this volume.

34. As I mentioned earlier, Jameson too notes the significance of the epic element for Adorno. See n. 17, p. 236. On the epic element, see also the discussion of the

epic particle in "Language: Its Murmuring, Its Darkness, and Its Silver Rib," in this volume. In a discussion analogous to the one of the epic element in Mahler's music, Adorno points to the role of the particle in the *Odyssey,* showing how it works to "slacken the train of thought" and counter the subsumptive force of the logical dimension inherent in language.

35. Cf. Adorno, "Notes on Kafka," 248–49; Benjamin, "Franz Kafka," 120–22.

36. Cf., on theater, Adorno, letter to Benjamin of Dec. 17, 1934, p. 108. On Kafka and enlightenment (and hence Ulysses, as in Adorno and Horkheimer's discussion of him in *Dialectic of Enlightenment*), see Adorno, "Notes on Kafka," 270.

37. Cf. *Aesthetic Theory,* 322/309 and 460/429.

38. As will be evident, I am deeply indebted to Linda Rugg and Robert Hullot-Kentor for some of the ideas in this section. Shock figures prominently in the Artwork essay and has inspired much commentary. See, for instance, Martin Jay, "Walter Benjamin, Remembrance, and the First World War," unpublished manuscript (1996). Jay foregrounds the way World War I forms a background to Benjamin's writings and puts the notion of shock in the context of Benjamin's refusal of a false, reconciling memorialization of the war dead. Benjamin was intent on keeping undenied the trauma of the 1914 antiwar suicides of Fritz Heinle and Rika Seligsohn. On shock and numbing, see also Susan Buck-Morss, "Aesthetics and Anaesthetics: Walter Benjamin's Artwork Essay," *October* 62 (fall 1992): 3–41. Adorno does not tend to figure in these discussions.

39. I have a vivid memory of this phrase but am unable to locate its source. For a comment similar in substance, see Adorno, "Benjamin the Letter-Writer," in *Notes to Literature,* vol. 2, p. 237, in which Adorno notes that Benjamin was "characterized by an utter and extremely gracious politeness."

40. Walter Benjamin, "A Berlin Chronicle," in his *Reflections,* 56–57.

41. See Linda Rugg, *Picturing Ourselves: Photography and Autobiography* (Chicago: University of Chicago Press, forthcoming). Rugg devotes a section of her book to Benjamin and demonstrates the progressive erasure of the personal in his autobiographical texts. She links the erasure with Benjamin's Jewishness.

42. Walter Benjamin, "Some Reflections on Kafka," in his *Illuminations,* 143. Hereafter cited in the text as "Reflections on Kafka." Benjamin begins the remarks just quoted with the statement, "Kafka lives in a complementary world," echoing Adorno's notion of Kafka as a photographer of the mundane world from the point of view of the redeemed world.

43. As noted above, Linda Rugg writes in a similar vein about Benjamin in *Picturing Ourselves.*

44. See Benjamin, letter to Gretel Adorno, 1933, in Walter Benjamin, *Briefe*, vol. 2, ed. Gershom Scholem and Theodor W. Adorno (Frankfurt am Main: Suhrkamp, 1978), 591, in which Benjamin refers to the "photographic" self-portrait contained in "The Mummerehlen."

45. This constellation of words, clouds, interiors, and violence has been explicated by Werner Hamacher in "The Word *Wolke*—If It Is One," *Studies in Twentieth-Century Literature* 11:1 (fall 1986): 131–61, using this miniature as well as others from *A Berlin Childhood*.

46. The version in the 1955 *Schriften* is equally suggestive regarding the connection between the mummerehlen and the cloudiness of snow: "[The mummerehlen] was the mute, loose, flocculent stuff that clouds up at the center of things like the snowstorm in the little glass ball" (609). According to Adorno, those little glass balls were a favorite of Benjamin's. See Peter Szondi, "Hope in the Past: On Walter Benjamin," *Critical Inquiry* 4:3 (spring 1978): 501. Szondi's piece contains one of the most extensive discussions of *A Berlin Childhood* available in English.

47. See Robert Hullot-Kentor, "What Is Mechanical Reproduction?" in Hans Gumbrecht and Michael Marinnen, eds., *Mapping Walter Benjamin* (Stanford: Stanford University Press, forthcoming).

Bibliography

Adorno, Theodor W. *Aesthetische Theorie. Gesammelte Schriften* 7. Ed. Rolf Tiede-mann and Gretel Adorno. Frankfurt am Main: Suhrkamp, 1970. English trans-lation, *Aesthetic Theory.* Trans. Christian Lenhardt. London: Routledge & Kegan Paul, 1984. (Retranslation, *Aesthetic Theory.* Trans. Robert Hullot-Kentor. Minnea-polis: Minnesota University Press, 1996.)

Adorno, Theodor W. "Die Aktualität der Philosophie." *Gesammelte Schriften* 1. Ed. Rolf Tiedemann. Frankfurt am Main: Suhrkamp, 1973. English translation, "The Actuality of Philosophy." *Telos* 31 (spring 1977): 120–33.

Adorno, Theodor W. "Aspects of Hegel's Philosophy." In Adorno, *Hegel: Three Studies.*

Adorno, Theodor W. *Beethoven: Philosphie der Musik.* Ed. Rolf Tiedemann. Frank-furt am Main: Suhrkamp, 1993.

Adorno, Theodor W. "Benjamin the Letter Writer." In Adorno, *Notes to Literature,* vol. 2.

Adorno, Theodor W. "Charmed Language: On the Poetry of Rudolf Borchardt." In Adorno, *Notes to Literature,* vol. 2.

Adorno, Theodor W. "The Essay as Form." In Adorno, *Notes to Literature,* vol. 1.

Adorno, Theodor W. *Hegel: Three Studies.* Trans. Shierry Weber Nicholsen. Cam-bridge, Mass.: MIT Press, 1993.

Adorno, Theodor W. "Im Jeu de Paume gekritzelt." *Ohne Leitbild.* Frankfurt am Main: Suhrkamp, 1967. (Also *Gesammelte Schriften* 10.1, 1977).

Adorno, Theodor W. "In Memory of Eichendorff." In Adorno, *Notes to Literature,* vol. 1.

Adorno, Theodor W. "Introduction to Benjamin's *Schriften.*" In Adorno, *Notes to Literature,* vol. 2

Adorno, Theodor W. *Kierkegaard: Construction of the Aesthetic.* Trans. Robert Hullot-Kentor. Minneapolis: University of Minnesota, 1989.

Adorno, Theodor W. "Looking Back on Surrealism." In Adorno, *Notes to Literature,* vol. 1.

Adorno, Theodor W. "Mahler." In Adorno, *Quasi una fantasia.*

Adorno, Theodor W. *Mahler: A Musical Physiognomy.* Trans. Edmund Jephcott. Chicago: University of Chicago Press, 1992.

Adorno, Theodor W. *Moments musicaux.* Frankfurt am Main: Suhrkamp, 1964. (Also *Gesammelte Schriften* 17, 1982.)

Adorno, Theodor W. "Motifs." In Adorno, *Quasi una fantasia.*

Adorno, Theodor W. "Music and Language: A Fragment." In Adorno, *Quasi una fantasia.*

Adorno, Theodor W. "Nachtmusik." In Adorno, *Moments musicaux.*

Adorno, Theodor W. "Nachwort." in Walter Benjamin, *Berliner Kindheit um neunzehnhundert.* Frankfurt am Main: Suhrkamp, 1987.

Adorno, Theodor W. *Negative Dialectics.* Trans. E. B. Ashton. New York: Continuum, 1987.

Adorno, Theodor W. "Neue Tempi." In Adorno, *Moments musicaux.*

Adorno, Theodor W. "Notes on Kafka." In Adorno, *Prisms.*

Adorno, Theodor W. *Notes to Literature.* 2 vols. Trans. Shierry Weber Nicholsen. New York: Columbia University Press, 1991, 1992.

Adorno, Theodor W. "On Epic Naiveté." In Adorno, *Notes to Literature,* vol. 1.

Adorno, Theodor W. "On Lyric Poetry and Society." In Adorno, *Notes to Literature,* vol. 1.

Adorno, Theodor W. "On the Classicism of Goethe's *Iphigenie.*" In Adorno, *Notes to Literature,* vol. 2.

Bibliography

Adorno, Theodor W. "On the Final Scene of *Faust*." In Adorno, *Notes to Literature*, vol. 1.

Adorno, Theodor W. "On the Question 'What Is German?'" Trans. Thomas Y. Levin. *Theory Culture & Society* 2:3 (1985): 121–31.

Adorno, Theodor W. "On the Use of Foreign Words." In Adorno, *Notes to Literature*, vol. 2.

Adorno, Theodor W. "Parataxis: On Hölderlin's Late Poetry." In Adorno, *Notes to Literature*, vol. 2.

Adorno, Theodor W. *Philosophy of Modern Music*. Trans. Anne G. Mitchell and Wesley V. Blomster. New York: Seabury, 1973.

Adorno, Theodor W. "A Portrait of Walter Benjamin." In Adorno, *Prisms*.

Adorno, Theodor W. "Presuppositions." In Adorno, *Notes to Literature*, vol. 2.

Adorno, Theodor W. *Prisms*. Trans. Samuel and Shierry Weber. Cambridge, Mass.: MIT Press, 1981.

Adorno, Theodor W. *Quasi una fantasia: Essays on Modern Music*. Trans. Rodney Livingstone. London and New York: Verso, 1992.

Adorno, Theodor W. "Reaktion und Fortschritt." In Adorno, *Moments musicaux*.

Adorno, Theodor W. "Schöne Stellen." *Gesammelte Schriften* 18. Ed. Rolf Tiedemann. Frankfurt am Main: Suhrkamp, 1984.

Adorno, Theodor W. "Schubert." In Adorno, *Moments musicaux*.

Adorno, Theodor W. "Schwierigkeiten." *Impromptus. Gesammelte Schriften* 17. Ed. Rolf Tiedemann. Frankfurt am Main: Suhrkamp, 1982.

Adorno, Theodor W. "Skoteinos, or How to Read Hegel." In Adorno, *Hegel: Three Studies*.

Adorno, Theodor W. "Spätkapitalismus oder Industriegesellschaft?" *Gesammelte Schriften* 8. Ed. Rolf Tiedemann. Frankfurt am Main: Suhrkamp, 1972. English translation, "Late Capitalism or Industrial Society?" Trans. Fred van Gelder. *Modern German Sociology*. New York: Columbia University Press, 1987.

Adorno, Theodor W. "Spätstil Beethovens." In Adorno, *Moments musicaux*.

Adorno, Theodor W. "Stefan George." In Adorno, *Notes to Literature*, vol. 2.

Adorno, Theodor W. "Thesen über die Sprache des Philosophen." *Gesammelte Schriften* 1. Ed. Rolf Tiedemann. Frankfurt am Main: Suhrkamp, 1973.

Adorno, Theodor W. "Titles." In Adorno, *Notes to Literature,* vol. 2.

Adorno, Theodor W. "Towards a Portrait of Thomas Mann." In Adorno, *Notes to Literature,* vol. 2.

Adorno, Theodor W. *Über Walter Benjamin.* Frankfurt am Main: Suhrkamp, 1970.

Adorno, Theodor W. "Verfremdetes Hauptwerk." In Adorno, *Moments musicaux.* English translation, "Alienated Masterpiece: The Missa Solemnis." *Telos* 28 (summer 1976): 113–24.

Adorno, Theodor W. "Vers une musique informelle," In *Quasi una fantasia.*

Adorno, Theodor W. "Words from Abroad." In Adorno, *Notes to Literature,* vol. 1.

Adorno, Theodor W. "Zu Benjamins Gedächtnis." In Adorno, *Über Walter Benjamin.*

Alexander, Christopher. *A Foreshadowing of 21st Century Art.* New York: Oxford University Press, 1993.

Alter, Robert. *Necessary Angels: Tradition and Modernity in Kafka, Benjamin and Scholem.* Cambridge, Mass.: Harvard University Press, 1991.

Barthes, Roland. *Camera Lucida.* New York: Hill and Wang, 1981.

Benjamin, Andrew, ed. *The Problems of Modernity: Adorno and Benjamin.* London and New York: Routledge, 1989.

Benjamin, Walter. *A Berlin Chronicle.* In Walter Benjamin, *Reflections.*

Benjamin, Walter. *Berliner Kindheit um neunzehnhundert. Gesammelte Schriften* 7:1. Ed. Rolf Tiedemann and Hermann Schweppenhauser. Frankfurt am Main: Suhrkamp, 1989.

Benjamin, Walter. *Berliner Kindheit um neunzehnhundert.* In Walter Benjamin, *Schriften,* vol. 1.

Benjamin, Walter. *Briefe,* vol. 2. Ed. Gershom Scholem and Theodor W. Adorno. Frankfurt am Main: Suhrkamp, 1978.

Benjamin, Walter. "Doctrine of the Similar." Trans. Knut Tarnowski. *New German Critique* 17 (1979): 65–69.

Benjamin, Walter. *Einbahnstrasse*. In Walter Benjamin, *Schriften*, vol. 1. Partial English translation in Walter Benjamin, *Reflections*.

Benjamin, Walter. "Franz Kafka." In Walter Benjamin, *Illuminations*.

Benjamin, Walter. *Illuminations*. Trans. Harry Zohn. New York: Schocken, 1969.

Benjamin, Walter. "The Image of Proust." In Walter Benjamin, *Illuminations*.

Benjamin, Walter. "On Some Motifs in Baudelaire." In Walter Benjamin, *Illuminations*.

Benjamin, Walter. "On the Mimetic Faculty." In Walter Benjamin, *Reflections*.

Benjamin, Walter. *Das Passagen-Werk*, vol. 1. Ed. Rolf Tiedemann. Frankfurt am Main: Suhrkamp, 1982.

Benjamin, Walter. *Reflections*. Trans. Edmund Jephcott. New York: Harcourt Brace Jovanovich, 1978.

Benjamin, Walter. *Schriften*. 2 vols. Ed. Theodor and Gretel Adorno. Frankfurt am Main: Suhrkamp, 1955.

Benjamin, Walter. "A Short History of Photography." Trans. Phil Patton. *Artforum* 15:6 (February 1977): 46–51.

Benjamin, Walter. "Some Reflections on Kafka." In Walter Benjamin, *Illuminations*.

Benjamin, Walter. "Surrealism." In Walter Benjamin, *Reflections*.

Benjamin, Walter. "Theses on the Philosophy of History." In Walter Benjamin, *Illuminations*.

Benjamin, Walter. "The Work of Art in the Age of Mechanical Reproduction." In Walter Benjamin, *Illuminations*.

Berman, Russell. "Adorno, Marxism, and Art." *Telos* 34 (winter 1977–78): 157–66.

Bernstein, J. M. *The Fate of Art: Aesthetic Alienation from Kant to Derrida and Adorno*. State College: Pennsylvania State University Press, 1992.

Birus, Hendrik. "Adorno's 'Negative Aesthetics'?" In *Languages of the Unsayable: The Play of Negativity in Literature and Literary Theory*. Ed. Sanford Budick and Wolfgang Iser. New York: Columbia University Press, 1989.

Bibliography

Blumenfeld, Harold. "Ad vocem Adorno." *Musical Quarterly* 75:4 (winter 1991): 263–95.

Bly, Robert. *Leaping Poetry: An Idea with Poems and Translations.* Boston: Beacon Press, 1975.

Bohrer, Karl-Heinz. *Plötzlichkeit. Zum Augenblick des aesthetischen Scheins.* Frankfurt am Main: Suhrkamp, 1981.

Bollas, Christopher. *Being a Character: Psychoanalysis and Self Experience.* New York: Hill and Wang, 1992.

Bowie, Andrew. "Music, Language, and Modernity." In Andrew Benjamin, ed. *Problems of Modernity.*

Bubner, Rüdiger. "Concerning the Central Idea of Adorno's Philosophy." In Huhn and Zuidervaart, eds., *The Semblance of Subjectivity.*

Buck-Morss, Susan. "Aesthetics and Anaesthetics: Walter Benjamin's Artwork Essay." *October* 62 (fall 1992): 3–41.

Buck-Morss, Susan. *The Dialectics of Seeing: Walter Benjamin and the Arcades Project.* Cambridge, Mass.: MIT Press, 1989.

Buck-Morss, Susan. *The Origin of Negative Dialectics.* New York: Free Press, 1977.

Cahn, Michael. "Subversive Mimesis: Theodor W. Adorno and the Modern Impasse of Critique." In *Mimesis in Contemporary Theory,* vol. 1. Ed. Mihai Spariosu. Philadelphia: John Benjamins, 1984.

Corbin, Henri. *The Man of Light in Iranian Sufism.* Trans. Nancy Pearson. Boulder: Shambhala, 1978.

Crimp, Douglas. "On the Museum's Ruins." In *The Anti-Aesthetic.* Ed. Hal Foster. Seattle: Bay Press, 1983.

Dahlhaus, Carl. "Zu Adornos Beethoven-Kritik." In Burkhardt Lindner and W. Martin Lüdke, eds., *Materialien zur aesthetischen Theorie.*

Dews, Peter. "Adorno, Post-Structuralism, and the Critique of Identity." In Andrew Benjamin, ed., *The Problems of Modernity.*

Eigen, Michael. "The Significance of the Face." In Eigen, *The Electrified Tightrope.* Northvale, N.J.: Jason Aronson, 1993.

Eigen, Michael. "Soft and Hard Qualities." In Eigen, *The Electrified Tightrope.* Northvale, N.J.: Jason Aronson, 1993.

Früchtl, Josef. *Mimesis: Konstellation eines Zentralbegriffs bei Adorno*. Würzburg: Königshausen & Neumann, 1986.

Habermas, Jürgen. "Moral Consciousness and Communicative Action." In Habermas, *Moral Consciousness and Communicative Action*. Trans. Christian Lenhardt and Shierry Weber Nicholsen. Cambridge, Mass: MIT Press, 1990.

Habermas, Jürgen. *The Philosophical Discourse of Modernity*. Trans. Frederick Lawrence. Cambridge, Mass.: MIT Press, 1987.

Hamacher, Werner. "The Word *Wolke*—If It Is One." *Studies in Twentieth-Century Literature* 11:1 (fall 1986): 131–61.

Hansen, Miriam. "Benjamin, Cinema and Experience: 'The Blue Flower in the Land of Technology.'" *New German Critique* 40 (winter 1987): 179–224.

Hewitt, Andrew. "A Feminine Dialectic of the Enlightenment." *New German Critique* 56 (spring–summer 1992): 143–70.

Hoffman, Rainer. *Figuren des Scheins: Studien zum Sprachbild und zur Denkform Theodor W. Adornos*. Bonn: Bouvier Verlag, 1984.

Hohendahl, Peter Uwe. *Prismatic Thought: Theodor W. Adorno*. Lincoln and London: Nebraska University Press, 1995.

Horkheimer, Max and Theodor W. Adorno. *Dialectic of Enlightenment*. Trans. John Cumming. New York: Seabury, 1972.

Huhn, Thomas. "The Kantian Sublime and the Nostalgia for Violence." *Journal of Aesthetics and Art Criticism* 53:3 (summer 1995): 269–75.

Huhn, Tom. "Kant, Adorno, and the Social Opacity of the Aesthetic." In Huhn and Zuidervaart, eds. *The Semblance of Subjectivity*.

Huhn, Tom, and Lambert Zuidervaart, eds. *The Semblance of Subjectivity: Essays in Adorno's Aesthetic Theory*. Cambridge, Mass.: MIT Press, 1997.

Hullot-Kentor, Robert. "Is Aesthetics Still for the Birds?" Unpublished essay.

Hullot-Kentor, Robert. "What Is Mechanical Reproduction?" In *Mapping Walter Benjamin*. Ed. Hans Gumbrecht and Michael Marinnen. Stanford: Stanford University Press, forthcoming.

Ingram, David. *Habermas and the Dialectic of Reason*. New Haven: Yale University Press, 1987.

Jameson, Fredric. *Late Marxism: Adorno, or the Persistence of the Dialectic*. London: Verso, 1990.

Jameson, Fredric. "T. W. Adorno: Or, Historical Tropes." In Jameson, *Marxism and Form*. Princeton, N.J.: Princeton University Press, 1971.

Jauss, Hans Robert. "Negativität und aesthetische Erfahrung. Adornos aesthetische Theorie in der Retrospektive." In Lindner and Lüdke, eds. *Materialien zur aesthetischen Theorie*.

Jay, Martin. "Adorno in America." In Jay, *Permanent Exiles*. New York: Columbia University Press, 1985, 120–37.

Jay, Martin. "Mimesis and Mimetology: Adorno and Lacoue-Labarthe." In Huhn and Zuidervaart, eds., *The Semblance of Subjectivity*.

Jay, Martin. "Photography and the Mirror of Art." *Salmagundi* 84 (fall 1989): 14–23.

Jay, Martin. "Walter Benjamin, Remembrance, and the First World War." Unpublished essay.

Jefferson, Ann. "Literariness, Dominance, and Violence in Formalist Aesthetics." In *Literary Theory Today*. Ed. Peter Collier and Helga Geyer-Ryan. Ithaca, N.Y.: Cornell University Press, 1990.

Johnson, Pauline. "An Aesthetics of Negativity/An Aesthetics of Reception: Jauss's Dispute with Adorno." *New German Critique* 42 (fall 1987): 51–70.

Kafka, Franz. "The Cares of a Family Man." In *The Penal Colony*. Trans. Willa and Edwin Muir. New York, Schocken, 1948.

Kafka, Franz. "Investigations of a Dog." In *Selected Stories of Franz Kafka*. Trans. Willa and Edwin Muir: New York: Modern Library, 1952.

Kauffman, R. Lane. "The Skewed Path: Essaying as Un-Methodical Method." *Diogenes* 143 (fall 1988): 66–92.

Kaufman, Robert. "Negatively Capable Dialectics: Keats, Vendler, Adorno, and the Theory of the Avant-Garde." Unpublished essay.

Kaufman, Robert. "Red Kant, or, The Persistence of the Third Critique in Adorno and Jameson." Paper presented at the Modern Language Association meetings, December 1995.

Krauss, Rosalind. *L'Amour Fou: Photography and Surrealism*. New York: Abbeville Press, 1985.

Bibliography

Krauss, Rosalind. "Notes on the Index." In Krauss, *The Originality of the Avant-Garde and Other Modernist Myths*. Cambridge, Mass.: MIT Press, 1986.

Lindner, Burkhardt, and W. Martin Lüdke, eds. *Materialien zur aesthetischen Theorie: Th. W. Adornos Konstruktion der Moderne*. Frankfurt am Main: Suhrkamp, 1979.

Mattick, Jr., Paul. "Mechanical Reproduction in the Age of Art." *Theory Culture & Society* 10:2 (May 1993): 127–47.

Missac, Pierre. *Walter Benjamin's Passages*. Trans. Shierry Weber Nicholsen. Cambridge, Mass.: MIT Press, 1995.

Mitchell, William J. *The Reconfigured Eye: Visual Truth in the Post-Photographic Era*. Cambridge, Mass: MIT Press, 1992.

Nägele, Rainer, ed. *Benjamin's Ground: New Readings of Walter Benjamin*. Detroit: Wayne State University Press, 1988.

Nicholsen, Shierry Weber. "Adorno in Postmodern Perspective." *Thesis Eleven* 34 (1993): 178–85.

O'Neill, Maggie, ed. *Adorno, Culture, and Feminism*. London and Newbury Park: Sage, forthcoming.

Osborne, Peter. "Adorno and the Metaphysics of Modernism: The Problem of a 'Postmodern' Art." In Andrew Benjamin, ed. *The Problems of Modernity*.

Paddison, Max. *Adorno's Aesthetics of Music*. New York: Cambridge University Press, 1993.

Paetzold, Heinz. "Adorno's Notion of Natural Beauty: A Reconsideration." In Huhn and Zuidervaart, eds., *The Semblance of Subjectivity*.

Puppe, Heinz. "Walter Benjamin on Photography." *Colloquia Germanica* 12:3 (1979): 273–91.

Roberts, David. *Art and Enlightenment: Aesthetic Theory after Adorno*. Lincoln and London: University of Nebraska Press, 1991.

Rosen, Charles. *The Classical Style: Haydn, Mozart, Beethoven*. New York: Norton, 1972.

Rugg, Linda. *Picturing Ourselves: Photography and Autobiography*. Chicago: University of Chicago Press, forthcoming.

Said, Edward. *Musical Elaborations*. New York: Columbia University Press, 1991.

Scheffler, Israel. *Beyond the Letter: A Philosophical Inquiry into Ambiguity, Vagueness, and Metaphor in Language*. London: Routledge & Kegan Paul, 1979.

Schultz, Karla. *Mimesis on the Move: Theodor W. Adorno's Concept of Imitation*. Berne: Peter Lang, 1990.

Shapiro, Henry. Review of T. W. Adorno, *Aesthetic Theory*. *Philosophical Review* 95 (April 1986): 288–89.

Sontag, Susan. *On Photography*. New York: Farrar, Straus & Giroux, 1977.

Subotnik, Rose Rosengard. "Adorno's Diagnosis of Beethoven's Late Style: Early Symptom of a Fatal Condition." In Subotnik, *Developing Variations*.

Subotnik, Rose Rosengard. *Developing Variations: Style and Ideology in Western Music*. Minneapolis: University of Minnesota Press, 1991.

Szondi, Peter. "Hope in the Past: On Walter Benjamin." *Critical Inquiry* 4:3 (spring 1978): 491–506.

Taussig, Michael. *Mimesis and Alterity*. New York: Routledge, 1992.

Wellmer, Albrecht. "Truth, Semblance, Reconciliation." In Wellmer, *The Persistence of Modernity*. Trans. David Midgeley. Cambridge, Mass.: MIT Press, 1991.

Whitebook, Joel. *Perversion and Utopia: A Study in Psychoanalysis and Critical Theory*. Cambridge, Mass.: MIT Press, 1995.

Wilke, Sabine. "Kritische und ideologische Momente der Parataxis: Eine Lektüre von Adorno, Heidegger und Hölderlin." *Modern Language Notes* 102 (April 1987): 627–47.

Wilke, Sabine, and Heidi Schlipphacke. "Construction of a Gendered Subject: A Feminist Reading of Adorno's *Aesthetic Theory*." In Huhn and Zuidervaart, eds., *The Semblance of Subjectivity*.

Wolff, Konrad. *The Teaching of Artur Schnabel*. London: Faber & Faber, 1972.

Wolin, Richard. "Benjamin, Adorno, Surrealism." In Huhn and Zuidervaart, eds., *The Semblance of Subjectivity*.

Bibliography

Wolin, Richard. "Mimesis, Utopia, and Reconciliation." In Wolin, *The Terms of Cultural Criticism: The Frankfurt School, Existentialism, Poststructuralism.* New York: Columbia University Press, 1992.

Wolin, Richard. *Walter Benjamin: An Aesthetic of Redemption.* Rev. ed. Berkeley and Los Angeles: University of California Press, 1994.

Zuidervaart, Lambert. *Adorno's Aesthetic Theory: The Redemption of Illusion.* Cambridge, Mass.: MIT Press, 1991.

Index

Adorno-Bejamin dispute, 181–188, 197

Adorno, Theodor W., works cited

"The Actuality of Philosophy," 4, 94–95

Aesthetic Theory, 3, 6, 8, 11, 17, 18, 20–21, 22, 23, 24, 49–50, 78, 95, 103–105, 110, 124–135, 137–138, 145–152, 158–166, 172–180, 182–184, 208, 246n33

"Alienated Masterwork," 44, 47–49

"Aspects of Hegel's Philosophy," 53

"Beautiful Passages" ("Schöne Stellen"), 5, 19–20, 25, 26, 28

Beethoven, 230n17, 233n20

"Beethoven's Late Style," 8, 41–43

"Benjamin the Letter Writer," 53–54

"Charmed Language: On the Poetry of Rudolf Borchardt," 62, 63–64, 65, 66, 70, 72–73, 74, 76, 77, 78

"Difficulties" ("Schwierigkeiten"), 44–47

"The Essay as Form," 9, 21, 23, 61, 91, 105–110, 111, 113, 123–125, 128–130, 174, 237n24

"In Memory of Eichendorff," 63, 64, 65, 68–69, 70, 74, 75, 86

Kierkegaard, 193, 194–195

"Looking Back on Surrealism," 187, 197–198

Mahler, 185, 216–217, 225, 246n25

"Mahler," 80, 209, 223

Minima Moralia, 55

Moments musicaux, 30, 43

"Motifs," 28–29, 30, 236n20

"Music and Language," 71–72, 73, 75, 81, 92, 246n33

Negative Dialectics, 4, 129, 235n12

"New Tempos," 37

"Night Music," 36, 38

"Notes on Kafka," 200, 202–203, 204, 210, 211, 224, 246n26, 247n36

Notes to Literature, 11, 61, 69–70, 71, 84, 91, 94, 96

"Notes Scribbled in the Jeu de Paume" ("Im Jeu de Paume gekritzelt"), 26–28

"On the Classicism of Goethe's *Iphigenie*," 88, 237n23

"On Epic Naiveté," 81–82

"On the Final Scene of *Faust*," 50, 55, 56, 67, 78

"On Lyric Poetry and Society," 61, 96

"On the Use of Foreign Words," 84, 87, 89

"Parataxis," 73, 83

"Presuppositions," 18, 44

Prisms, 111–112

"Reaction and Progress," 33

Adorno, Theodor W. (cont.)
  "Schubert," 38–40
  "Skoteinos," 20, 44, 61, 91–93,
    237n24
  "Stefan George," 74, 76, 77–78, 82–
    83, 85, 97–100
  "Theses on the Language of the Phi-
    losopher," 60–61, 90
  "Titles," 55, 56, 69–70, 80, 110–122,
    124–126, 137, 201, 202
  "Toward a Portrait of Thomas
    Mann," 52–53
  "Vers une musique informelle," 7,
    44
  "Words from Abroad," 56–57, 67,
    84, 85, 86–88, 102
Aging of works of art, 31–40
Alexander, Christopher, 243n24
Allegory in language, 65
Alter, Robert, 244n3
Aragon, Louis, 38
Arrangement (dispositio). See Imagina-
  tion; Presentational form
Atget, Eugene, 189, 196
Aura, 28–29, 34, 43, 155-158, 164,
  181–225
  in Adorno-Benjamin dispute, 181–
    185
  and early experience, 28–31, 34, 43
  and the face, 188–194
  and mimesis, 152–157
  negative or para-, 186–187, 203,
    211, 221–222
  perversion of, 194–196
  and shock, 201–203

Bach, J. S., 26
Bacon, Francis, 4, 94
Barthes, Roland, 187, 190, 200
Beauty, 156–167
Beckett, Samuel, 69, 112, 126, 164
Beethoven, Ludwig, 7, 26, 39, 41–43,
  45, 47–49, 78, 132–133, 207, 208
Benjamin, Andrew, 228n3
Benjamin, Walter, 57, 68, 85, 134–
  135, 148, 150, 174, 177–178, 180,
  198–199, 207

conception of mimesis, 139–145
conception of photography, compared with Adorno's, 181–187
on enigma and aura in mimesis,
  152–158
Entäusserung in, 52–54
on gesture in Kafka, 203–205
on the history of photography, 188–
  197
on hope, 223–225
language and constellational form
  in, 167–173
reception in the United States, 1–2
relation to Adorno, 9–10, 137–139
self-sacrifice in, 211–222
on shock, 200–202
works cited
  Arcades Project, (see Passagen-Werk)
  Berlin Childhood, 57, 142–145, 152–
    154, 155, 157, 169–171, 172, 174,
    186, 187, 192, 195, 212–218, 219–
    220, 221, 222, 241n12
  Berlin Chronicle, 42–44
  "Doctrine of the Similar" (see "On
    the Mimetic Faculty")
  "Franz Kafka," 181, 199–200, 211–
    212, 219, 222
  Goethe's Wahlverwandtschaften, 54
  "The Image of Proust," 154–155,
    168, 178, 241n10
  One-Way Street (Einbahnstrasse),
    177–178, 236n22, 242n18
  "On the Mimetic Faculty," 138–
    142, 152, 157, 167–168, 169, 173,
    242n18
  "On Some Motifs in Baudelaire,"
    155–157
  Origin of German Tragic Drama,
    238n4
  Das Passagen-Werk, 144, 172–174,
    193, 194–195, 245n20
  "Short History of Photography,"
    182, 188–192, 194, 196–197, 199,
    214, 217, 221
  "Some Reflections on Kafka," 214–
    215, 247n24
  "Surrealism," 196

"Theses on the Philosophy of History," 172, 242n15
"Work of Art," 182–183, 200, 201–202, 214, 215–216, 220–221, 222
Benn, Gottfried, 91
Berg, Alban, 46
Bergson, Henri, 159
Berman, Russell, 227n3, 231n1, 239n9
Bernstein, J. M., 228n5, 230n15, 231n4
Birus, Hendrik, 238n3
Blumenfeld, Harold, 227n2
Bly, Robert, 232n6
Bohrer, Karl-Heinz, 239n12
Bollas, Christopher, 237n27
Borchardt, Rudolf, 60–61, 62, 63, 70, 72–73, 74, 77, 85, 91
Botstein, Leon, 227n2
Bowie, Andrew, 235n13
Brecht, Bertolt, 75, 207
Bubner, Rüdiger, 229n13, 240n3
Buck-Morss, Susan, 2, 227n1, 227n3, 234n2, 235n11, 244n2, 247n38

Cahn, Michael, 175–176
Chopin, Friedrich, 30–31
Clarity, vs. intelligibility, 91–92
Configurational form, 3, 9–10, 60–62, 83–84, 90, 94–95, 96–101, 103–135, 167–180
  in Adorno's aesthetic essays, 110–124
  in Aesthetic Theory, 124–135
Constellational form. See Configurational form
Convolution. See Mimesis
Corbin, Henri, 244n9
Correspondence. See Mimesis
Crimp, Douglas, 244n2

Dahlhaus, Carl, 233n17
Dews, Peter, 228n3
Dreamworld. See Mimesis

Eichendorff, Joseph, 64, 65, 68–69, 74, 75, 85–86, 91

Eigen, Michael, 236n15, 244n10
Émigré, 56, 61, 80, 84, 115–120, 217–220
Enigma, 150–152, 152–154, 170. See also Mimesis
Entäusserung (divestiture, externalization), 51–58, 63
Epic, 79–83, 207–211
Equivocation, 9, 93, 107–110. See also Essay form
Erschütterung, 23, 40
Essay form, 103–110. See also Configurational form
Exile. See Émigré
Exoticism, 194–195, 216–217. See also Émigré
Experience. See also Subjectivity
  Adorno's own as basis for his work, 31
  artistic, 131–133
Expression, 121–122, 161, 163–164

Face, 188–199, 217. See also Aura; Gaze
Fame, 51–58
Film. See Photography
Foreign words, 56–58, 61, 84–91, 101–102
Früchtl, Josef, 240n3

Gaze, 155–158, 164, 186–187. See also Aura; Face
George, Stefan, 74, 76–77, 78, 82–83, 85, 97–100
Gesture, 203–211
Geulen, Eva, 228n4
Goethe, J. W., 50, 67, 78, 88, 91

Habermas, Jürgen, 5–7, 229n13, 235n8, 235n9, 239n12
Hamacher, Werner, 248n45
Hansen, Miriam, 244n2
Harte Fügung, 79, 83. See also Parataxis
Hegel, G. W. F., 7, 52–53, 61, 91–93, 102, 125–128, 130, 131–133, 222
Heidegger, Martin, 56–57, 90

Historical trajectory of aesthetic experience. *See* Aging of works of art
Hoffman, Rainer, 237n26
Hohendahl, Peter, 228n3, 228n5, 234n2, 234n3
Hölderlin, Friedrich, 73, 81, 83–84
Homer, *Odyssey* of, 81
Hope, 54–58, 222–225
Huhn, Tom, 228n3, 228n5, 231n4, 232n7, 242n13, 245n10
Hullot-Kentor, Robert, 221, 228n2, 229n6, 232n11, 238n5

Imagination
exact, 4–5, 19–20, 26, 94–95
productive, 20
Imitation. *See* Mimesis
Ingram, David, 239n12
Inorganic, work of art as, 31–40
Interior, 191–196, 203
Inwardness. *See* Interior

Jameson, Fredric, 2, 7, 137–139, 145, 176, 228n4, 229n6, 231n1, 232n4, 235n17, 237n26, 243n21, 246n34
Janouch, Gustav, 200–201
Jauss, Hans Robert, 231n1
Jay, Martin, 227n3, 234n27, 240n3, 244n2, 247n38
Jefferson, Ann, 240n5
Jewishness, 217–220
Johnson, Pauline, 231n1
Joyce, James, 62
Jung, Carl, 94

Kafka, Franz, 59, 60, 80, 111–122, 181, 183, 185, 186, 187, 192, 199–211, 212, 214–215, 217, 219, 223–224
Kant, Immanuel, 16, 21, 73, 108, 121, 126–128, 130, 150, 160
Kauffman, Lane, 238n4
Kaufman, Robert, 229n12, 231n1, 231n4
Kierkegaard, Sören, 5, 193–194, 203

Klages, Ludwig, 94
Kraus, Karl, 112, 157
Krauss, Rosalind, 189, 245n12, 245n23

Language, 59–102. *See also Rauschen*
Adorno's use of, 95–102
authentic or expressive dimension of, 66–73
and configuration, 90–91, 94–95
figurative, 10, 33
in Hegel, 91–94
illogical particles in, 79–83
music and, 68–73, 75, 80–81, 83
and philosophy, 89–102, 165–167
and will, 76–79
Languagelike quality of art, 22, 161–165
Late style, in Beethoven, 7–8, 41–42. *See also* Late work
Late work, 7–8, 40–51, 133–135
Lessing, G. E., 112
Linguistic criticism (*Sprachkritik*), 60, 91–95, 98–99
Logic
and art as tour de force, 207–210
slackening of in language, 79–84, 92, 98 (*see also* Essay form; Parataxis)
Logicity (Adorno), 22, 25, 124, 177
Lukács, György, 238n4

Mahler, Gustav, 80–81, 185, 186, 208–209, 216–217, 218, 222–225
Mallarmé, Stéphane, 243n23
Mann, Thomas, 52–53
Mattick, Paul Jr., 244n2
Mendelssohn, Felix, 70
Meyer, Theodor, 64
Mimesis, 137–180
in aesthetic experience, 16–19
in *Aesthetic Theory*, 145–150
Benjamin's conception of, 138–142
in language, 141, 167–180
and late work, 43–44
and natural beauty, 158–167

as nonsensuous similarity, 141, 167–180
Missac, Pierre, 11, 230n22, 242n16
Monet, Claude, 134
Mozart, W. A., 45
Music. *See also* Beethoven; Mahler
and aura, 28–31
and epic, 207–211
and language, 70–73
and subjective aesthetic experience, 44–49
and tour de force, 130, 207–210
Musical materialism, 32–33

Nägele, Rainer, 2, 222n1
Name, 55, 68–69, 89, 112–113. *See also* Language
Nominalism. *See* Nonidentical
Nonidentical, the, 207–211

Object, primacy of, 3, 17
Odradek (Kafka), 59–60, 63, 66, 94, 201, 206, 211, 219, 220
O'Neill, Maggie, 228n3
Organicism, critique of. *See* Inorganic
Osborne, Peter, 231n4

Paddison, Max, 228n5, 229n8, 233n13, 233n17
Paetzold, Heinz, 241n13
Painting, 26–28
Parataxis, 79–84, 96–99, 104, 195–199
Particle. *See* Language
Personality, transcendence of. *See* Entäusserung
Photography, 117–118, 181–225
and Adorno-Benjamin dispute, 181–188
aura in, 181–225
Benjamin's history of, 188–196
and hope, 222–225
as index, 189, 210
and shock, 199–205
and Surrealism, 196–199
Picasso, Pablo, 132

Picture puzzle. *See* Enigma
Presentational form (*Darstellungsform*), 3, 104, 107, 124–125, 129, 175

Rationality. *See also* Logic
communicative (Habermas), 5–6
nondiscursive, 3–5
Rauschen (murmuring), 59–71, 74–75
Ravel, Maurice, 118
Reading, and nonsensuous similarity, 168–169, 180
Reflection, second, 166
Reger, Max, 20
Renoir, Pierre-Auguste, 27
Resemblance. *See* Mimesis
Rhetoric. *See* Essay form
Rilke, Rainer Maria, 70, 72, 78, 164
Roberts, David, 228n5
Rose, Gillian, 227n3
Rosen, Charles, 227n2, 239n14
Rugg, Linda, 213, 247n38, 247n41, 247n43

Said, Edward, 227n2, 233n17, 239n13
Sanders, August, 189, 196
Scheffler, Israel, 238n7
Schenker, Heinrich, 76
Schlipphacke, Heidi, 228n3
Schönberg, Arnold, 7, 26, 32, 46
Scholem, Gerschom, 214
Schopenhauer, Arthur, 192
Schubert, Franz, 26, 38–40, 162
Schultz, Karla, 240n3
Schumann, Robert, 70
Shapiro, Henry, 230n19
Shapiro, Jeremy J., 237n29
Shock
and photography, 196–205
and sacrifice in Benjamin, 211–222
and Surrealism, 196–199
and violence, 199–211
Sontag, Susan, 244n2
Speculative ear (Kierkegaard), 19–20, 99. *See also* Imagination

266

Index

Sprachkritik. See Linguistic criticism
Strauss, Richard, 28–29, 34
Subjectivity
  in aesthetic experience, 4, 15–51,
    115–151
  in essay form, 105–113
  in experience of configurational
    form, 118–124, 124–135
Subject-object paradigm, 5–7, 9, 16,
  165
Subotnik, Rose, 233n17, 237n25
Suhrkamp, Peter, 111–112
Surrealism, 196–199
Szondi, Peter, 248n46

Taruskin, Richard, 227n2
Taussig, Michael, 240n5
Tonality, language of, 44–47
Toulouse-Lautrec, Henri, 28
Tour de force, 130, 207–211. *See also*
  Music
Tractatus form, 177–178
Trakl, Georg, 22, 70, 72, 81

Valéry, Paul, 155–156, 173
Violence, 199–211
  dialectic of in language, 76–79

Weber, Max, 6–7
Webern, Anton, 45, 162, 166
Wellmer, Albrecht, 3–7, 8, 104–105,
  124, 134, 230n15, 239n12, 241n9
Whitebook, Joel, 230n15
Wilke, Sabine, 228n3, 235n19
Wolff, Konrad, 242n14
Wolin, Richard, 227n3, 230n22,
  240n3, 243n1

Zuidervaart, Lambert, 228n3, 228n5,
  230n15

Studies in Contemporary German Social Thought
Thomas McCarthy, general editor

Theodor W. Adorno, *Against Epistemology: A Metacritique*

Theodor W. Adorno, *Hegel: Three Studies*

Theodor W. Adorno, *Prisms*

Karl-Otto Apel, *Understanding and Explanation: A Transcendental-Pragmatic Perspective*

Seyla Benhabib, Wolfgang Bonß, and John McCole, editors, *On Max Horkheimer: New Perspectives*

Seyla Benhabib and Fred Dallmayr, editors, *The Communicative Ethics Controversy*

Richard J. Bernstein, editor, *Habermas and Modernity*

Ernst Bloch, *Natural Law and Human Dignity*

Ernst Bloch, *The Principle of Hope*

Ernst Bloch, *The Utopian Function of Art and Literature: Selected Essays*

Hans Blumenberg, *The Genesis of the Copernican World*

Hans Blumenberg, *The Legitimacy of the Modern Age*

Hans Blumenberg, *Shipwreck with Spectator: Paradigm of a Metaphor for Existence*

Hans Blumenberg, *Work on Myth*

James Bohman, *Public Deliberation: Pluralism, Complexity, and Democracy*

James Bohman and Matthias Lutz-Bachmann, editors, *Perpetual Peace: Essays on Kant's Cosmopolitan Ideal*

Susan Buck-Morss, *The Dialectics of Seeing: Walter Benjamin and the Arcades Project*

Craig Calhoun, editor, *Habermas and the Public Sphere*

Jean Cohen and Andrew Arato, *Civil Society and Political Theory*

Maeve Cooke, *Language and Reason: A Study of Habermas's Pragmatics*

Helmut Dubiel, *Theory and Politics: Studies in the Development of Critical Theory*

John Forester, editor, *Critical Theory and Public Life*

David Frisby, *Fragments of Modernity: Theories of Modernity in the Work of Simmel, Kracauer and Benjamin*

Hans-Georg Gadamer, *Philosophical Apprenticeships*

Hans-Georg Gadamer, *Reason in the Age of Science*

Jürgen Habermas, *Between Facts and Norms: Contributions to a Discourse Theory of Law and Democracy*

Jürgen Habermas, *Justification and Application: Remarks on Discourse Ethics*

Jürgen Habermas, *On the Logic of the Social Sciences*

Jürgen Habermas, *Moral Consciousness and Communicative Action*

Jürgen Habermas, *The New Conservatism: Cultural Criticism and the Historians' Debate*

Jürgen Habermas, *The Philosophical Discourse of Modernity: Twelve Lectures*

Jürgen Habermas, *Philosophical-Political Profiles*

Jürgen Habermas, *Postmetaphysical Thinking: Philosophical Essays*

Jürgen Habermas, *The Structural Transformation of the Public Sphere: An Inquiry into a Category of Bourgeois Society*

Jürgen Habermas, editor, *Observations on "The Spiritual Situation of the Age"*

Axel Honneth, *The Critique of Power: Reflective Stages in a Critical Social Theory*

Axel Honneth, *The Struggle for Recognition: The Moral Grammar of Social Conflicts*

Axel Honneth and Hans Joas, editors, *Communicative Action: Essays on Jürgen Habermas's* The Theory of Communicative Action

Axel Honneth, Thomas McCarthy, Claus Offe, and Albrecht Wellmer, editors, *Cultural-Political Interventions in the Unfinished Project of Enlightenment*

Axel Honneth, Thomas McCarthy, Claus Offe, and Albrecht Wellmer, editors, *Philosophical Interventions in the Unfinished Project of Enlightenment*

Studies in Contemporary German Social Thought

Max Horkheimer, *Between Philosophy and Social Science: Selected Early Writings*

Tom Huhn and Lambert Zuidervaart, editors, *The Semblance of Subjectivity: Essays in Adorno's Aesthetic Theory*

Hans Joas, *G. H. Mead: A Contemporary Re-examination of His Thought*

Michael Kelly, editor, *Critique and Power: Recasting the Foucault/Habermas Debate*

Hans Herbert Kögler, *The Power of Dialogue: Critical Hermeneutics after Gadamer and Foucault*

Reinhart Koselleck, *Critique and Crisis: Enlightenment and the Pathogenesis of Modern Society*

Reinhart Koselleck, *Futures Past: On the Semantics of Historical Time*

Harry Liebersohn, *Fate and Utopia in German Sociology, 1887–1923*

Herbert Marcuse, *Hegel's Ontology and the Theory of Historicity*

Larry May and Jerome Kohn, editors, *Hannah Arendt: Twenty Years Later*

Pierre Missac, *Walter Benjamin's Passages*

Shierry Weber Nicholsen, *Exact Imagination, Late Work: On Adorno's Aesthetics*

Gil G. Noam and Thomas E. Wren, editors, *The Moral Self*

Guy Oakes, *Weber and Rickert: Concept Formation in the Cultural Sciences*

Claus Offe, *Contradictions of the Welfare State*

Claus Offe, *Disorganized Capitalism: Contemporary Transformations of Work and Politics*

Claus Offe, *Modernity and the State: East, West*

Claus Offe, *Varieties of Transition: The East European and East German Experience*

Helmut Peukert, *Science, Action, and Fundamental Theology: Toward a Theology of Communicative Action*

Joachim Ritter, *Hegel and the French Revolution: Essays on the* Philosophy of Right

William E. Scheuerman, *Between the Norm and the Exception: The Frankfurt School and the Rule of Law*

Studies in Contemporary German Social Thought

Alfred Schmidt, *History and Structure: An Essay on Hegelian-Marxist and Structuralist Theories of History*

Dennis Schmidt, *The Ubiquity of the Finite: Hegel, Heidegger, and the Entitlements of Philosophy*

Carl Schmitt, *The Crisis of Parliamentary Democracy*

Carl Schmitt, *Political Romanticism*

Carl Schmitt, *Political Theology: Four Chapters on the Concept of Sovereignty*

Gary Smith, editor, *On Walter Benjamin: Critical Essays and Recollections*

Michael Theunissen, *The Other: Studies in the Social Ontology of Husserl, Heidegger, Sartre, and Buber*

Ernst Tugendhat, *Self-Consciousness and Self-Determination*

Georgia Warnke, *Justice and Interpretation*

Mark Warren, *Nietzsche and Political Thought*

Albrecht Wellmer, *The Persistence of Modernity: Essays on Aesthetics, Ethics and Postmodernism*

Joel Whitebook, *Perversion and Utopia: A Study in Psychoanalysis and Critical Theory*

Rolf Wiggershaus, *The Frankfurt School: Its History, Theories, and Political Significance*

Thomas E. Wren, editor, *The Moral Domain: Essays in the Ongoing Discussion between Philosophy and the Social Sciences*

Lambert Zuidervaart, *Adorno's Aesthetic Theory: The Redemption of Illusion*